Stepping Out of LINE

Some Recent Titles from the *Perspectives on Gender* Series
Series Editor: Myra Marx Ferree, University of Wisconsin, Madison

Black Feminist Thought: Knowledge, Consciousness, and the Politics of Empowerment
Patricia Hill Collins

Feminisms and the Women's Movement: Dynamics of Change in Social Movement Ideology and Activism
Barbara Ryan

Black Women and White Women in the Professions: Analysis of Job Segregation by Race and Gender, 1960–1980
Natalie J. Sokoloff

Gender Consciousness and Politics
Sue Tolleson Rinehart

Mothering: Ideology, Experience, and Agency
Evelyn Nakano Glenn, Grace Chang, and Linda Rennie Forcey, Editors

For Richer, For Poorer: Mothers Confront Divorce
Demie Kurz

Integrative Feminisms: Building Global Visions, 1960s–1990s
Angela Miles

Rock-a-by Baby: Feminism, Self-Help, and Postpartum Depression
Verta Taylor

School-Smart and Mother-Wise: Working-Class Women's Identity and Schooling
Wendy Luttrell

Community Activism and Feminist Politics: Organizing Across Race, Class, and Gender
Nancy A. Naples, Editor

Grassroots Warriors: Activist Mothering, Community Work, and the War on Poverty
Nancy A. Naples

Complex Inequality: Gender, Class, and Race in the New Economy
Leslie McCall

Maid in the U.S.A.: 10th Anniversary Edition
Mary Romero

Home-Grown Hate: Gender and Organized Racism
Abby L. Ferber, Editor

Regulating Sex: The Politics of Intimacy and Identity
Elizabeth Bernstein and Laurie Schaffner, Editors

Stepping Out of LINE

Becoming and Being Feminist

CHERYL HERCUS

ROUTLEDGE
NEW YORK AND LONDON

Published in 2005 by
Routledge
270 Madison Avenue
New York, NY 10016
www.routledge-ny.com

Published in Great Britain by
Routledge
2 Park Square
Milton Park, Abington
Oxon OX14 4RN
www.routledge.co.uk

10 9 8 7 6 5 4 3 2 1

Library of Congress Cataloging-in-Publication Data
    Hercus, Cheryl, 1954-
        Stepping out of line: becoming and being feminist/Cheryl Hercus.
            p. cm. — (Perspectives on gender)
        Includes bibliographical references (p.) and index.
        ISBN 0-415-93032-4 (hardback: alk. paper) — ISBN 0-415-93033-2
    (pbk.: alk. paper)
        1. Feminists—Australia. 2. Feminism—Australia. 3. Feminists—
    Attitudes. I. Title. II. Series: Perspectives on gender (New York, N.Y.)

HQ1823.H47 2004
305.42'0994—dc22   2004007497

Table of Contents

Acknowledgments

This book could not have been written without the support and contributions of many people. Although they cannot be named, the women who made the book possible by sharing their knowledge, views, and life stories with me must be thanked. These women gave willingly of their time and of themselves. Over time, some have become close friends and I thank them in particular for their continuous support and interest. Thanks are also due to Dale Spender for her encouragement at the start of the project, and to Betty McLellan for her assistance and support. Senator Margaret Reynolds provided valuable information on feminist activism in Townsville during the 1970s, and I thank her for her time and input.

The research on which this book is based was carried out while I was a postgraduate student at James Cook University. Research funds provided by the university supported the data collection stage of the project, while a study leave during 2002 provided an opportunity to concentrate full-time on the process of rewriting the dissertation into a book. Over many years, colleagues from James Cook University and elsewhere have provided invaluable support, encouragement, and guidance. In particular, I would like to thank Claudia Knapman, my PhD supervisor, for her guidance, patience, professionalism, and support throughout the entire project. The late Stephen Crook provided excellent feedback on the dissertation and, until his untimely death in 2002, continued to encourage and support my work. Kerreen Reiger helped me clarify my thoughts by gently but persistently asking over lunch, "Cheryl, just what is your research about?" Marion Stell read parts of the manuscript and provided valuable feedback. Bronwyn Davies has always been very supportive and has provided an excellent sounding board for some of my crazier ideas. I also appreciate the ongoing support I have received from Janet Greeley and Rohan Bastin, the current Head of the School of Anthropology, Archaeology, and Sociology, James Cook University.

In 2002, I spent two months as a Visiting Fellow in the Department of Sociology at the University of Wisconsin—Madison. The intellectual stimulation, friendship, and encouragement I experienced during my visit provided a much-needed boost and I would like to thank everyone who made my stay so enjoyable and rewarding. Special thanks go to Myra Marx Ferree, who has been a wonderful mentor. Her guidance and friendship have been invaluable in the writing of this book. I would also like to thank Ilene Kalish, my editor at Routledge, for her helpful advice and enthusiasm.

Friends and family are also essential to the successful completion of a project like this. I thank my women friends, including those in the Townsville Feminist Collective, who over many years have shared the highs and lows, the tears, the frustrations, the laughter, the wine, and the sense of achievement. There are too many to thank individually, but I would particularly like to mention Shirley Morrisey, Penny Barkas, Karen Greig, Jane Thomson, Shelley Greer, Rosita Henry, Celmara Pocock, Morgan King, and Catherine Spencer.

The research conducted for this book would never have started or finished without the support of Grant Whiteman, who has always encouraged me to believe in myself. Special thanks also go to my mother, who provided a workspace free from distractions during crucial stages of writing. She cooked for me, juiced fresh oranges each morning, and provided company when I was not working. My father, Fraser Hercus, died in 1998 before I completed the dissertation. He was a man with many interests, who read widely and valued knowledge not only for its instrumental uses, but also for its own sake. Although he would have liked me to pursue a career in the biological sciences, I know he would be proud of my achievement in writing this book; I dedicate it to his memory. My sisters, Dianne and Kerrie, my brother, Bruce, and my sister-in-law, Gabrielle, all helped by caring for my children during holidays so I could work. I thank them and my brothers, Robert and Colin, for their general support and encouragement. My children, Michael and Caitlin, lived for many years with their mother's dissertation hanging over their heads. Then, when they thought it was all finally over, it transformed into "the book" she was writing. Through it all they have remained supportive of my goals and have provided balance and happiness in my life. Although they have now grown up and left home, they are as relieved as I am that the book is finally finished.

Introduction:
"I'm not a feminist . . . or am I?"

A young woman in a university class makes a strong statement about male domination in international politics, but she follows up immediately with "not that I'm a feminist or anything."[1] Why does she say this? Is the answer to be found in a cartoon by feminist cartoonist Judy Horacek: "I'm not a feminist, but . . . that's because I'm a doormat?"[2] This seems unlikely. Here is a young woman, studying for a degree in politics, speaking boldly about the issues under discussion. She does not sound like anybody's doormat, but she rejects or does not see a connection between her views of the world, which could be described as feminist, and her own self identity. In this she is not alone. During the 1990s, the refrain "I'm not a feminist, but . . ." became a cliché for the widespread phenomenon of women expressing support for feminist goals such as equal opportunity and equal pay, access to affordable child care, and freedom from sexual harassment and assault, yet at the same time distancing themselves from any sort of feminist identification. Some commentators noted that even women who had actively fought for women's rights were often reluctant to label themselves feminist.[3]

While in the 1990s feminists pondered the "I'm not a feminist, but . . ." phenomenon, in the 1970s and 1980s they were more commonly writing about the "click" phenomenon: that moment when they first recognized the subordinate status of women, their own oppression, and the possibility of change. The term came from an article titled "Click! The Housewife's Moment of Truth" first published in *Ms. Magazine* in 1972.[4] In this article, the click is defined as "A moment of truth. The shock of recognition. Instant sisterhood," and numerous anecdotes of click situations are described. The article suggested that click experiences were "coming faster and faster" to American women in 1972. In reality, the click was not only occurring for American women; British, European, and Australian women were also recognizing the click. Sensitized by media coverage of the Women's Liberation movement and its issues, women were noticing little things that their husbands did or that their bosses said that confirmed their subordinate status as women. One example from the *Ms.* article was of a woman who had placed a pile of toys on the stairs ready to be put away. Her husband complained in an annoyed voice, asking why they were there. "Click! 'You have two hands,' she said, turning away."[5]

The click was often the result of this type of personal experience and sometimes was quite dramatic in its intensity. Sonia Johnson labeled the experience an epiphany when she finally faced and accepted the reality of women's oppression in society at large, and in particular in the Mormon Church. She had attended a talk given by a Mormon religious leader in the hope of hearing some intelligent justification for the church's opposition to the Equal Rights Amendment (ERA). But the speaker's patronizing tone and trivializing of the issue forced her to confront "[w]hat it means to be female in a male world." She wrote, "I knew instantly what the women's movement was all about; I knew it in my very bones." That night she finally said what she had been resisting saying for a long time. "I am a feminist."[6] For other women, the click was brought about by reading one of the classic works of the Women's Liberation period. For instance, Dale Spender described experiencing it when she read Germaine Greer: "Initially, reading *The Female Eunuch* was like reading a horror story: all those clues I had ignored, all those awful connections I'd never dared make, all that evidence I had not been brave enough to examine; all put together, and pushed at me with great force . . . The world turned on its head!"[7]

For me, the click came in 1977 while on a three-day train trip up the Australian east coast. I traveled with my boyfriend of the time, an education student at the University of Sydney, who brought along a few books to while away the long hours. One of these—presumably assigned by a feminist professor—was Shulamith Firestone's *The Dialectic of Sex*. We took turns reading and discussing each chapter. He read the chapter on love and predicted I would hate it. Although I had been raised to believe that women and men were equal, that education was just as important for females as males, and that women could do anything as well as men, I was also raised on fairy-tales, dolls, and protestant Christianity. Consequently, at that point in my life I was still in thrall to the romantic myth. I fully expected to find Mr. Right in the next year or two, get married, and settle down to domestic life. Despite this background, I did not hate the chapter. Instead, "the scales fell from my eyes" and I "saw the light." The romantic myth I had been so well schooled in was shattered. Firestone showed how women had been taught to believe that love was their primary purpose and goal in life, whereas for men it was a facet of their lives, a pleasant diversion from more important goals and accomplishments. Indeed, male-dominated society was parasitic on the emotional labor women performed in the name of love.

Two weeks after the train trip I took a job as a cook and deckhand on a prawn trawler, and there came across my second feminist book. The book had been left behind by the previous cook and inside the front cover was a handwritten message of woman-to-woman solidarity, the exact words of which I cannot remember. In this collection of Women's Liberation essays and manifestos, I read about the "Society for Cutting Up Men," about the oppression of women in the church, and about the myth of the vaginal orgasm. I knew then that I was onto something that would change my life.[8] I returned south and enrolled at university where I studied sociology and women's studies.

By mid-1978 I had adopted feminism as my worldview and started calling myself a feminist. For many years, my commitment to feminism was expressed primarily through academic pursuits and my general approach to life rather than through involvement in feminist activist groups. Although I chose to marry and have children, I no longer saw this as my primary goal in life, and the list of characteristics I sought in a partner expanded to include sensitivity to feminist issues and a commitment to equality. On a personal level, I considered my lifestyle to be consistent with feminist principles. My partner and I shared childcare and domestic labor, attempted to raise our children in a nonsexist manner, and gradually I dropped my religious beliefs. Studying for a Diploma of Education in 1986, I continued my interest in feminism, particularly in relation to education.

Reflecting on my own discovery of feminism, I have often wondered over the years what direction my life would have taken if I had not serendipitously come across the writings of these early Women's Liberationists. On the one hand, I probably would have found my supposed prince and made a valiant attempt at living out the myth of the "lived happily ever after" life of a conventional stay-at-home mother, never quite knowing why I did not feel as satisfied as I was supposed to. Then again, I may have discovered feminism through some other route, maybe through a magazine picked up in a doctor's waiting room. I may have discovered feminism later in life, driven by the experience of an unhappy marriage. Or maybe I would have become one more voice in the "I'm not a feminist, but . . ." chorus. On the other hand, if I had made contact with feminist activists at that time, I may have become far more outwardly active and radical than I did. At a women's peace camp in 1984 I met a group of women from an alternative community whose lifestyle was very appealing to me. If I had met these women in 1978 before marrying and having children, I may have gone to live with them instead of returning to the university.

These musings on my own experiences of becoming and being feminist, on the lives of other women who experienced the click, and on those who claim not to be feminist while endorsing feminist goals underscore the questions that I explore in this book. What is a feminist? What is feminist identity and how does identity change? What features of the broader social, cultural, and political environment support the process of becoming feminist, and which ones lead women to disclaim feminist identity while supporting feminist goals?

The answers to these questions are more complex than the concept of the click suggests. Even though I have often recounted the story of reading *The Dialectic of Sex* as a classic click experience—"I boarded the train an antifeminist, and three days later got off a feminist"—in reality the process was not that simple. To begin with, the seeds of feminist consciousness and practice were built into my childhood. Although she never would have called herself a feminist, my mother believed in gender equality and enacted this equality in crucial areas of family life. She expected her sons and her daughters both to wash dishes and help with meal preparation and, although I played with dolls, my brothers also had dolls and my sisters and I played with toy cars and trucks. My parents held high expectations of their daughters in relation to education and professional careers, albeit careers that could accommodate the responsibilities of motherhood. Via the media, I was also aware of the Women's Liberation movement and was sympathetic to a number of issues. I could not see why women should be barred from "male" occupations and believed women should receive equal pay. However, I held these views without recognizing the tension that existed between them and the images of marriage and motherhood to which I aspired.

If my life prior to the train trip was not so unambiguously nonfeminist, neither was the transformation to being feminist quite so instantaneous. The two books I read on the train and on the trawler certainly influenced me in profound ways, but feminist consciousness and identity did not operate like a switch being turned on. For several months I was still unsure about whether I wanted to call myself a feminist. I did not personally know any other feminists and so did not know if I was like them. Furthermore, there were some feminist ideas I was not prepared to accept, such as Firestone's suggestion that women would achieve liberation through artificial procreation. As it happens, I was not alone in my reaction against this idea. Feminists have in fact been some of the strongest critics of reproductive technology as it has developed over recent decades. Thus, it was only after returning to the university and reading much more about feminism that I began to call myself a feminist.

The Research Project: Laughing and Singing at the Revolution

When in 1991 I moved to Townsville and enrolled in a postgraduate research degree, my own personal biography in relation to feminism fed into my developing ideas for a research project.[9] A few months into my candidacy, I became aware of an upcoming feminist weekend workshop and the specific idea for this study arose. The workshop was facilitated by Dale Spender, a well-known Australian feminist researcher and writer, and was entitled *Laughing and Singing at the Revolution*.[10] It was described in the 1991 Winter Institute program as "an opportunity for feminist women to get together to examine the present status of the revolution we call the Women's Movement."

The workshop was held at a church-owned campsite located adjacent to a National Park at Crystal Creek, 70 kilometers north of Townsville. Activities began on the Friday evening with a getting-to-know you session and continued throughout Saturday and Sunday with a variety of activities based on a range of feminist issues. One session dealt with humor as a way of dealing with sexism and another looked at the question of political and ideological differences within feminism. Dale Spender talked about her research and writing, including her work on the historical silencing of women writers and their contributions to literature. On Saturday night everyone joined in for a lively feminist concert that included poetry reading, singing, chanting, and tap dancing.

As a participant at the workshop I talked with others, and with Dale Spender, about my ideas for a research project. During the final group session on Sunday afternoon, I more formally raised the possibility of conducting research based on the experiences of the women present. The suggestion was greeted positively, and following the session a number of women approached me individually to offer their support. The research participants thus came with the topic. However, features of the group made these women particularly suitable for a study exploring the processes and experiences of becoming and being feminist. The 49 women who attended the workshop (including the coordinator of the workshop, the facilitator, and me) came from a wide geographical area and previous involvement in feminist activities ranged from those who could be described as highly committed activists to women who had virtually no prior contact with feminist activism or ideology. Thus, the process and context of becoming involved, and the variety of factors that might lead to increased or decreased involvement, could be explored through these women.

In the weeks following the workshop I began contacting women for interviews and the positive reception to the proposed project translated into an excellent response rate. Forty-five workshop participants agreed to be interviewed and only one declined. Of these, the majority (60%) lived in Townsville. Another significant group (29%) came from Mackay, a coastal town about four hours drive south of Townsville. Two women traveled up from Brisbane, and three came from towns in central Queensland. Participants also varied in terms of age, lifestyle, and life experience. When the study commenced, 17 were living with a male partner, 13 lived alone, 7 were lone parents, and 8 lived in shared households or with a female partner. In terms of sexual identification, 25% self-identified in the interview as lesbians.[11] Their ages ranged from early twenties to over 60. The majority (82%) fell between the ages of 31 and 50, with a mean age of 41. The sample was highly educated relative to the general population. Fifty-one percent held degrees or equivalent and 13% had completed certificate or diploma qualifications. Eighty-nine percent were in some form of paid employment, with a significant proportion occupying mid- to high-level professional and white-collar positions in the community service sector. The group was not ethnically diverse, however. No Aboriginal women were included and although two women were born outside Australia, both were from European backgrounds. This feature of the sample reflects the ongoing lack of relevance of mainstream feminism for Indigenous and migrant Australian women, which is discussed in Chapter 2.

Qualitative in-depth interviewing was chosen as the primary method of data collection because of its consistency with feminist research principles and because my particular questions about becoming and being feminist could not be answered adequately using quantitative methods.[12]

I initially interviewed each of the participants between September and December 1991. I asked them about their experience attending the workshop, their identification with feminism, their prior involvement in feminist activism, their confrontation with any obstacles in terms of feminist involvement, and their discussions with significant others prior to and following the workshop. Preliminary analysis of these initial interviews indicated that the weekend workshop was a very significant, transforming event in the lives of some participants, particularly those whose previous contact with feminism was limited. I was interested to see whether the enthusiasm generated by the workshop had translated into further involvement for these women in the year that followed as well as the pattern of involvement for the longer-term "feminists" in the group. Consequently, follow-up interviews were conducted toward the end of 1992.[13] These were more structured than the initial interviews. They explored the extent and nature of feminist involvement and any changes in thoughts and feelings about feminism during the period between interviews.

Interviews lasted between 30 and 90 minutes, with the follow-up interviews being generally shorter than the initial interviews. All interviews were transcribed and analyzed with the aid of a computer-based qualitative data analysis program. In addition to the interviews, I participated in and observed other feminist events held in the region during the study period. I also spoke with Dr. Betty McLellan, who organized the Winter Institute for Women, and with Senator Margaret Reynolds.[14] Both provided valuable background information on feminist activities in the Townsville region during the 1970s and 1980s.

In line with feminist research principles I approached this research with a commitment to build open and ethical relationships with participants. Participation was voluntary and confidentiality was assured through the use of pseudonyms in any reports on the research, including this book. Once analysis was under way, aspects of the study were presented in forums where women from the study were in attendance. On those occasions, feedback was sought and provided. Nonetheless, the research could not be described as participatory in the fullest sense. The account provided in this book reflects my analysis of participants' lives. It goes beyond "giving voice" to participants while, hopefully, doing justice to their understandings and to the rich complexity of their lives.

Outline of the Book

In Chapter 1 I provide a brief review of the feminist and social movement theory, as well as research that fed into the study. I then describe, explain, and illustrate a model of becoming and being feminist, based on a concept of fractal subjectivity, which is elaborated throughout the rest of the book. In combination with Chapter 1, Chapter 2 provides the contextual background that is necessary to fully appreciate the stories I tell in later chapters about the experiences of the women I interviewed. In this chapter, the focus is on the field or environment in which women become feminist. In particular, it considers the historical and geographical dimensions of feminism as a social movement.

Chapters 3, 4, and 5 concentrate on the process of becoming feminist. Chapter 3 examines the paths traveled in becoming feminist. Becoming feminist involves intertwined processes of coming to "know" the world and oneself in feminist terms, and of taking up a position within feminist discourse and networks. In this chapter the various routes through which women gained access to these resources for the development of feminist subjectivity are outlined. Variations in the women's biographical accounts of becoming feminist are analyzed and discussed. The tensions and contradictions faced by interviewees in terms of their involvement in feminism and the processes of becoming and being feminist are addressed in Chapter 4. The issue of personal autonomy versus a sense of collective identity or belonging is a central theme in this chapter. In Chapter 5, the focus is on the opposition women face as feminists. Opposition to feminist identity and involvement was encountered in a range of settings, creating a largely hostile environment for the development of feminist identity and activism.

Chapters 6 and 7 document the range and extent of feminist action engaged in by participants. Chapter 6 describes the broad range of participation in feminist organizations and events reported by women in the study, and discusses the significance of these activities for the women concerned. Broader implications for the study of social movements involvement are drawn out of the themes that emerge from this data. In Chapter 7 the focus shifts from participation in organizations and events to the myriad ways in which women establish a feminist presence in daily life. Various themes, related to the rewards and outcomes of participation discussed in Chapter 6, are picked up in Chapter 7 as strategies for activism in daily life. I argue that a relationship exists between these two arenas of activism, where knowledge, energy, and identity are enhanced through participation in events and organizations, but also deployed in daily life.

In the final chapter I explore what my findings add to our understanding of the feminist women's movement and of the processes of becoming and being involved in feminist collective action. The empirical findings are reviewed in light of a fractal model of feminist subjectivity, and the implications of my findings for existing social movement theory and for feminist theory and practice are discussed.

CHAPTER 1

Developing a Model of
Feminist Becoming and Being

Although for many feminists the concept of the "click" resonates power-fully as a pivotal moment in their becoming feminist, it is limited as an explanation of the transformation of consciousness, emotions, identity, and action that are involved in this process. If not as a single click, how, then, might we explain the process of becoming and being feminist? In my quest to answer this question, to understand both my own personal journey and the lives of the women whose stories form the empirical basis of this study, I have found both feminist and social movements research and theory to be helpful.

Anthony Giddens, in *New Rules of Sociological Method*, writes about two interacting levels of sociological understanding, which he labels the double hermeneutic.[1] The first level involves understanding social life from the perspective of social actors. This requires a closeness or immersion in the lives of those being researched and is achieved through ethnographic ob-servation, interviews, and other forms of qualitative research. The second level involves stepping back from immersion in social action, to a position outside, from where the phenomenon under study is interpreted using the concepts and theories of social science.

When this model of sociological understanding is applied to my re-search, feminist writings on consciousness and identity and on what it means to be a woman and a feminist contribute to the first level of under-standing implied by the double hermeneutic. Reading this material, which emanates from within the feminist women's movement, forms part of my understanding of the movement, as an actor who is part of the movement. The second level of understanding in the double hermeneutic, comes from the "outsider" view taken by sociological theories of social movements, and my position as a sociologist who tries to understand general processes relating people to social movements.

In an increasingly reflexive world, however, the boundary between these two positions —in this case, of being inside the movement and identifying with feminism while also being outside and drawing upon a rich sociological tradition of scholarship on social movements—is not clear cut. As Giddens points out, there is a two-way interaction between these two levels of interpretive understanding. In modern society, meanings generated by social actors inform the meanings generated by social science and vice versa. From a position within feminism, I see sociology as a discipline where male voices and male perspectives have been, and still are, dominant. Thus, feminist theory can become the outside position from which I reflect on social movements theory. I envisage this as being like two mirrors—or, more precisely, two multifaceted mirrors, representing the variety of perspectives within both feminist and sociological theory—arranged facing each other, endlessly reflecting each other into infinity. The position from which I write is located between these two sets of mirrors. The concepts and theories from both feminist and social movements literature, reflecting on each other, offer a fuller understanding, if also a more complex picture, of what it is to be a feminist and how women become feminist.[2] It can also illuminate the way participants in any social movement are actively involved in constructing the movement and its meaning.

In this chapter, my first goal is to review feminist and social movements literature to show how these two "mirrors" inform my understanding of the process, particularly as it relates to the central questions addressed by the study. Following this, I outline a model of feminist becoming and being, based on a metaphor of fractal geometry.

Reflections from the Feminist Literature

Since the 1970s, feminists have been writing about issues of consciousness and identity, and how they relate to social and political change. They wrote initially in a celebratory fashion as they tried to explain the powerful sense of injustice, but also the feeling of liberation associated with becoming feminist.[3] Later they wrote in a more reflective fashion, as differences between women were explored in the context of difficult attempts to forge feminist solidarity.

In the early days of the women's liberation movement, in the late 1960s and 1970s, many women in the Western world underwent the type of awakening distilled in the concept of the click through participating in consciousness-raising (CR) groups. In CR groups, they met together, talked about their personal experiences, and collectively discovered the social and political causes of their problems. Inspired by their own profound personal transformation, some began to write and theorize about CR. Since many early participants had begun their political lives through involvement in the New Left, they turned to familiar Marxist concepts of class consciousness and false consciousness to explain the process of becoming and being feminist. It was argued that women generally were unaware of the effects of male domination or patriarchy because of "its ability to masquerade as the 'natural' and inevitable form of social organization."[4] CR was the means by which this masquerade, or false consciousness, was shown for what it was, and the truth revealed.[5]

It was generally assumed that feminist identity and feminist activism were the direct result of feminist consciousness. All women were oppressed in a patriarchal society and thus shared a set of experiences as women. Becoming feminist was the result of a woman having her consciousness raised to a point where she recognized her oppression as a woman and her common interests with other women, expressed as sisterhood.

The practice of CR in groups formed solely for this purpose dissipated in most Western societies by the late 1970s. Nonetheless, women continued to come into contact with feminist ideas and become feminist through the texts and organizations that grew out of this period. The strong sense of unity and strength experienced by many participants in the early days of women's liberation did not continue, however, and cracks among the sisterhood began to appear. Ideas about what it meant to be a feminist and, indeed, what it meant to be a woman, came under scrutiny.[6] The universalizing nature of much feminist discourse came under fire as women from ethnic and racial minorities, lesbians, and working-class women argued that their experiences were often quite different from those of the white, heterosexual, middle-class women who initially constituted the public face of the movement.

During the 1970s and 1980s, the notions of false consciousness and of the universal nature of women's oppression were called into question, but the privileging of personal experience as the basis of "true" consciousness was retained. In the words of Nickie Charles, the result was a turn to identity politics. Discussing the British context, she suggests that "the dominant feminist identity of the . . . women's liberation movement became split into many identities—of lesbians, of black feminists, of Irish feminists, of working class feminists, of Jewish feminists—and recognized as being specific to a particular group of women."[7] As was the case in earlier formulations, consciousness and identity were still viewed as flowing directly from experience, although now differences of experience and resultant consciousness and identities were recognized. Where this might leave a woman who was, say, lesbian, black, and Jewish, was not asked.

Beginning in the 1980s and extending into the 1990s, a more profound challenge to the conceptualization of experience as the basis of feminist consciousness and identity was mounted by poststructuralist feminists. Claiming that all experiences are already textually mediated interpretations, poststructuralist writers came to view the concepts of consciousness and identity as being hopelessly enmeshed in humanist notions of the stable, rational self. Rather than being transparent reflections of reality, consciousness and identity, according to poststructuralists, are aspects of subjectivity created through "positioning" and "discursive practices" that create the fiction of a unified, knowing, self.[8]

A danger with poststructuralist analyses, however, is the tendency to depoliticize the women's movement since the deconstruction of feminist consciousness, identity, and experience, indeed, of the very categories of "gender" and "women," leaves no basis on which to organize collectively. Radical and socialist feminists have expressed concern that the possibility of political action is lost as the existence of any reality beyond the text is denied by poststructuralists.[9] For example, Somer Brodribb, writing from a radical feminist perspective, argues that the problems of dualism—reason/emotion, nature/culture, mind/body, and male/female—are inappropriately resolved in postmodern/poststructuralist theory through a denial of female difference. In her view, rather than dismantling these binary oppositions, the deconstruction of the category "woman," which is central to such theories, actually represents the ultimate triumph of reason over emotion, culture over nature, and mind over body. Postmodern theory "claims to lift identity right off the skin, the body . . . Mind will no longer need to make reference to body in its identity claims; unchained at last from the sensations and limitations of the flesh."[10] From a different perspective, Iris Marion Young finds the deconstruction of the categories "gender" and "women" compelling, but nonetheless paralyzing since they do not address the "pragmatic political reasons for insisting on the possibility of thinking about women as some kind of group."[11] An important pragmatic reason for retaining some conceptualization of women as a collective, according to Young, is the necessity of maintaining some point of view beyond liberal individualism that generally operates to obscure the systematic and structured nature of oppression.

The debate between postmodern/poststructuralist feminists and feminists coming from radical and socialist feminist traditions has not been resolved. While the deconstructive work of the poststructuralists is compelling, many feminists still cling to a desire for a theory that can ground personal identity and political action. While some feminists are busy doing deconstructive work, others feel threatened by a project that appears to destroy categories that support identity and solidarity. In this book I hope to contribute toward a way out of this impasse. In my view, a shortcoming of the debate is that it has largely been carried out at a theoretical level among feminist academics. Little attention has been paid to the possible contribution that could be made to the debate by ordinary women doing actual politics. Empirical research into feminist subjectivity and politics as they are experienced and practiced by women in grassroots settings removed from prestigious women's studies departments, shows how women respond to feminist discourse in its myriad forms, how they come to share a collective sense of "being" women engaged in a common political project, and how they respond in specific ways to the diversity of their experience.

In the fractal model I outline later and develop throughout this book, I have chosen to use the term feminist subjectivity to depict being feminist at the broadest level. This is consistent with feminist poststructuralist approaches; however, alongside numerous other feminist writers, I reject textual foundationalism.[12] I do not view subjectivity as solely discursive, but as consisting of multiple components, including both psychological and biological aspects. Embodiment is integral to this conceptualization of subjectivity. Feminist consciousness, emotions, identity, and action, which I examine in this book, are all embodied aspects of subjectivity. Thought occurs in the brain (a part of the body) just as emotion is both the increased beating of the heart as well as the cognitive processes that interpret this beating. We do things like marching in a protest or signing a petition with our arms and legs, we speak to others and chant slogans with our voices, but we form the intentions and thoughts embodied by these actions in our minds. And our bodies can sit with a group in a room, or march with them in a protest, while our minds are elsewhere.

Reflections from the Social Movements Literature
Representing the second mirror, issues similar to those discussed above have been addressed by social movements scholars in their attempts to understand how people are drawn into and participate in social movements. Diverse theoretical perspectives within the field are based on varying assumptions about the nature of social movements and the nature of the "self" who participates in them. From a feminist perspective, these underlying assumptions are not inconsequential. For instance, most social movement theory and research has until recently reproduced a range of binary oppositions such as reason/emotion, public/private, culture/nature, male/female that, although central to Western social and political thought,

have been extensively critiqued by feminists as providing justification for gendered power relationships.[13] There is a risk, therefore, that women's experiences of getting involved and participating in social movements may be marginalized and their voices silenced if mainstream theoretical orientations are adopted uncritically. In the following brief review of theoretical positions within this field, the value of each approach to an understanding of women's experiences is paramount.

During the first half of the twentieth century, the collective behavior approach dominated the sociological study of social movements. Although two strands developed, one associated with symbolic interaction and the other with structural functionalism, the structural-functionalist version as elaborated by Neil Smelser has been particularly influential and problematic. In Smelser's formulation, social movements represent the irrational and emotional response of marginalized individuals to structural strain. Concomitantly, movement participants are viewed as psychologically disturbed individuals manipulated by clever movement leaders who formulate and disseminate generalized beliefs as "short-circuited" exaggerations of reality. In the absence of effective social control, such generalized beliefs are translated into irrational episodes of collective behavior.[14] Inherently conservative, the collective behavior approach has functioned to discredit movement participants and their ideas.[15] It has proved particularly problematic for analyses of women's activism given the historical association of women with emotion and irrationality.[16] Despite being largely discredited and superceded by more recent approaches, the historical context of this perspective sheds light on the neglect of emotion in subsequent theories of social movements' emergence and participation.

The resource mobilization approach to social movements presents a quite different picture. Developed during the 1970s and 1980s in opposition to the collective behavior approach, resource mobilization theory (RMT) looked beyond the grievances of marginalized groups for an explanation of movement emergence and growth. It focused instead on the availability of resources and political opportunities for mobilization.[17] Turning to questions of recruitment and participation, RMT rejected psychological descriptions of movement involvement as pathological. Instead, individuals who became involved in social movements came to be viewed as rational agents who weighed the costs and benefits before choosing to join social movements organizations (SMOs) and/or participate in protest events. Links to other movement members through informal movement networks facilitate this process of micromobilization.[18] Consistent with the introduction of rational choice assumptions to the study of collective action, researchers working within the RMT framework focused their attention on the organizational-level analysis of SMOs and their strategies.[19]

From a feminist perspective, the RMT emphasis on instrumental goals and the inherent rationality of movement involvement appears initially as an advance on the collective behavior approach that reinforced images of (feminine) irrationality. However, the underlying assumptions of RMT present their own problems. By reversing, but not discarding, reason/emotion dualism and by focusing on instrumental goals of movement organizations, RMT has difficulty explaining precisely those features of women's collective action and movement identities that are most distinctive and interesting.[20] The emotional dimension of movement involvement, which is so evident in the stories told to me by the women in this study, is excluded from analysis, as are cultural and informal forms of political action in everyday life. A major theoretical contribution of the women's liberation period of feminism was the reconceptualization of politics to include recognition of the political nature of personal life; any adequate model of feminist subjectivity and feminist involvement must take this into account.

RMT also falls short in terms of theorizing structural inequality and power relations at a macro level, due to its organizational (meso-level) focus.[21] Despite these shortcomings, I have found it useful to draw on some concepts from RMT. In particular, I have found the concept of micromobilization useful for drawing attention to the microstructural conditions necessary for recruitment and participation in collective action.

During the 1990s, the dominance of the resource mobilization approach waned. Cultural and social psychological dimensions of movement involvement, including emotion, found their way back into the study of social movements under the combined influence of social constructionism and new social movements theory (NSMT). NSMT also reinstated an interest in the macro-historical and structural context of social movements.

The social constructionist approach, exemplified by the work on framing by David Snow and his colleagues, revives a symbolic interactionist version of collective behavior theory, thereby refocusing attention on the social-psychological aspects of recruitment and involvement in social movements.[22] Snow, Zurcher, and Ekland-Olson foreshadowed their interest in framing in a 1980 article that suggested that recruitment requires cognitive states to be aligned with a movement's value orientations.[23] Snow, Rochford, Worden, and Benford developed the idea further by proposing the concept of frame alignment, defined as "the linkage of individual and SMO interpretive orientations, such that some set of individual interests, values and beliefs and SMO activities, goals, and ideology are congruent and complementary."[24] Movement organizations facilitate frame alignment —a necessary precondition for movement participation, according to this approach—through a variety of strategies. Collective action frames mobilize collective action by performing three core framing tasks: first, diagnosing an aspect of social life as problematic; second, outlining a proposed solution; and third, providing a rationale for action. A significant feature of diagnostic framing is the attribution of causality or blame, with problems and grievances being defined in terms of injustice.[25]

With the recent trend toward emphasizing the cultural dimensions of collective action, interest in the framing activity of movement organizations and their opponents has continued. However, a major shortcoming of this approach is the top-down nature of the model. Movement organizations and leaders are viewed as strategic actors who persuade, solicit, and coax relatively passive individuals to adopt movement frames and participate in movement activities. In this sense, it parallels models of socialization where, in the past, children have been viewed as passive recipients of a one-way process. In this study I have found the concept of framing useful for understanding the cognitive dimension of becoming and being feminist. It provides a tool for analyzing feminist consciousness as socially constructed, thereby avoiding the imputation of false consciousness to nonfeminist women and to women prior to their becoming feminist. Nonetheless, I have found it necessary to extend the concept of framing to account for emotional aspects of movement involvement and to examine the way in which individuals actively select and rework existing frames in the process of constructing feminist subjectivity. Thus, I view framing work as a bottom-up as well as a top-down activity. For this, I have found another type of social movement theory is useful.

In Europe, the development of what has come to be known as NSMT drew upon and provided an alternative to Marxist analyses that had previously dominated European sociology.[26] Even as the work of scholars associated with NSMT is not homogeneous, a number of general themes are evident. NSMT reintroduced a concern with macro-level analysis, viewing the emergence of new movements as the result of major structural changes associated with the transformation from industrial to postindustrial society where the production of knowledge and symbolic manipulation are more central than material production. Postindustrial or late-industrial societies require individuals who are capable of autonomous action, but they also need to avoid the risk of social disintegration. New conflicts and new social movements arise out of the contradiction inherent in this situation.[27] The political paradigm of the "new" movements goes beyond concerns with economic growth, distribution, and security to focus on cultural production.[28] This focus on cultural processes—on language, discourse, identity, consciousness, and emotions—within NSMT is clearly consistent with the practices and theory of feminism. Not surprisingly, a number of feminist social movements scholars have responded positively, although not uncritically, to NSMT.[29]

A key concept for NSM theorists, and one that is important to the fractal model of movement involvement developed in this book, is that of collective identity, the sense of unity, the "we" feeling, or the sense of belonging associated with being involved in collective action. The concept of collective identity provides a link between structural conditions and collective action. However, collective identity cannot be assumed to exist simply on the basis of structural location; rather it is an achievement of social actors. Melucci argues that the social construction of collective identity is continually occurring within the submerged networks of movement communities in a process that involves both cognitive and emotional dimensions. Ends, means, and the field of action are defined cognitively, while individuals' emotional investments in collective identity create a feeling of community. Melucci's call for movement scholars to shift their "attention from the top to the bottom of collective action" from the discourse of leaders and visible forms of action to "the more invisible or hidden forms" and "the more silent voices" is taken seriously in the analysis of feminist involvement provided here.[30] In this book, the voices presented are not those of the leaders in the movement, but those of "ordinary" women as they encounter and respond to feminist discourse and practice in a variety of settings and ways during the process of becoming and being feminist.

A Fractal Model of Becoming and Being Feminist

The fractal model of becoming and being feminist presented in this book draws upon both feminist and social movements theory and research, and it integrates a range of concepts from these fields. It employs a biographical perspective and presents movement involvement as a complex, interactive process, whereby the construction of feminists and feminism occurs as a simultaneously individual and collective process. Participants in feminist activism biographically construct feminist subjectivity at the same time as they construct feminism as an ever-changing social movement.

The fractal label for the model reflects the use of a metaphor taken from fractal geometry, a new kind of geometry first fully articulated by the French mathematician, Benoit Mandelbrot, in 1975. While fractals and fractal geometry are well known in the natural sciences, the theoretical possibilities opened up by fractal geometry are only recently being explored by social scientists.[31]

Often found in nature, fractals are shapes that exhibit some interesting characteristics that until the 1970s presented problems for mathematicians because they could not be understood within the terms of Cartesian coordinate geometry. Two major defining features of fractals are that they exhibit *self-similarity* at various scales, and that they are created through processes of *iteration*. Self-similarity means that as you zoom in and focus on any part of a fractal shape or object, you will see the original shape repeated at a smaller scale. A good example from nature is a fern. If we look closely at a portion of a fern frond, we see that the shape of the entire frond is repeated on a smaller scale, and repeated again on an even smaller scale. Working in the opposite direction, a small portion of the frond contains within it the shape of the whole. The iterative process through which fractals are produced involves repeatedly carrying out a particular operation and feeding the result back into the next iteration of the process. Mathematically, the process of iteration can continue infinitely; however, with most fractals in nature this recursive process fades away as the scale becomes infinitesimally small.[32]

Fractal geometry provides a useful metaphor for thinking about subjectivity, particularly subjectivity as it exists in late-modern society. Articulating a position common among feminist postmodern/poststructuralist writers, Jane Flax hopefully imagines "subjectivities whose desires for multiplicity can impel them toward emancipatory action. These subjectivities would be fluid rather than solid, contextual rather than universal, and process oriented rather than topographical."[33] Based on a type of geometry that came into being because previous Euclidian and Cartesian geometries were not up to the task of understanding the complexities of the Information Age, the concept of fractal subjectivity meets this requirement.

According to the fractal model developed in this book, the process of becoming and being feminist involves four intertwined components of subjectivity—knowing (consciousness), feeling (emotions), belonging (identity), and doing (action)—each of which exists not only at the personal level, but also at the collective level. Ways of knowing, feeling, belonging, and doing are constructed collectively as discourses and practices by movements and by institutions and groups within the field or environment of action. These collective discourses and practices become available to individuals as resources for constructing subjectivity/biography and for acting in the world. While these four components do not comprise the sum total of subjectivity, I have focused on them because of their centrality to understanding how movement-related subjectivities are created.

The process of becoming and being feminist first involves thinking about or knowing the world in a certain, feminist way. This is the aspect of feminist subjectivity that has generally been referred to as feminist consciousness, a shared way of understanding or *knowing* the world that includes an awareness of and rejection of gender inequality as being unjust, unnecessary, and worth fighting against. Women encounter feminist ideas in a variety of settings (micromobilization contexts) and at different life stages. But, whenever and however this occurs, part of becoming feminist is coming to accept a set of beliefs (frames) that define women's problems (and problems one faces personally as a woman), at least partially in structural terms as a gendered form of social injustice. This does not imply a lack of recognition of other axes of injustice, but to be feminist there must be awareness of gender-based injustice.

Second, feminist subjectivity involves experiencing certain *feelings* about the world that can be identified as feminist. This is an aspect of feminist subjectivity that, although often implied in the concept of feminist consciousness, has not been extensively analyzed. Of the emotions that have received attention, anger is the most prominent. There has been much written about anger associated with feminist consciousness. For example, Verta Taylor has written about the way in which feminist organizations transform negative emotions such as shame and depression into anger and action.[34] More recently, other emotions associated with feminist subjectivity have been receiving attention from feminist and social movements scholars. The positive emotions of empathy and affection for other women promoted by feminism have been noted.[35] These agentic emotions of anger and empathy/love (when directed toward other women) have been identified by feminists as "outlaw emotions."[36]

The third component of feminist subjectivity involves identifying yourself as *belonging*, or claiming to belong, to the group or category of people called feminists. As we have seen, social movements scholars have referred to this as the "we" feeling of sharing a collective identity with others in the movement.[37] In much early feminist work, this "we" feeling was expressed through the term "sisterhood," and it was assumed to flow automatically from feminist consciousness. However, in this fractal model, identifying with feminist groups or organizations or with feminism as a social movement is not synonymous with possessing feminist consciousness or feminist emotions. As feminist poststructuralists and NSM theorists have noted, being a "we" is a necessarily complex and constructed process. For the individual, coming to see oneself as part of a "we" is also complex. The "I'm not a feminist, but . . ." phenomenon indicates that many women incorporate aspects of feminist consciousness into their understanding of the world without defining themselves, publicly or privately, as feminists. The stigma attached to feminism as a label of identity in the broader society is one reason for this, but interpersonal tensions between women and between groups of women—misreadings, misunderstandings, and misrecognitions—all play a part.

Finally, being feminist involves *doing* feminist types of things. In this book, I argue that this involves more than the usual activities associated with being an activist, that is, organizing and/or attending protests or rallies, signing petitions, and so on. It also includes a myriad of actions taken in daily life, not *just* in or through movement organizations that are designed to challenge gender assumptions and the subordinate status of women. From buying women's music, books, and artwork, through producing newsletters, to volunteering as rape crisis counselors, women from this study demonstrated their commitment to other women and to feminism. They also worked to disrupt gender hierarchy through the way they raised their children and through the way they conducted paid work, leisure, and volunteer work. Thus, for the women in this study, doing feminism was about using feminist knowledge and emotions to change the world and improve the lives of women in all areas of their lives. As with the other components of feminist subjectivity, some aspects of doing feminism, as I define it, are practiced by women who do not identify themselves as feminist, and who are not self-consciously aware of any feminist thoughts and emotions directing such action.

The process of becoming and being feminist can be initiated by experiences that impact upon any one of the four dimensions of subjectivity described previously. Participation in movement events (doing) may precede and even lead to changes in knowing. For example, a number of women in this study attended the workshop with very little prior knowledge of feminism as either a movement or an ideology. They signed up for the weekend because a friend suggested they do so, or because they saw an advertisement for it and simply liked the idea of spending a weekend away from home. Some of these women were actively seeking new experiences that would potentially open up new ways of being.

For other women, their emotional response to a particular life event was the starting point for becoming involved in feminism. The need to work through the emotional trauma of rape led one woman to the local women's center for counseling, where she came into contact with feminist women and feminist ideas. For some, emotions associated with negative experiences of marriage—disappointment, boredom, loneliness, and resentment—prompted an active search for alternative understandings of the world and of themselves. Others described a sense of belonging to a collectivity of women that extended back into childhood and led them, as adults, to gravitate toward feminist networks and overt forms of activism.

This feature of the fractal model—that the process of becoming feminist can begin from knowing, feeling, belonging, or doing—differentiates it from other models in the social movements' literature that present the process of becoming involved in collective action (recruitment) as linear and as necessarily emerging in a specific order. In models consistent with RMT and its rationalist conception of the self, this order has usually prioritized change in consciousness as the first step in the process.[38] In the collective behavior approach, an emotional reaction to structural strain was the starting point, while for NSMT, belonging to a network in a specific milieu is prioritized. Feminist models are similarly limited in this respect. The feminist click models and consciousness-raising models, like RMT, prioritize changes in consciousness. Identity-based models prioritize belonging to a particular category of people, either women in general or more limited categories such as Black women, lesbian women, working-class women, and so forth. Finally, postmodern approaches tend to focus on individualized resistance, thus prioritizing a form of doing feminism that is divorced from knowing and feeling as collective phenomena, and, more particularly, from belonging to a collectivity of others who are also acting to bring about change. To sum up, approaches that are linear or that prioritize one component of subjectivity over others are like the blind man and the elephant, describing one possible way of seeing the process that is not so much wrong as dramatically incomplete.

Another core feature of the fractal model of becoming and being feminist presented in this book is the emphasis placed on the structured nature of the field of action in which these processes take place. I argue that the ongoing processes of self-construction inherent in becoming and being feminist must be understood as occurring within the context of the struggle between movements (in this case, feminist women's movements) and the various individuals, groups, and institutions that make up the wider social, cultural, and political environment. The collective beliefs, emotions, identities, and actions constructed by movements conflict with and contest those generated by institutions and groups such as families, workplaces, the media, and state agencies. This conflict takes place within a structured environment where power is unevenly distributed. The significance of this often hostile environment is evident in the stories of the women interviewed for this study and is stressed theoretically in terms of its impact on possibilities for personal change and the development of feminist subjectivity. Just as people make history, but not under conditions of their own choosing, people create themselves as subjects of their own biography, but not under conditions of their own choosing and not just as they choose. Movements matter to people not because they create ready-made biographies/subjectivities for them to adopt—although movement leaders do sometimes attempt to do so—but because they alter the conditions within which individuals can create biography/subjectivity.

Returning to the fractal nature of the model, I contend that whether we are talking about consciousness, emotions, identity, or action, the construction of movement-related subjectivities and collective action are fractal-like in that they are produced iteratively and they exhibit elements of self-similarity at different scales. A narrative or biographical approach demonstrates the iterative nature of human subjectivity. People make sense of subjectivity—their own and that of others—through biographically constructing themselves and others as beings with a past, present, and future. The past, the present, and the future are connected through recursive processes of iteration; thus, change and continuity are both inherent in the process. Collective and historical narratives of identity are continually told, retold, and relived through the lives of individuals.

Self-similarity is also evident. If we consider the subjectivity/biography of one individual in all its particularity, we can see in it the patterns of the society, culture, and times they are a part of. Alternatively, if we zoom out to look at society and culture on a macro level, we see many of the same patterns, tensions, and contradictions evident at the individual level, played out in society at large. Thus, the fractal metaphor is useful for envisioning micro and macro levels of analysis, and structure and agency models of the self, not as dichotomous alternatives, but as fundamentally related aspects of the same process. The personal is political and the political is personal.

CHAPTER 2

Feminist Movements:
Past, Present, Local, and Global

In their analysis of social movements, new social movements theorists have drawn attention to the vast macro-level social, political, and cultural changes that have taken place during the twentieth century as western nations have been transformed from modern, industrial societies to late-modern, postindustrial societies. There is not space nor necessity here to provide a full description of these changes. However, the implications these changes have, not only for our understanding of subjectivity, but also for the subjective possibilities that late-modern society makes available to individuals, dictate the need to examine these changes briefly, particularly as they intersect with the history of feminist women's movements. In other words, if we are to understand how feminist women's movements matter to the individuals who become involved in them, we must have some understanding of where these movements have come from, how they spread, and how they fit within the broader social, geographical, and historical fabric.

Women today have inherited the legacy of earlier waves of feminist activism that have contributed to the culture and politics of modern Western societies. Past gains in legislative reform, changed collective consciousness, and continuing organizations all form part of the social environment in which Australian, British, and American women today discover feminism and become feminist. However, in this chapter my focus is primarily on Australian feminist movements and their achievements as the contextual background for the case study material presented in the rest of the book. My goal is to situate the study group as representative of 1990s feminism as constituted by local women's movement communities that exist as nodes within a larger, global, and historical network of relationships and information flows.

An Old "New" Movement

Although new social movements theorists have included feminism as one of the "new" movements that arose in the late 1960s, feminism as a global movement has roots that stretch back long before that time. The account I present here begins in the late nineteenth century, a time of heightened social ferment and reform throughout the Western world, with both labor movements and women's movements contributing to the ongoing process of modernization. In relation to women's place in society, influential works such as Mill's *The Subjection of Women* and Wollstonecraft's *Vindication of the Rights of Women* circulated widely and influenced the thinking of political elites in Europe and in settler societies such as the United States, Canada, New Zealand, and Australia.[1] Within this climate, women's movements addressed a range of issues concerning the status and rights of women. Central issues included legal impediments women faced in relation to marriage, divorce, child custody, and property rights; questions of sexual morality and temperance (in particular the need to regulate male behavior in these areas); the rights of working women; the detrimental effects of women's economic dependence on men; and the right of girls and women to receive an education. While womanhood suffrage was an important symbolic goal and rallying point for activism, nineteenth century feminists sought access to the ballot box in order to bring about broader legal, social, educational, and cultural reform. In Australia, as elsewhere, the range of issues associated with the "woman question" provided a focus for women's activism in suffrage societies, in labor organizations, and in the Woman's Christian Temperance Union, an international movement organization that gained strong support from Australian women.

From the beginning, Australian feminism incorporated a strong international focus. Australian feminists were not only aware of feminist literature emanating from Britain and the United States, they were also linked into international networks through travel, migration, and lecture tours. Ideas, campaigns, and protest tactics were transported through these international links. Australian attempts to reform marriage and to see the enactment of Married Women's Property legislation, for example, followed and reflected similar campaigns in the United States and Britain. Prominent Australian activists attended meetings of the League of Nations, the Pan-Pacific Women's Conferences, and international women's suffrage congresses. Some Australian feminists even participated in marches organized by suffragettes in London.[2]

Australian women gained the vote and the right to stand for political office in 1902, decades before either their British or American counterparts.[3] Once this fight was won, the focus of feminist activism changed as new women's organizations were formed to mobilize the woman's vote. Throughout the twentieth century, feminist activism continued on a number of fronts. The fight for equal pay became a major focus of struggle as lower wages for women were institutionalized through Australia's centralized system of industrial awards. In 1937, trade unions and women's organizations joined forces to establish a Council of Action for Equal Pay that campaigned nationally.[4] Spurred on by the higher wages earned by women during the Second World War, the campaign for equal pay continued throughout the postwar years. The international focus of Australian feminism remained strong following the Second World War, particularly among left-wing women who regularly celebrated International Women's Day with programs of events that were actively internationalist.[5]

Gains were made throughout the first half of the twentieth century. However, by the late 1960s, on the eve of the eruption of the women's liberation movement, women still faced significant discrimination and disadvantage in the workforce and elsewhere. Economically, despite years of activism and some minor improvements, lower rates of pay for women were still officially sanctioned, and direct and indirect discrimination in employment was rife. Increasing numbers of women entered the paid workforce during the 1950s and 1960s, but they were largely concentrated in female-dominated industries and occupations that were less well paid and enjoyed lower status than male-dominated areas. Still viewed primarily as the dependents of male breadwinners, women were barred access to many technical and trade-based occupations. Cultural expectations required women, particularly those who were mothers, to prioritize domestic duties over paid work. Consequently, childcare services were limited and expensive.

Consistent with the secondary position occupied by women in the labor market, the education of girls was not highly valued. In the early 1970s, researchers found that parents, teachers, and girls themselves held lower academic expectations of girls than of boys.[6] Girls were streamed into gender-specific areas of study, both at secondary school and university. In politics, Australian women had not progressed as far as they might have been expected either, given that Australia was the first nation where women gained not only the right to vote, but also the right to stand for election. Two women were elected to the Australian Parliament in 1943, but in 1972 there were no women members of the House of Representatives.[7] Overall, women and their contributions to Australian society were undervalued and this was further reflected in the narrow stereotypes of women portrayed in the media and advertising.

New Waves

A new phase of feminist activism began with the emergence of women's liberation. Australia, along with most other Western democracies, experienced a period of intense social movement activity during the late 1960s and early 1970s. In particular, the anti-Vietnam War movement radicalized diverse groups of people, including the women who started the first women's liberation groups in the U.S. and in Australia. These young university women felt frustrated over the limited roles available to women in the New Left and over the often blatant sexism of their male colleagues. Women's liberation groups were established in Australia in Sydney in 1969, and then in Melbourne, Adelaide, and Brisbane early in 1970.[8] Almost simultaneously with the emergence of women's liberation among Australian university students, Zelda D'Aprano—an older woman who was a member of the Communist Party and a long-term activist in the union movement —staged a sensational protest for equal pay by chaining herself to a government building in Melbourne. Publicity surrounding the chain-up led other women to join her and shortly thereafter a Women's Action Committee was formed as "a women-only activist group dedicated to alleviating the oppression of women in all aspects of their lives."[9]

From this beginning, the new women's liberation movement spread rapidly with small groups being formed throughout the country, first at the universities and in the capital cities, and then in the suburbs and regional towns. These groups published newsletters and ran consciousness-raising sessions. They drew extensively on overseas literature and were particularly influenced by radical feminist ideas emanating from the United States and Britain.[10] They eagerly accepted the idea that "the personal is political" and, along with the practice of consciousness raising, adopted new models of organization based on nonhierarchical and collective principles. Within a year there were 34 groups in Melbourne alone, with several thousand women involved in the Women's Action Group by 1972.[11]

Another significant development was the establishment of the Women's Electoral Lobby (WEL) in February 1972. The American National Organization for Women (NOW) inspired the setting up of WEL, and in terms of ideology and political strategy, WEL was similar to NOW. WEL began with the initial goal of surveying political candidates in the 1972 federal election to ascertain their views on a range of issues of importance to women. WEL grew rapidly and by year's end had a national membership of nearly 2,000 in branches across the country. As membership grew, WEL enlisted increasing numbers of mainstream, middle-class women who were attracted to its reformist strategies, and the membership, organizational structure, and strategies of WEL increasingly diverged from women's liberation.[12]

Most of the women who became involved in women's liberation groups or WEL saw little connection between their protests and the activities of earlier feminists. They lacked knowledge of the struggles fought by their predecessors; indeed, they rejected the label of feminist because of the negative, staid images feminism brought to mind. Despite this less than positive appraisal, the goals of the new movement were not that different from those pursued by earlier feminists. Women's liberationists criticized the institution of marriage, attacked the double standard of sexual morality that sanctioned the sexual exploitation of women, and demanded economic, social, and educational change. They diverged from the first wave by also criticizing the institution of motherhood, by rejecting the sexual division of labor (both within the home and the paid workforce), and by couching their concerns regarding the sexual exploitation of women within a generally more sexually permissive context. They demanded the right to control their own bodies and fertility through contraception and access to safe abortions, and the right to explore and freely express their own sexual needs.

As was the case for earlier feminist activists, economic issues were viewed as fundamental by women's liberationists. Drawing on Marxist analysis, they argued that equality between the sexes could only be based on women's entry into and equality within the paid workforce. Education was also linked to the issue of economic independence since the education received by girls was seen to channel them into "feminine" occupations that generally attracted lower status and lower pay. Working-class activists in the movement knew from personal experience the importance of economic equality for women. The difficulty they faced paying rent and supporting themselves on women's wages underpinned their commitment to equality in the workforce. For middle-class women's liberationists, it was access to the satisfaction of a career, in addition to economic independence, that motivated their demands in this area.[13] Although not always to the same extent, or in the same ways, limited employment options, institutionalized discrimination, and pay differentials disadvantaged all women, whether they were working class, middle class, married, or single.

Although the issues and demands of women's liberation were closer to those of earlier feminists than most participants acknowledged, the strategies of protest adopted by the new groups were more militant than those of their immediate predecessors. Talking about the women's organizations active in Australia in the decades following World War Two, Curthoys suggests that they, "including those in which communists were active, were generally respectable in tone, using traditional and polite forms of protest, and—working in a generally hostile environment—setting moderate targets."[14] In contrast, the women's liberation movement embraced militant direct action. In addition to chain-ups—in public bars and over the equal pay issue—marches, rallies, and public protests proliferated. Following the example of women's liberationists in the United States, public protests were staged in opposition to beauty contests and women marched in the street to demand abortion law reform. Australian feminists also adopted *Reclaim the Night* in 1978. Originating in Italy in 1976, they were held in Britain in 1977 and in the United States (using the name "Take Back the Night") in 1978.[15] Held at night, demonstrators marched through the streets protesting against violence against women.[16]

As the decade of the 1970s progressed, new developments emerged and the label women's liberation was generally dropped in favor of feminism. Rallies and protest marches, to mark International Women's Day and *Reclaim the Night,* proliferated alongside the development of new strategies that directly addressed women's problems and needs. In Australia, as elsewhere in the Western world, women's centers and women's services sprang up, first in the major cities and then in regional centers around the country.

Multipurpose centers or houses were the earliest form of women's services to grow out of this period of activism.[17] The first feminist women's centers in Australia opened in the early 1970s. The Sydney Women's Liberation House and the Adelaide Women's Liberation Centre both opened in 1970, and in 1972 a women's liberation center opened in Melbourne.[18] Later, these became the starting points for more specifically focused services such as refuges, rape crisis, and women's health services. The first feminist women's refuge, Elsie, was established in Sydney in 1974 when a group of women broke in and took possession of two vacant houses owned by the Church of England.[19] At around the same time, Control, a women's health collective in Sydney, received government funding to establish a women's health center. The opening of that center—the Leichhardt Community Women's Centre—marked the "beginning of what would, over the next decade and a half, become a significant new feature of the Australian primary care landscape: state-funded feminist women's health centers, run by women for women."[20] Throughout the rest of the 1970s and into the 1980s and 1990s, the refuge movement, the Women's Health Movement, and the development of feminist sexual assault services went from strength to strength.

Related to the growth of feminist women's services in Australia is the unique relationship that developed between feminism and the state. This relationship began with the election of the Whitlam Labor government in 1972, the establishment of a National Advisory Committee, and the appointment of a Women's Advisor in 1973.[21] From this beginning, various women's units, advisory committees, and equal opportunity offices were established in both federal and state bureaucracies. Thus, throughout the 1970s and 1980s feminists entered the bureaucracy in increasing numbers, where they attempted to implement feminist agendas by shaping government policy and legislation, and by directing funding to women's services.

Finally, the growth of women's cultural and intellectual pursuits constitutes another major component of Australian feminism in the 1970s and 1980s. Feminism provided a boost to women's confidence and contributed to a revaluation of women's creative abilities. This was expressed through an outpouring of women's writing, theater, radio, filmmaking, and academic scholarship.[22]

Ideology, Divisions, and Differences

Drawing on overseas literature and images, Australian women's liberationists saw themselves as part of an international women's movement based on a supposedly shared notion of sisterhood. However, here, as elsewhere, the ideal did not always translate easily into practice. Anne Summers described a sense of disillusionment occurring as early as 1970, following the first women's liberation conference held in Melbourne.[23] The causes of the divisions and hostility that arose within the movement were complex and it is difficult to deal with them succinctly. Ideology was one basis of difference and this also led to debates over strategy.

Philosophical commitments to different ideologies and strategies were behind many of the conflicts and crises that have beset feminist women's health and welfare services.[24] Tensions also arose between feminists in the bureaucracy and those in the broader women's movement. In the words of Anna Yeatman, there was "considerable ambivalence within the grassroots women's movement about women who [were] able to make well-paid careers out of feminism, and who turn[ed] its ideology into the arcane dialects of public bureaucracy on the one hand, and academe on the other."[25] This ambivalence was reflected in the initially derogatory terms "femocrat" and "femocracy" used to describe feminists working within state bureaucracies. The classification of feminists into liberal, socialist, and radical camps, although somewhat outdated now, was common in the 1970s and 1980s and contributed to the animosity between some grassroots activists and femocrats. On the other hand, there has been recognition from some quarters of the feminist commitment of femocrats, the hostile environment they have worked in, and of the gains they have achieved for women.[26] Dale Spender claims femocrats "are worth their weight in gold to Australian women."[27]

In Australia, as elsewhere, divisions also emerged based on the diverse life experiences of women, and on perceived and real exclusions. Lesbians, Aboriginal women, immigrant women, and working-class women all expressed concern that the movement agenda was being driven by the interests of heterosexual, middle-class Anglo-Australian women.

Lesbians have played a central role in the women's movement in Australia with many women's refuges, health centers, and rape crisis services benefiting from their active involvement. Lesbians have also made a major contribution to the building of women's culture and feminist theory. However, despite this significant contribution, the relationship between lesbian and heterosexual women in the movement has often been uneasy and tense. Anti-lesbian attitudes and behaviors have been experienced by many lesbians in the movement.[28] On the other hand, claims by some political lesbians that heterosexual women are "collaborators with the enemy" and that "serious feminists have no choice but to abandon heterosexuality" could not be expected to contribute to harmonious relationships between heterosexual and lesbian feminists.[29]

During the early years of women's liberation in Australia, concerns that paralleled those of "women of color" in the United States and Britain were raised about the relevance of the movement to the situation of Aboriginal women. Roberta Sykes, a prominent Black activist who grew up in north Queensland, was critical of white liberationists' ignorance and lack of concern for the specific oppression faced by Aboriginal women. She called upon white women to recognize both the racist and sexist nature of the oppression faced by Aboriginal women and to take action against racism.[30] Frustration expressed by Aboriginal women in relation to the white women's movement frequently concerned the prioritizing of sex oppression over race oppression and the feeling that Aboriginal women were expected to choose between loyalty to black men as partners in the fight against racism, or loyalty to white women in the fight against sexism. Time and again, Aboriginal women have pointed out the primacy, for them, of racist oppression and the need for solidarity with Aboriginal men in fighting this.[31] Lessons were learned slowly and painfully, and tensions persist today.

The tendency within feminist theory to universalize the experiences of white, middle-class women has not only been problematic from the perspective of Aboriginal women, but also from that of non-Anglo immigrant women. According to Kaplan, the women's movement discovered migrant women as "victims" in the 1970s, but did not accept them as equal partners.[32] In the face of ethnocentrism and exclusion, non-English speaking background women have formed their own organizations and women's services.[33]

Finally, as Bulbeck suggests, "one of the most vitriolic and long-lasting debates within feminist scholarship contests whether feminism has served largely white middle-class women or also responds to the needs of working-class" women.[34] However, it is not clear to what extent such criticisms have come from working-class women themselves or from middle-class women applying a class analysis. Zelda D'Aprano's response to the debate is interesting in this regard. D'Aprano, a founding member of the Women's Action Committee in Melbourne and a woman whose working-class credentials cannot be questioned, felt frustrated and angry over constant references to the movement as middle class. She wrote the following in the November 1973 edition of the Women's Liberation Newsletter:

> There are women who are not industrial workers who proceed to tell all of us so-called "middle-class" women what working-class women want. In my anger, I have asked myself why am I ignored even though all the women know I am an industrial worker? . . . Why are all the women in the Movement who work in offices, shops etc. being told they are middle class?[35]

Although the movement has not removed inequalities based on class, campaigns for equal pay and for antidiscrimination and equal opportunity legislation have improved the prospects of working women across the board. For example, despite critics' accusations that the federal Sex Discrimination Act, passed in 1984, would primarily benefit middle-class career women, in fact it has been widely utilized by working women employed in small businesses and shops. Quentin Bryce, the second Commonwealth Sex Discrimination Commissioner, reported that young women had told her "about getting a copy of the Act or one of our brochures and taking it and saying to their employer 'you can't DO that to me, it's against the law.'"[36] Furthermore, many working-class women have been part of the movement and have been empowered through their involvement. Nonetheless, as D'Aprano pointed out in a 1995 edition of her autobiography, as "more working women enter the Movement and become aware and articulate, they cease to be seen as working class and the cry continues, 'Where are the working-class women?'"[37]

Local Connections
Queensland women have participated in all phases of the women's movement since the late nineteenth century. Suffrage organizations existed in Brisbane and in regional centers, including the north Queensland towns of Charters Towers and Townsville. During the 1930s and 1940s, communist women in north Queensland developed a strong and independent movement based on autonomous women's groups. The novelist, communist, and militant feminist, Jean Devanny, played a significant role in establishing Women's Progress Clubs throughout north Queensland during this time.[38] These clubs interspersed political activities with social work and

feminist activism. Townsville women were also among the foundation members of the Union of Australian Women (UAW), a left-wing organization that lobbied for equal pay and government subsidies for child care centers. Significantly, the UAW was one of the women's organizations that provided continuity between earlier women's activism and the emergence of women's liberation in Australia.[39]

Building on this long history of left-wing activism, women in north Queensland were involved in the union movement, the peace movement, and the movement for Indigenous rights during the 1960s. These movements paved the way for the women's liberation movement that reached Townsville by the early 1970s. Women's liberation ushered in a vibrant period at the local level with women active across a range of organizations from the more conservative Country Women's Association and National Council of Women, through the moderate Family Planning Association and Women's Electoral Lobby, to radical women's liberation consciousness-raising groups.[40] During International Women's Year, 1975, International Women's Day was celebrated with marches in towns and cities across the country, including Townsville.

In Townsville, as elsewhere, an outcome of this period of feminist activism was the setting up of women's centers and services. A women's resource center was established in 1973 with funding from the newly elected Labor government. Although a change of government led to a loss of funding and closure of the center in 1975, during the two to three years of its existence, it served as a base for a food co-op, a craft co-op, WEL meetings, and women's liberation meetings. Women from a range of organizations worked together on specific issues, and a few women held multiple memberships and worked across groups.[41] Such cooperation between more conservative, established women's organizations and the spontaneous new women's liberation groups is noteworthy and may be a particular feature of activism in smaller, regional centers in contrast to large capital cities. A more interconnected set of networks probably existed between groups in this local environment, leading to less rigidly defined boundaries.

From the late 1970s into the 1980s, several efforts were made to reestablish a women's center and services in Townsville. One such attempt followed a successful women's conference held in 1984. The Townsville Women's Centre operated on donations of money and time for 18 months before achieving external funding. It provided space for women's activities and services, an organizational base for coordinating campaigns and rallies, and a venue for visiting feminists.[42] Despite relocation to new premises and some periods of instability and internal conflict, this center still exists today.[43]

Conclusion

A general agreement exists among social movements scholars that structurally, social movements consist of "networks of informal interaction between a plurality of individuals, groups, and/or organizations, engaged in a political and/or cultural conflict."[44] These networks, as we have seen in relation to feminist movements, are not only geographical, linking the local with the global, but also they are historical, linking the past with the present. In keeping with the fractal metaphor, whichever point in this network we choose to focus upon, the movement as a whole and the individuals, groups, and organizations that make up the network are related. Clearly, feminism as a social movement is not the same everywhere and at all times, but nonetheless similar patterns can be found in the issues, strategies, difficulties, and achievements of feminist women's movements across time and space and at macro and micro levels. Aspects of the movement as an international phenomenon are reflected in the local and vice versa. The past is reflected in the present, and the past is interpreted and understood in light of the present. Not only does the movement exhibit self-similarity in this way, but it can be seen to be generated through iterative processes whereby beliefs, emotions, identities, and ways of acting spread throughout the network between the past and the present and the local and the global. Thus, although the women I interviewed for this study live in a part of the world that is remote from the capital cities and centers of feminist activism in Australia, the United States, and Europe, their experiences of discovering feminism, of becoming feminist, and of practicing feminism reflect and are reflected in the historical, contemporary, local, and global feminist women's movements.

CHAPTER 3

Becoming Feminist:
Paths and Passages

The women in this study arrived at an understanding of feminism from a variety of routes and at different points in their lives. The settings in which they encountered feminism ranged from universities, through religious organizations and personal growth workshops, to lesbian and gay political groups. Some first encountered feminism in their youth, while others did so in middle age. Through exploring the paths and passages they followed in their journeys to becoming feminist, this chapter aims to demonstrate the variety of ways in which the four components of feminist subjectivity —knowing, feeling, belonging, and doing—come together in the lives of individual women and how the social, cultural, and political environment shapes this process.

The first major section of the chapter looks at the pattern of social settings or micromobilization contexts through which the women initially encountered feminism. Several locations were identified through the data as offering a social context conducive to drawing women towards feminist involvement. These micromobilization contexts are described and illustrated with examples from the interview material. Patterns also emerged in the way women talked about the process of adopting feminist subjectivity and of taking up a position within feminist networks. These biographical accounts of becoming feminist are presented in the next section. The following section considers changes in feminist subjectivity between the initial and follow-up interviews, and examines the links between micromobilization contexts, biographical trajectories, and the level of feminist identification.

Postmodern society is sometimes characterized as providing a myriad of resources for interpreting the world and for defining a sense of self. However, the grievances behind the identity claims made by social movements must not be ignored. Feminist frames, ontological narratives, and networks that support feminist subjectivity are more readily available to some women than others. Age cohort, social class, education, and geographical location are all important factors in determining access to feminist ideas and networks. The final section of this chapter discusses these issues in light of the data presented in this chapter and of the fractal model of movement involvement outlined in Chapter 1.

Making Contact through Micromobilization Contexts

Micromobilization contexts are defined by Doug McAdam as small group settings where "processes of collective attribution are combined with rudimentary forms of organization to produce mobilization for collective action."[1] They are settings where subjective meanings and movement identities are constructed. Most social movements scholars agree upon the importance of social networks in drawing people into movement involvement.[2] People with links to existing movement members are more likely to be targets of recruitment efforts and are more likely to become involved than those outside such networks. Movement networks play a central role in providing a context for processes of consciousness-raising, identity construction, and motivation building.[3] While macro political conditions are the source of the grievances around which movements mobilize, these conditions do not automatically produce collective action. They only offer "a certain objective 'structural potential' for collective political action. Mediating between opportunity and action are people and the subjective meanings they attach to their situations."[4]

Collective consciousness does not arise spontaneously from one's structural location. While oppression may be an objective fact, this fact is often obscured. Thus, "cognitive liberation" is a necessary step in bringing about social change. Movements researchers have identified the social psychological processes of attribution and framing as central to this process. The concept of micromobilization context captures this aspect of movement networks, providing a conceptual "bridge" between micro and macro levels of analysis.

Movement organizations and events can provide the context for mobilization, but many other settings also operate as micromobilization contexts. Preexisting political groups, informal friendship networks, and nonpolitical groups such as clubs and churches can provide suitable environments for facilitating the development of movement subjectivity and recruitment to activism. Meyer and Whittier introduced the concept of "social movement spillover" to capture the way in which the "ideas, tactics, style, participants, and organizations of one movement often *spill over* its boundaries to affect other social movements."[5] In a similar manner, Katzenstein has described a process of unobtrusive mobilization whereby feminist ideas have infiltrated mainstream institutions such as education, the church, and the military.[6] Through spillover and unobtrusive mobilization, groups and organizations not specifically identified as feminist may function as micromobilization contexts for the development of feminist consciousness and identity.

It could also be said that feminist ideas have entered mainstream discourse via the mass media, thus providing another avenue through which women can become aware of feminist ideas. In contemporary Western societies (and some non-Western societies), varieties of feminist discourse circulate widely via television, movies, magazines, popular books, newspapers, and the Internet. However, these avenues are limited in terms of drawing women into feminist involvement. First, media representations often provide a distorted view of feminism and feminists.[7] Second, and more importantly, the mass media do not provide links to feminist networks and groups that can support the process of becoming feminist. Where women in this study did mention the influence of television reports, magazine articles or popular feminist books on their view of the world and of their place as women in society, they usually also talked about the difficulty of making contact with other like-minded women. Thus, while media sources are able to provide minimal access to resources for knowing the world and the self in feminist terms, they do not provide access to the movement networks needed to become more fully involved or to develop a sense of belonging to a collective of feminist women. They do not provide the micromobilization contexts that are central to the process of recruitment.[8]

Despite the variety of avenues through which individuals can come into contact with feminist discourse and networks, not all women have the same access to these resources. Access to knowledge and identity resources, like other resources, is socially structured and reflects the grievances behind the identity claims of movements such as feminism. In this study, social location is reflected in the micromobilization contexts through which participants came into contact with feminist discourses and networks. The three most common settings mentioned as pivotal to the process of becoming feminist were educational institutions, the personal growth movement, and feminist service organizations. Together, these three micromobilization contexts accounted for more than 80 percent of cases. The remaining women encountered feminism through settings as varied as a women's church group, travel, and family relationships.

Higher Education—"That was the turning point . . . that was
when I really started to think about issues"

Since the 1970s, feminism has established a significant presence in universities, both within student politics and in the academic arena. This has provided a major route to feminism for the women in this study. The
experience of studying at university, either as a young woman or as a mature-age student, provided contact with feminism and contributed to the development of feminist consciousness and identity for 16 women (35 percent).

Campus politics and feminist student groups played a part in providing
access to both feminist ideas and networks, as did specific courses of study.
Alex said, "I went to university . . . and took on that whole feminist culture
from there." A number of women talked about joining feminist collectives
and rape crisis collectives on campus. Others described first encountering
feminism through attending campus-based events or meetings. The ideas
presented on such occasions articulated their own feelings of frustration
and resentment at the way women are treated in society. Emma recalled, "I
remember going to some of the meetings, and it was something I could relate to. It was sort of that feeling that, you know, 'this really makes sense.'
. . . It just explained lots of things that I didn't feel comfortable with."
Similarly, Laurie talked about the way in which feminist ideas encountered
at university meshed with her growing awareness of gender inequality.
Throughout childhood she had recognized and resented the fact that boys
had certain rights and status that were denied her. At university she responded readily to feminist campus politics:

> I think it was only by the time I got to university, first year, that I was
> able to give a word to what I had been unable to articulate all those
> years. That perception that something was not right, and not fair . . .
> That articulated for me that socialized discrimination that I had cer-
> tainly been aware of and sensitive to all my life.

Courses of study taken at university provided another avenue of access to
feminist ideas. Two women completed Women's Studies majors. Others
came across feminist ideas through courses in a range of disciplines including history, education, and welfare studies. As with student-based
events, course material often clarified and confirmed existing feelings and
beliefs. Talking about her time at university, Jocelyn suggested, "that really
changed things for me. That's when I started to get the academic theories
to my feelings."

For a small number of women, study resulted in a major shift in beliefs
and ideas. Toni, who studied as a mature-age student, talked about struggling to write a history paper and being loaned a feminist book by the
tutor that, she said, "helped me make sense of my world." Louise described

becoming "a rabid feminist" and, for a period of time, having little to do with her husband or sons, as a result of doing Women's Studies courses. For Louise, Women's Studies was "the eye opener," revealing "how women have been treated over the years." The language of having one's eyes opened was also used by Lorna to describe the impact on her life of discovering feminism through a university course on minority groups:

> I discovered feminism and I began to have to challenge my past attitudes and beliefs and just, I think it's built on from there . . . That was the turning point. That was when I really started to think about issues . . . It was such a struggle for me to give up some of the beliefs that I had at the time, about what [were] appropriate roles and language, you know, sexist language. I couldn't sort of—I used to get caught up in those arguments about "Oh, it's just trivial to be sort of focusing on arguing that if we use 'man' all the time as the neutral, that's somehow damaging," you know. It was really—and once your eyes are opened, and that might take a hell of a lot of prizing open, but once they are, it's like as if you can't ever close them again, never, never, never can you go back to being as unaware as you were before.

While university or college was the most common context in which the women in this study encountered feminism, it only accounted for around one third of the sample. Given their age profile, approximately one half of the women completed their schooling at a time when access to post-school study was limited in Australia, particularly in regional areas and particularly for women. Higher education expanded massively from the mid-1970s and beyond, when the Whitlam Labor government abolished fees and introduced student living allowances. Consequently, throughout the 1980s a greater proportion of young women went on to university or college following high school. Access for mature-age students also improved at this time. Consistent with this expansion of higher education, a larger proportion of the younger women I interviewed attended university straight from high school.

Aside from the question of opportunity, not all women desire to undertake study at university or college, so, if they are to come into contact with feminism, other avenues are necessary. For the women in this study, community-based personal growth organizations provided another avenue.

Personal Growth Movement—"That was where it all started for me"

The personal growth and self-help movements have been criticized by some feminists for providing psychologized, individualized forms of emotional support that represent a depoliticization of the women's movement.[9] However, in this study, the personal growth movement can be seen to have provided a bridge to feminist ideas for a significant number of women.[10] After higher education, it was the next most common setting in which interviewees accessed feminism. Twelve women (27 percent) were exposed to feminist ideas and developed links to feminist networks through attending personal growth workshops or courses. Most of these workshops and courses were not explicitly feminist, nor were they affiliated with feminist organizations. Many were sponsored by community or church-based welfare organizations as part of their training program for volunteers and employees. However, feminist content was often introduced and links facilitated with feminist networks.

Participation in these activities was motivated in some cases by a desire to help others. Alternatively, it was in response to dissatisfaction with life and a desire to change and grow. Either way, the impact on these women's lives was often substantial. Margaret's description of her introduction to feminist thought highlights the impact feminist input into this type of activity can have:

> I'd only been here a couple of months when the Lifeline course [for volunteer telephone counselors] was advertised, and I knew that was an area that I wanted to work in . . . That was where it all started for me, . . . the whole concept of group discussions and all that sort of thing, . . . and some really good things happened there. And then, of course, Betty was employed there shortly after I started working there, . . . and she'd just come back from America, and she'd been very involved in feminist work there, so she was very keen to pass on all this information and it just sort of grew from there.

Stella also described her developing commitment to feminism as arising through involvement in a wide variety of personal growth and voluntary welfare organizations.

> I started getting involved in women's groups around 1979. And I went off to lots of group things, like . . . Gestalt workshops . . . Then I joined Lifeline and did all this lovely self-awareness, personal development stuff and thought "Gee, this all fits so well" and just through being exposed, I realized yes, there is a name for all this, and that's called feminism and rights, and personal power, yeah. So, probably, it's through the Lifeline movement and meeting other women who were prepared to stand up and be counted.

A further example that demonstrates the significance of personal growth groups is that of two women who attended the 1991 Winter Institute Weekend as a result of participating in a "rebuilding course" designed for women who had recently experienced a broken relationship. These women did not have any prior contact with feminism and their attendance at the Winter Institute Weekend was a direct result of encouragement from the course facilitator. For one, the weekend contributed to major changes in her life.

The discourse of personal growth shares with feminism the idea that the individual woman is of value, and that pursuit of personal growth is not a selfish pastime, but a worthwhile and acceptable activity. Through the involvement of women with explicitly feminist views in the personal growth movement, feminist analyses of personal problems become available to a broad range of women through a process Snow, Rochford, Worden, and Benford call frame extension.[11] Through frame extension a number of women in this study came to perceive personal problems in structural terms consistent with feminist analyses. They began to see their own problems as being based on gender inequality and not personal failing, thus setting them on the path to feminism.

Feminist Organizations—"I found it in the women's center"

For nine women (20 percent), feminist organizations or groups played a direct role in their "recruitment" to feminism. One woman came to identify with feminism through involvement with feminist groups in London in the early 1970s. The other eight were all exposed to feminism much more recently, either through the Mackay Women's Health and Information Centre, the Townsville Women's Centre, or the Winter Institute for Women.

Sarah became involved with the Mackay center after many years of community involvement and action related to her children's schooling and leisure activities. Talking about this time she said, "Because I was a woman, no one would take any notice of me . . . I stood my ground on different things but felt quite powerless most of the time. Powerful every now and again, but most of the time powerless because I was a woman." Within this context, an organization that focused on women's needs and issues was attractive:

> When I first got involved in the women's center here . . . it was the best thing since sliced bread for me . . . I thought "I need a bit of relief," and I found it in the women's center. We have these "You, beaut!" nights once a month and I would just feel completely relaxed and floating after being there. I mean we basically didn't— nothing much at all except talk, felt free to talk and air our views.

Sarah was exposed to feminist ideas and her growing identification with feminism was nurtured.

Judy responded directly to a newspaper advertisement for an Introduction to Feminism course offered by the Townsville Women's

Centre. From there she heard about the Winter Institute for Women and progressively became more involved. Responding directly to advertisements in this way was unusual. A more common situation involved friends either passing on information and brochures or encouraging participation in specific events. Catherine, whose first exposure to feminism was the 1991 Winter Institute Weekend, explained how she came to attend:

> I read a newspaper cutting from the year before . . . A friend from Mt. Isa days, who now lives in Townsville, cut it out of the *Bulletin*, and sent it to me. And when I saw the title—something about Angry Women, Gentle Women, I immediately thought, "If I have any chance at all, I'm going to get to that next year." . . . I kept the piece of paper and carted it round with me. I do this sort of thing if I want to do something badly enough, and I kept looking at it, and I rang Betty up occasionally and said, "Is it going to be on this year?" And when it got closer to the date she sent me the information.

Four women first heard about and participated in the Winter Institute for Women through this type of personal contact.

Other Contexts

The settings through which interviewees came into contact with feminism varied widely. While educational institutions, the personal growth movement, and feminist organizations together accounted for 37 women (82 percent), another eight (18 percent) encountered feminism in other settings. Consistent with the social movement spillover concept, involvement in other social movement activity was one avenue. The alternative lifestyle movement and environmental protest provided the context in which Rose encountered feminism, while Monique described initially becoming involved in lesbian and gay politics and, through this, becoming aware of feminist issues and networks:

> At that time I was involved in gay politics and organizing, beginning to organize a commercial for a conference . . . And then I got to know the women on the feminist collective on the radio station and they, I suppose, that period of time prompted my opinion.

Kathleen talked about the significance of her long-term involvement in the Grail, a laywomen's group associated with the Catholic Church. Talking about the role this group played in her movement towards feminism, she said

> It has been a very big factor in empowering me as a woman . . . It was very instrumental in my development and there were strong

friendships I formed with women who were in that group . . . People from the Grail are involved in different things like Women-Church, in Sydney, which brings out an absolutely magnificent magazine with alternative liturgies, say, for the baptism of girls and for breaking up of relationships, and oh, just really provoking, wonderful things.

The Grail Movement began in Europe in 1929 and was introduced to Australia in 1936. From its inception, it was based on radical ideas about the role of women within the church. It operated independently of the clergy and encouraged "members to be individual and innovative in attitude and practice."[12] As Kathleen points out, specifically feminist concepts and practices were introduced to the Grail in Sydney through the active involvement of members in Women-Church, an international Christian feminist movement that "grew out of the need shared by many feminists in the Church to find a home and identity within Catholicism."[13] Kathleen encountered feminist ideas and developed a feminist identity through the increasing presence of these feminist voices within the Grail. In this example, we see the significance of unobtrusive mobilization, with feminist discourse crossing the boundaries of religious institutions and organizations. Women-Church may have begun as a home for feminists within the church, but subsequently it has become more than that. It has created a feminist presence that provides opportunities for other churchwomen to come into contact with feminist ideas. Women who would be unlikely to get involved directly through feminist organizations may become aware of feminism through such channels.

Family relationships provided access to feminist ideas and networks for Jacqui. She explained that two of her sisters were social workers and that her ideas about feminism had been influenced by their input. Kate was introduced to feminist ideas through attending lunchtime seminars organized by the Equal Employment Opportunity Office at the university where she worked as a clerk. Finally, a handful of women talked about coming into contact with feminism, and developing feminist awareness, through travel and reading.

To sum up this section, women in this study came into contact with feminist ideas and networks through a variety of micromobilization contexts— university study, personal development groups, feminist organizations, and other settings such as a community radio station and a women's church group. In these settings they encountered feminist frames that made sense in terms of their own experiences. Many talked about a long-term but somewhat vague awareness of gender oppression in their lives, and associated feelings of frustration and dissatisfaction, but it was within the social contexts described here that they discovered a language with which to express these feelings and begin to change their lives. In these settings, their experiences and feelings were legitimated and, in the company of other women for whom feminist frames also made sense, they were encouraged to develop a feminist sense of self.

Becoming Feminist: Biographical Accounts

The way in which interviewees described the process of becoming feminist varied not only in relation to the micromobilization contexts through which they accessed feminist cognitive and relational resources, but also in terms of how readily available such resources were and how actively they were sought. This variation is evident in the biographical stories the women told about how they became feminist. Looking at these stories, a range of trajectories is evident.[14] A minority (20 percent) saw themselves as having always been feminist, while the rest described a process of transition. Some described this transition as gradual and evolutionary, simply part of the development and unfolding of their lives. Others described a more active search for meaning and identity.[15] I have labeled these trajectories as "always feminist," "evolving feminist," and "personal quest" accounts.

In recent times biographical approaches to movement identities have gained prominence, just as narrative approaches to identity have been put forward more generally as an alternative to static constructions of social identity prevalent in orthodox social psychology.[16] In the construction of a biographical account of becoming feminist, identity is not achieved through categorization as in social identity theory, but through locating oneself in a process that is historical and relational. The biographical stories told by the women in this study share a set of features, common to all narratives, that make them a particularly useful way of looking at individual identity, collective identity, and the link between the two. Biographical or ontological narratives are stories with a plot that specify relationships and connections, and selectively appropriate events, turning them into episodes embedded in time and space. They are not fixed or static. Biographical narratives construct the individual whose story is being told as a subject with a past, present, and future. Narratives preserve continuity within change for both individuals and collectivities. As Polletta argues, they "explain what is going on in a way that makes an evolving identity part of the explanation."[17]

Importantly, biographical analysis constructs subjects as agents who actively shape their own lives.[18] Nonetheless, actors cannot create biographies at will. Biographical narratives are a means of making meaningful the opportunities and barriers of lived experience, not a means of ignoring them. Grievances are not arbitrary. Social relations based on inequality and domination shaped the construction of biography and of collective and individual identity for the women in this study.

Always Feminist—"I think it came from as early as I remember"

Nine women said they had always held views and had feelings consistent with feminism. These women all mentioned the influence of childhood experiences that contributed to their feminist disposition. The strong role model provided by mothers was a common theme, with numerous descriptions of mothers who coped with adversity, stood up for themselves, pursued personal interests, including careers, and encouraged their daughters to follow their example. Alex commented, "My mother's a really forceful woman. She's always sort of done what she wanted to do, and that's sort of, I suppose that's been my main role model." Lisa expressed similar sentiments, "Oh, well, my mother's a feminist, so I suppose it's just a natural thing for me to progress into." While Julie and Emma both suggested their mothers would not have called themselves feminists, they described them respectively as "strong" and as "a liberated woman [who has] always worked, and always been a bit angry about what men do." Emma further commented that her mother's feminist attitudes were reflected in their mother/daughter relationship. "There's never really been any pressure on either my sister or myself to get married and have children . . . and that's just because of her attitudes mainly."

Linked to the theme of strong mothers, a few women talked about the significance of being raised in an "all-female" or "female-dominated" household. Again, this was associated with positive views regarding women's independence, high expectations with regard to education and careers, and, in some cases, a negative opinion of men:

> I don't think there's actually a date that I can put on it. In some ways, I think I've always been a feminist, in a curious kind of way, because I was brought up in an all-female household . . . And so I've always had that model of women being able to do anything and everything, and always treating men with slight sort of contempt and disdain in that way . . . So in that way, I think I've always kind of had that slant and always kind of found it curious that anyone would think that women weren't able to do whatever they wanted to.

An early awareness of social injustice, particularly the injustice experienced by women, was a final theme that arose in interviews with these women. Lisa said, "Ever since I've been a young girl I've always been confronted with understanding of the women's situation of today or of the past. I've always been aware of that—of women." Helen's turbulent childhood, overshadowed by domestic violence, created a keen interest in social justice and women's issues during her high school years. These interests stayed with her as she entered university, influencing both her choice of study and career and her developing identity as a lesbian feminist. Similarly, for Vicki, an awareness of social injustice was evident and acted upon from an early age:

> Sometimes I think I was born one [a feminist], because I feel as though I've been a bit of a radical all of my life, been a bit different all of my life . . . I have been aware of injustice most of my life. Early in my life I can remember incidents in primary school where I took up issues and stuff . . . In grade five, we had a really violent teacher . . . and we eventually had that teacher suspended . . . So I've had these fights, you know . . . and eventually that got sorted into some gender inequity as well, which led to my calling myself a feminist. So that started in the later years of high school when I did sociology, and I looked back at the assignments I did and they were on women's work and child care, women's issues, even then when I was 15 and 16, so I guess it's been with me for a while, though, it certainly wasn't put in a feminist model or anything like that.

In becoming feminists, these women did not report experiencing dramatic changes in values, beliefs, or in their sense of self. The process they described was not so much one of personal transformation, but of becoming aware of the language or discourse of feminism as a vehicle for expressing already held beliefs about the world and about themselves, and of linking up with other women who shared their outlook. For all but one of these women, the setting in which they found support for feminist identity was university, which they attended in their youth. It is interesting to speculate as to why this was the case. It seems likely that their upbringing predisposed them to attend university following high school and that, once there, they were receptive to feminist activities on campus.

Evolving Feminist—"It was a slowly developing and growing awareness"

For 19 women, becoming feminist was described in the language of evolution or development. As in the case of those women who saw themselves as having always been feminists, these women did not experience a dramatic "conversion" or personal transformation. They described a gradual growth in awareness of women's or feminist issues, and a parallel development of feminist identity. For example, "I think it was a slowly developing and growing awareness, so it's hard to pinpoint something specific" (Marie), and "I think it's probably been a gradual process for me" (Michelle). Stella, a lesbian feminist who had previously been married said, "It's not something that I decided one day that I was a feminist . . . Lots of things contributed to that change." Although Patricia recalled reading *The Dialectic of*

Sex by Shulamith Firestone when she was 17, she also described the process of becoming feminist as a series of stages:

> I guess I first was aware of feminist thinking when I was about 17 and my sister brought home a book which she thought was all about sex from the library and it turned out to be all about feminism, and I read it instead of her, so I guess the seeds were always there. I think I read *The Second Sex* in my first year at uni[versity] and then I didn't read anything for a long time afterwards of a feminist nature, but I do agree totally with a lot of the thinking so it was more a matter of I had certain stages of, you know, accepting "Yes, this is one really valid way of looking at the world." And then a few years later I did another course . . . and it just widened my perceptions and I think, you know, initially . . . that was it. I knew I was on the right track from those few texts.

The evolving nature of feminist involvement and identification is also clearly evident in this account from Sandra:

> How did I become a feminist? I think in my final . . . year at uni[versity] . . . The first three years, you know, I hadn't sort of really got involved in much political activity at all, but in my Honors year I seemed to have a lot more energy for other things and started getting a bit involved in politics around campus. Just sort of quite, fairly peripherally with the women's group and the union, and then the next year I moved to Sydney, in '76, into a house I shared with a woman and a man. And the woman who lived in the house had been a feminist for a few years then, and she'd been a member of a consciousness-raising group in Sydney since the early '70s. We discussed a lot of political issues and belonged to a reading group looking at wonderful things like the dialectic of historical materialism (laugh).

Although the descriptions of "becoming feminist" provided by these women share much with those of women who saw themselves as "always feminist," some differences are discernible. The emphasis on mothers as strong role models was not evident, and there was a greater tendency to describe a childhood (if it was discussed at all) within a traditional nuclear family, with fathers who were dominant, even if also caring and protective. While this type of upbringing sometimes produced an awareness of discrimination and differential treatment—for example, Marie "was always aware of different treatment and opportunities that [her] brothers had"—the language with which to articulate these feelings was not so readily available.

On average, the women grouped here tended to identify less strongly with feminism than those who saw themselves as having always been feminist, although four of them identified strongly prior to the workshop. They also tended to be older when they came to identify with feminism. Generally, they talked about being in their late 20s or 30s before they began to see themselves as feminist. For example, Muriel said

> By the time I was about 30, I started to think differently. I'd been brought up in a very traditional family, where the father was very caring and protective, and head of the house, and Mum had her role, and so on . . . We were brought up to believe that men ruled the world as it were, and we were subservient to that. Well, that really irritated me, and I think I really thought about that as an adolescent, even though I might not have been able to put that into words, but I always had the feeling that nobody's going to dominate me. I couldn't take that. It's probably why I stayed single I think . . . I really couldn't stand to have someone, you know, making demands on you, where you just couldn't get out of it . . . By the time I'd reached my thirties I suppose I had studied a bit more, and interacted a bit more, and traveled a bit more and whatnot. I'd read a bit more on this too, and I thought "Oh, these girls have really got the same ideas as I have" (laugh), and you know, I read a bit more then and got involved in groups.

Personal Quest—"I was forced into going, looking for options"

For 16 women, the process of becoming feminist involved a more difficult search for meaning and identity than was evident for other respondents. For these women, becoming feminist was a journey of discovery where they actively, and often against considerable barriers, sought out new understandings of the world around them and of themselves. More than three-quarters of these women were married with children before encountering feminism. This contrasts with less than one half of those who described an evolutionary process and none of those who said they had always been feminist.

Typically, the stories told by these women included references to feelings of dissatisfaction that prompted an active search for alternatives. A major theme was disappointment and unfulfilled expectations of marriage and motherhood. Mixed with this, in some cases, were feelings of boredom and a general lack of meaning in life. Anne recalled her predicament as a young wife and mother at home with two children and a husband who did not return home until 8.00 pm each evening after visiting the pub. She said, "I guess that I started to resent this and think, you know, 'Why is it, that I'm in this situation?'" Louise talked about her naivete in thinking "that when you got married, you lived happily ever after." She described how the reality of married life did not live up to her expectations:

> I basically couldn't understand why things didn't work out the way I wanted them to . . . Within four years I'd met my husband, got engaged, got married, had the kids, moved to Queensland, left all my family behind, and was desperately lonely, and really wasn't fitting in anywhere, and, of course, didn't really understand that I had to take responsibility.

Rachel had "been indoctrinated with the idea of man's superiority, for most of [her] life," but she wanted to rebel:

> I couldn't understand why it is that the man is considered better, because I could see that a lot of his ideas were not particularly wonderful. And yet I was well indoctrinated in the belief that I obey my husband and I do everything to please him . . . which made it seem that I was being disloyal when I thought my own thoughts, which were different to his . . . So you could say I've had quite a turnaround and there was a point of time where I decided that I'd had enough of all this. I wanted to know something different; I wanted to be different, and behave differently, and stand up for myself in general.

For a couple of women, issues of sexual identity were intertwined with their search for alternatives. As Judy put it, "What's been a big issue for me, up till now, was dealing with my homosexuality, and I suppose a lot of the feminist readings and interest I have, has come out of reading things in that area. It's come from there." For Toni, choosing to live a lesbian lifestyle was part of a process of politicizing her ideas:

> Feminism—"het" feminism, helped me towards lesbianism. Het feminism made the idiocy of heterosexuality undeniable to me and enabled me then, I suppose, to act on my impulses towards women which I've always had and set aside. I just reached the point where I could no longer sleep with men, and then I just couldn't live that double standard.

For Barbara, a religious sister, the stifling nature of the institutional church provided the impetus for exploring feminist ideas. She talked about her "desire to become more aware of issues and take some affirmative action" as being prompted by being publicly named derogatorily as a militant feminist in a church publication. "I just had to say to myself I'm not. I wish I was, but I'm not."

For all of these women, the dissatisfaction they felt with life led to a search for alternatives. Each in her own way sought to expand her horizons and options. Anne picked up a book called *Male Chauvinism in the Office*. This book provided her with evidence that she was not alone and that her problems and dissatisfaction were related to broader social structures. Louise enrolled in a Women's Studies degree externally. Rachel embarked on a project of personal development through participating in personal growth workshops and joining various groups. Toni enrolled in university as a mature-age student, and Barbara began reading and going to workshops held at the local women's center. For Rose, seeking alternatives led to more drastic measures. Rose married a violent man and bore four sons before leaving him. "I left him and I survived for about seven years in what you'd call the ordinary, mainstream society—I mean, just survived physically." But life as a single mother in central Queensland was not easy and Rose was driven further in search of new opportunities:

> Finally, I guess, I was lucky, because about this time the Nimbin experience was starting to get in the *Women's Weekly* and things like that—'76, '77, '78, '79.[19] And I mean, this culture, this central Queensland culture is just so barren and so emotionally cruel to women that in desperation, and I mean in *desperation*, I got to thinking, "Well, people who want to build their own houses and grow their own vegetables and just live in their house and cause no harm couldn't be that bad. They couldn't be as bad as you people." That was my (pause)—I was forced into going, looking for options. And that was just a terrible time in my life, but that was sort of, July '79 was the watershed, and really the turning point . . . I ended up in Nimbin . . . You see there was no support for women. None. And it was a terrible life. So, anyway, to turn up in Nimbin was the start of the difference.

The journey, once embarked upon, was seldom straightforward or easy for these women. In a number of cases the process was long and difficult and support for a developing feminist identity was difficult to find. Jocelyn's awareness of and "secret" attraction to alternative ways of being preceded active involvement by many years due to the isolation she experienced as a young mother largely restricted to the family sphere:

> When I was first married in the '60s, that was when Women's Lib first came out . . . Items would come up, say, on the news . . . One of the things I specifically remember was in '65 round about, when women started to protest about their being banned from . . . public areas in hotels. When that would come up on a news item on the television, my family, whoever was there, if it was my father or my husband or

neighbors or whatever, they would all say "Oh, how disgusting. Why would women want to go into those places?" and "Look at them, they're all strident and badly dressed." And I would be sitting there with this absolutely secret kind of "Hooray! Oh good on them!" and "I wish I was there!" and, you know, they'd show you marches up the street, especially the peace marches—I'd think "I wish I was there." I loved it, but I saw myself as this kind of nobody, you know, I was a mother, I was kind of pregnant and had toddlers, and I just really saw myself as a nobody. I just had been told for so long I was unintelligent and all that sort of stuff, that I just, like I would just get a secret thrill from those things, but wasn't, didn't know what that meant. I've only just started to put that into context for myself.

Others described similar experiences. They talked about being aware of the existence of women who lived very different lives from their own, women who were active and involved in protest. Margaret talked about being aware through the mainstream media of women's groups such as the Women's Electoral Lobby that she watched from a distance:

That was the first start for me, of thinking "Well, women actually get together and they talk about issues," and that sort of stayed in my mind for a little while and I was interested to pursue it a little bit further, later on, though none of my friends at that time were particularly interested.

From beginnings such as these, the path to feminist involvement and identity was not easy or smooth for most of these women. Anne, for instance, described successive attempts to gain support from those around her for the interpretation of her problems that became available through reading the book on male chauvinism. She initially mentioned these ideas to her doctor. "I was going to him for depression and not sleeping and I mentioned it, you know, that male chauvinists and whatever—I started discussing these things as perhaps why I—and he seemed to think that was a bit of a joke." Later she joined a women's speaking club where she again sought confirmation of her views:

I started trying to express my views on women's role in society at that club, but I was sort of greeted with "Oh, here's Anne," you know, "going on again about this," and the women there weren't really very much interested in what I had to say on that. It was just "Oh, here she goes again on it." So I never really got much support there at all.

Although Jocelyn became involved in community action, "helping Aboriginal people get onto the rolls and vote," while living in Western Australia during the 1970s, it was not until she moved to Townsville that she made contact with specifically feminist networks and organizations. For Jocelyn, the interstate move threatened to destroy the person she had become through her involvement in political action:

> It was terrible for me coming here. I didn't want to come and so I was back to kind of just trying to set up a household here and keep the family together and get the kids into school 'cause they were still quite young at that stage, and I went into quite a decline, because leaving was very difficult for me; it wasn't my choice. I left behind— for the first time, there was this person called "Jocelyn" who was doing things. It was just amazing things. I was just, it was like I was "born again" (laugh), and so coming to Townsville actually put me back to how I was, back in the early days of being married and having kids . . .
>
> When we first came here, in 1979, I enrolled in the Associate Diploma in Community Welfare, and that really changed things for me. That's when I started to get the academic theories to my feelings, and then I moved into women's services, and so that's just strengthened and strengthened and grown. So I now call myself a feminist.

Through a variety of avenues, each woman became aware of feminist ways of viewing the world, made connections with feminist networks, and eventually arrived at the point where she defined herself, to a greater or lesser extent, in feminist terms. These women, like those who described an evolutionary path to feminism, tended to describe conventional upbringings and expectations—"there was always this kind of expectation that I would be this working-class conventional Australian woman" (Jocelyn), and "I'd never been encouraged to read, nor did I mix with women who were feminist. I'd never really been exposed to feminism, more's the pity" (Toni). Making contact with the ideas and networks of the women's movement was not always easy, even for those who were aware of its existence.

Levels and Changes in Identification with Feminism
Prior to the 1991 Winter Institute Workshop, participants varied in terms of the strength of their identification with feminism.[20] Fifteen women identified strongly as feminists, stating that feminism was either central to or a highly significant aspect of their lives. All 15 were happy to use the term "feminist" to describe themselves and three identified openly as lesbian feminists. Typical comments from these women were "Feminism came together

for me as being totally my view of the world when I was in my late 20s," and "I am a feminist, and that's who I am and how I relate to people." The 1991 workshop provided confirmation and amplification of feminist consciousness, emotions, and identity for these women.

The largest group, 20 women, identified with feminism to a moderate degree prior to the workshop. They were willing to say they were feminists, but their answers were often qualified in some way. A number said they did not like labels or did not like being categorized. Some distanced themselves from "other" feminists who were labeled as "rabid," "radical," "militant," or "extreme." Among this group, two were lesbians. In general, the workshop had a greater impact on this group than it did for those who were already highly committed activists. Many talked about the workshop having an impact on their willingness to openly wear the label feminist in future. Almost three-quarters went on to increase their involvement in feminist activities and their identification as feminists throughout 1992. Tracy talked in the follow-up interview of clarifying her views and feeling stronger as a result. Stella said she felt "less concerned about what people think of my feminist views." Similarly, Michelle said she felt more comfortable with herself and with radical segments of the movement.

Finally, 10 women attended the 1991 Winter Institute Workshop despite having little or no identification or involvement with feminism prior to the workshop. They attended for a variety of reasons and with varying knowledge of what the workshop would involve. Three of these women identified themselves as lesbian. All these women reported experiencing the workshop positively, although only nine identified as feminist at the time of the follow-up interviews.

In relation to the process of becoming feminist, six of the 15 women who were categorized as high on feminist identification saw themselves as having always been feminist in their orientation, and four described an evolutionary process. Grouped together, these 10 women were, on average, nine years younger than the study group as a whole. At the time of the first interview, only two were married (one of whom was living apart from her husband) and three were living in de facto relationships with men. Two were mothers with one young child each. What is most striking about this group, however, is that all 10 attended university as young women, most immediately following high school. Furthermore, university study provided the micromobilization context in which feminist awareness and identity were developed by all, bar one, who came to feminism via lesbian and gay politics. For the remaining five women in the category of high identification and commitment, accounts of becoming feminist represented a personal quest. Becoming feminist occurred at a later age and was a slower and more transformational process than for the others. All five were married with children prior to becoming feminists and, at the time of interviewing, had a mean age of 48, seven years older than the overall mean. University study was also significant for three of these women, but interestingly this study came at a later time in their lives and was part of an active journey of self-discovery. Finally, two encountered feminism through personal growth activities.

The micromobilization contexts that brought the 20 moderate feminists into contact with feminism were more diverse than for the women initially categorized as highly committed. The personal growth movement was the most common setting (six women), but university (four women), feminist organizations (four women), and a range of other contexts (six women) were also significant. Only three of these women described themselves as having always been feminist. Much more common was an account of feminist identity developing and unfolding over a period of time. Twelve women gave this type of account. For a further five, becoming feminist was part of a personal quest. An important difference between this moderately identified group and those categorized as highly identified was their overall level of education. They were much less likely to have completed degrees compared to the highly committed group, and less likely to have encountered feminism through study.

Turning to the 10 women who were low on identification initially, it is interesting to note that, in contrast to the other groups, only one had graduated from university and none discovered feminism through formal study. Four encountered feminism through the personal growth movement, five through direct contact with feminist organizations, and one through attending lunchtime women's seminars at the university where she worked. None described themselves as having always been feminist. Three gave evolving accounts of becoming feminist, six gave accounts consistent with the idea of a personal quest, and one chose not to define herself as a feminist. For most, the Winter Institute workshop contributed to an increase in feminist consciousness, involvement in activities, and feminist identification that was still evident 12 months later.

Changes in lifestyle were major for Rhonda and Judy. Rhonda, a lesbian who prior to the workshop was not "out," moved to live in Sydney where she felt it would be easier to pursue her developing feminist interests and to live openly as a lesbian. She arrived in time for the Sydney Lesbian and Gay Mardi Gras, and through notice boards in a feminist bookstore she contacted and joined a variety of lesbian feminist groups, including one called OWLS—Older, Wiser, Lesbian Support group. Judy, also a lesbian, moved in with a feminist partner and at the time of the second interview described her life as follows:

> Feminism permeates every single facet of my personal life . . . I
> mean, the house—not only do we live on basic feminist principles,
> I suppose, but to their fullest extent I think you'd say. Almost to the
> extreme . . . Our household is almost on a separatist level. The only
> male that really we mix with regularly now is Danielle's ex-partner
> who we're both very fond of. He comes over . . . mainly when he
> drops the kids off.

The weekend workshop had a major impact on Kate and Elaine also, but
the changes they made in their lives did not include increased involvement
in specifically feminist activities and groups. The workshop provided Kate
with an important sense of self-validation, as she put it, "confirmation that
I'm okay, that I'm not strange, weird, or abnormal." Through the workshop
she arrived at an understanding that "women don't have to be normal." So,
despite only a moderate increase in feminist activities and identification,
the overall impact on Kate's sense of self was significant. This was also the
case for Elaine. She described the weekend as wonderful, and as having
"made a change in me," which was noticed and commented upon by her
friends. She said following the weekend she had "more guts" and was more
able to make decisions for herself. She summed up the difference this way:

> I think that's what the weekend's done [it's] sort of made me feel
> that I'm human, that I'm not just a bit of nothing, that I am human,
> and I can say—whether I say something stupid or not, you know.
> That's why I would never talk before, because everything I'd say, he'd
> say, "Oh shut up, you don't make any sense." But now I say, "Oh well,
> if it doesn't make sense, I know it makes sense." If nobody else does,
> I don't care.

When asked during the initial interview whether she saw herself as a feminist, Elaine gave a long reply concerning her awareness of how badly
women are treated and concluded, "Probably, I suppose, I'm turning into a
feminist—I don't really give much of a shit for men anymore." Following
the workshop, she made a major life decision to return to high school study
with the goal of eventually attending university and completing a degree.
Despite the fact that she did not continue an active involvement in feminist
activities, mainly due to time and financial constraints, 12 months later she
still described the workshop as a major turning point in her life. Living
feminism, for her, meant asserting herself and achieving an education in
spite of obstacles and barriers placed in her way.

Networks, Emotion, Consciousness, and Identity

The evidence presented in this chapter supports the central importance of social movement networks in drawing individuals into collective action. Only a handful of women became involved directly through feminist organizations and some of these had prior personal contact with individual feminists who encouraged their involvement. Most encountered feminism through participation in a range of nonmovement organizations and social settings, indicating the significance of unobtrusive mobilization and social movement spillover in creating suitable micromobilization contexts.

In the literature on micromobilization, however, little is said about how people come to participate in the small group settings that constitute micromobilization contexts. People just happen to be part of these groups and from there are recruited to movements. Not only is the agency of subjects downplayed in this conceptualization, but also the variation evident in accounts of becoming involved that characterize the biographies of the women in this study is missed. A feature of these, which is particularly evident for those women I have categorized as embarking on a personal quest, is the specific and conscious action they have taken to seek out and explore social contexts that might lead them to new understandings of the world and of themselves. These women sought out situations that would provide knowledge, affirmation, and identity resources that were not immediately available in their environment. As Rachel so vividly describes, it was her desire to "*know* something different . . . to *be* different, and *behave* differently" that led her to the personal growth workshops where she first came across feminist ideas.

Feelings of dissatisfaction with her life led Rachel to seek changes. Such feelings or emotions are central to the process of becoming and being feminist. Pauline Johnson argues that the modern women's movement arose from a widespread "experience of radical dissatisfaction and sense of frustrated potential with the life choices available to women."[21] Social movements scholars refer to this sense of dissatisfaction and frustration as grievances. While grievances may have a cognitive dimension, it is clear that they are apprehended through emotion. Arlie Hochschild suggests that the display of emotion can perform a signal function, reflecting buried perspectives and providing clues to others about how a person might act.[22] Feelings can also perform this function for the self, initiating a search for alternatives. This was particularly evident in the accounts of becoming feminist I described as a personal quest. Negative emotions associated with marriage and motherhood in a patriarchal society—dissatisfaction, anger, shame, and depression—provided the impetus for a number of women to seek alternatives.

In terms of the framing of issues and the development of feminist consciousness, the significance of system attributions is another obvious feature of the data presented here. Dominant ideologies in Western societies individualize problems and tend to blame the oppressed for their own suffering. Thus, people may suffer hardships but not define them as grievances because they attribute problems to their own failings. Collective action frames and movement discourse more generally replace such self-attributions with system-attributions which de-legitimate the system and thus provide the impetus for sustained social action.[23] Feminist knowing or consciousness involves the framing of women's problems in structural terms as a form of social injustice based on gender. Such framings were widespread among these women.

A significant dimension, in terms of which accounts of becoming feminist differed, was the timing and contexts through which participants became aware of the language of social justice and system attributions. For those who described themselves as "always" feminist, the tendency to view a range of issues, both personal and social, in terms of system attributions rather than personal failings is at the core of their claim to always being feminist. They claim a continuity in their perception of injustice in the world and in particular of injustice towards women.[24] For these women, their childhood environment and experiences contributed to a basic orientation that was consistent with such system attributions and, in some cases, also provided the language for expressing such views. To a lesser extent, this language also appears to have been available to those who described an evolving feminist subjectivity. Many talked about being aware of injustice from a young age; however, their accounts were more likely to describe this as a feeling or emotion rather than cognitively as a political view of the world. There was an awareness that aspects of their own and others' lives were not fair—for example, Marie "was always aware of different treatment and opportunities that [her] brothers had,"—but they were less likely to have access to language with which to express this until later in life. This was also the case for those women for whom becoming feminist was part of an active search for personal change. On one level they were aware of injustice, but within their environment the cognitive resources needed to interpret and act on this were not available. As Kate said, she had realized that women were confined and bound by gender roles, but she had no way of interpreting this other than as a "sad" state of affairs until she attended the Winter Institute seminars and workshop. Kate's story, along with others in this group, demonstrates the uphill struggle that is often involved in achieving "cognitive liberation." Searching for, and discovering, a discourse through which to express the feelings associated with social injustice was a significant feature of all the personal quest accounts.

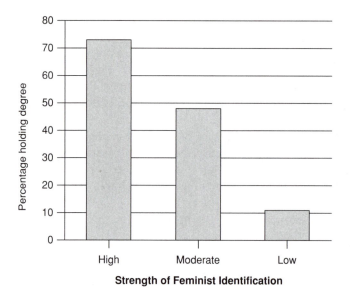

Figure 3-1 Percentage of interviewees holding degrees, by strength of feminist identification.

An interesting feature of the data is that the strength of feminist identification prior to the workshop was strongly associated with the level of education (see Figure 3-1). Seventy-three percent of the highly identified women held degrees. Forty-eight percent of the moderate identifiers did and only 11 percent of the low identifiers did. The centrality of "knowing" to the experience of becoming and being feminist is supported by this finding and by the fact that the single most common context through which women in this study came into contact with feminism was higher education.

It is also worth noting that differences in levels of education reflect other aspects of structural location such as social class, age, and geographical location. Social class is clearly related to education, with working-class women being much less likely to have had the opportunity to pursue higher levels of education. One working-class woman in this study expressed anger at the lack of educational opportunities available to her as a young woman. Another talked about her lack of literacy skills, which presented a considerable barrier to her desire to gain greater knowledge of feminism and to pursue alternative career options.

The women in the study who had grown up in rural and regional areas had less access to education than their sisters who had lived in major cities, as did the older women in the group. Access to post-school education has expanded significantly in Australia during the past 25 years, so it is not surprising that the younger women in the study were more likely to have completed degrees and to have accessed feminism through university study.

As I outlined in Chapter 1, individual involvement in collective action revolves around four dimensions of subjectivity: knowing, feeling, belonging, and doing. For the women who described themselves as "always feminist" there is a sense of unity between these dimensions that stretches back into the past and is also projected into the future. For those who described themselves as "evolving feminists," integration between the four dimensions developed over time, but their accounts still have a strong theme of continuity, both in terms of past feelings and past activities. In contrast, the struggle involved in forging feminist subjectivity was most obvious for the women whose biographical accounts were categorized as a personal quest. They talked about earlier times when they had felt "stuck" in lives that were unsatisfying. Who they felt they were, or who they wanted to be, had not always been consistent with what they were doing. Integrating knowing, feeling, belonging, and doing represented a hard-won achievement for these women. Once they began on the journey to feminism, the resistance they faced from those around them made the transition more obvious than it was to the "evolving feminist" and "always feminist" women. Nonetheless, they recognized both continuity and change in their lives. The feelings that led them to question assumptions concerning their place in the world provided a continuing thread in the biographical narratives through which they defined their sense of self.

It may be asked, have these women merely created the *fiction* of a unified self? Although I would agree that their sense of self is a creation, I argue that it is not a fiction. As Jane Flax suggests, "The subject *is* a shifting and always changing intersection of complex, contradictory, and unfinished processes," but "[s]ubjectivity is not an illusion."[25] Lived experiences, along with the public narratives produced by the women's movement come together in the construction of feminist selves. The biographical narratives women create from these resources allow them to make sense of their lives and to engage in feminist action to change the world. Still, the process of becoming feminist is complex. The framing of issues and the narratives of identity produced by the women's movement are multiple, and they are not the only public narratives involved in the complex interactions that produce subjectivity. Narratives of identity are constructed by a whole range of collective actors, including the media, other movements, government institutions, churches, and families. The women in this study are placed differently in relation to each of these. In the following chapter, some of the tensions and contradictions inherent in the complex process of constructing feminist subjectivity are addressed.

CHAPTER 4

Tensions and Contradictions in the Construction of Meaning and Identity

Chapter 3 explored the various paths to feminism traveled by the women in this study. The micromobilization contexts through which they came into contact with feminist ideas and networks were identified and accounts of their personal journeys toward feminism examined. Through a variety of settings and routes, participants encountered feminist narratives for both knowing the world and knowing the self, and, to a greater or lesser extent, they adopted these narratives to make sense of their world and of themselves. For all but one the outcome at the time of the study was a more-or-less strongly defined feminist sense of self. At a minimum, they shared a level of feminist consciousness that attributed problems women face in the world, including many they experienced in their own lives, to structural forces. Complexity enters the picture, however, when the multiplicity of feminist discourses and practices, and of discourses and practices that circulate within the broader society, is recognized. The complexity, tensions, and contradictions inherent in the process of becoming feminist are the subject of this chapter.

The first section of the chapter presents data concerning interviewees' responses to feminist discourses for "knowing the world" as encountered in various settings. It examines the way these women related to and appropriated feminist collective beliefs and finds that responses to feminist narratives were shaped by a critical and reflexive approach to the texts and discourses of feminism and by a desire for knowledge that was perceived as empowering. A level of skepticism was evident in the way participants responded to feminist narratives, whether encountered as oral or written texts. They did not automatically accept feminist collective beliefs, even when women who were admired as intelligent, educated, and knowledgeable presented them. The second section is concerned with how identity is constructed in interpersonal interactions in movement settings. It is in such settings that individuals encounter movement frames and the "we" of collective identity. What happens when the "I" or "me" of personal identity confronts the we? From this data it is evident that interpersonal dynamics and discursive positioning within feminist groups and organizations influence the way in which women feel about themselves, their feminist identity, and feminist involvement. The tensions and contradiction that arise in such encounters are discussed. The next section addresses the issue of multiple identities. What other identities coexist with feminist identity for these women? How do they experience and deal with the tensions and contradictions of multiple identities? In the last section of this chapter theoretical implications are discussed.

Responding to Feminist Narratives of Knowing

Questions concerning the nature of the relationship between individual consciousness and collective consciousness are central to the study of social movements. Adopting a Marxist position, a number of theorists have dealt with consciousness at the cultural level as ideology or discourse. However, such accounts tend to ignore the possibility of an active agent of collective action and in the process replicate structure/agency dualism.[1] A more satisfying approach conceptualizes consciousness "as the interplay between two levels—between individuals who operate actively in the construction of meaning and socio-cultural processes that offer meanings that are frequently contested."[2] Gamson suggests that the concept of framing meets this requirement. However, to date, most of the work that has adopted the framing approach has presented collective action frames as the products of movement organizations and leaders who persuade, solicit, and coax individuals to adopt the movement point of view. The frame alignment processes and core framing tasks described by Snow and his colleagues are a case in point.[3] These are strategies utilized by movement organizations, and little is said about the responses of those to whom they are directed.

When collective consciousness is viewed as being imparted through a process of socialization, as Taylor and Whittier suggest in their discussion of identity construction in lesbian feminist communities, there is again the danger of losing sight of an active agent contributing to the process.[4] There is a problematic tendency in socialization theory to construct "the person doing the socializing as the active agent and the person being socialized as passive recipient, the 'object' or the 'raw material of socialization.'"⁵ In the data presented here, these top-down approaches are balanced by a view from the bottom-up as I examine how participants responded to feminist ideas as they encountered them through workshops, seminars, lectures, and written texts.

"I don't believe everything they tell me"

Participants clearly asserted a sense of agency in adopting feminist ideas. Rachel, for instance, talked about admiring strong women and of being influenced by the ideas encountered at seminars and workshops she had attended: "I've been absolutely amazed at some of the ideas put out by women." The material presented by such women spoke to her experiences as a woman and "opened up the way to new thinking." However, she clearly asserted her independence and autonomy in the process of selecting feminist ideas. She said in the initial interview:

> I don't always believe everything they tell me; I want to think about it; decide how I feel about it. I'm not just walking along saying "yes, that's right, because she said so." You've got to use your own imagination and work things out.

Rachel described the 1991 Winter Institute workshop as a movement forward in terms of her understanding of feminism and an opportunity to hear a feminist message from someone whom she had not heard before. She talked about the insights that could be gained from a speaker "with a lot of education who's done a lot of teaching and writing." Referring to the range of feminist speakers she had heard at various workshops and seminars, she concluded, "They may basically say a lot of similar things, but it's said differently, and it opens up new avenues of thought."

Michelle also insisted on a level of agency in accepting new feminist ideas. For her, becoming feminist has been about emerging as a woman who acts confidently in the world. She talked about feeling good about herself now and having the confidence to tackle situations that she once would have found daunting. She said, "I can talk to people, and I can stand up and talk to people as a group. I still get nervous, but I feel good." This confidence was linked to her growing identification with feminism, but it was feminism on her terms:

> I certainly have become a lot more aware of women's issues. But I've slotted them in to fit me. And I think you only take in what you sort of want to take in at the time and leave the rest, and you might sift through a bit more of that later.

Michelle identified a point in time, about two years prior to the 1991 workshop, when she first began to think of herself as a feminist, "A lot of the ideas that I had put forward to me, I thought well that fits, that feels okay, I can accept that."

Kate described her approach to feminist ideas in terms of rejecting a stance that she perceived as fanaticism and "going overboard." She said, "A lot of things are good, religion's good, a lot of things are good, but when you go overboard and you get fanatical, I think that's probably the fear that I would have had about joining anything." In the follow-up interview she said, "I still see feminism as an individual thing . . . as how it relates to me, how it affects me, or how I can use it to become, to have a choice, to make choices and not to be victimized." From Kate's point of view, if feminism is taken up fanatically it becomes another set of rules that reduce choice and the ability to construct a self that is not victimized. Susan, a long-term feminist, also valued autonomy in relation to accepting or rejecting feminist ideas. Explaining her reasons for not joining a feminist reading group she said, "I like my own interpretation. Being opinionated, I'd prefer to read and not sit and discuss it."

The view that each woman should be free to interpret feminism for herself without being judged by others was expressed by a number of women and indicated a desire for flexibility in the definition of feminist subjectivity. Julie, for example, suggested that "everyone's different," and they have "to go through their own education and come up with what they're comfortable with." She characterized her own definition of feminism as fluid, but at the same time unchanging in terms of a core position, "I don't have a clear definition. I don't think my ideas have changed; I've always kind of had a tolerant view of what feminism is, it's basically a view of support and concern and affection for women. And that hasn't changed."

"It's a growing thing anyway, feminism; you never actually get there"

The fluidity of feminist consciousness and identity was commented upon frequently. Women commented that feminism was "not cut and dried," that being feminist was "always a struggle," and that "to keep true to your feminism" you needed to keep it "growing and alive." These ideas were also associated with the notion that feminism was something that had to be worked at as an ongoing project. These types of comments were made by women who were relatively new to feminism and also by those who were long-term and highly committed feminists.

Jacqui expressed this position clearly when talking about her developing interest and involvement in feminism, and the significance of having the right words to name her feelings:

> I didn't have the feminist information. I had the feelings but I couldn't label them and define them and that sort of thing. So that's probably a twelve-month to two-year thing. I mean it's a growing thing anyway, feminism, you never actually get there. You're always on the road to it.

For Jacqui, feminist knowledge or consciousness is not an unchanging set of beliefs that one either subscribes to or rejects completely. Reading, listening to speakers, thinking, arguing, accepting, and rejecting various ideas are all part of a never-ending process.

The visit to Townsville of revolutionary feminist Sheila Jeffreys, for the 1992 Winter Institute, provides a good example of the way in which many women in this study responded to new and challenging ideas. While in Townsville, Jeffreys spoke at a variety of public venues including the Townsville Women's Centre and James Cook University. She also facilitated a weekend workshop for lesbian feminists. She expounded her views on pornography, sadomasochism, and political lesbianism, and spoke about her own journey from heterosexual feminism to lesbian separatism. She asserted that for as long as women continue to expend energy on men and support male egos, women will not achieve liberation. According to her analysis, heterosexuality is incompatible with radical feminist practice. Clearly, Jeffreys' ideas challenged heterosexual feminists, implying that heterosexual women either suffer from false consciousness and are victims, or from a lack of moral courage, colluding in their own oppression and that of others.

Sharon, a long-term and highly identified feminist, welcomed the challenge presented by Jeffreys' controversial views: "Sheila Jeffreys was really good because I felt she did provide a very challenging viewpoint which makes you think about your lifestyle." For Sharon, fluidity, change, and growth within feminism is an ideal to be strived for:

> As a feminist you can't ever stop and be contented about the way you are and the way your partner is, and how things are in the world. It's a kind of constant shifting . . . I think if as a feminist I didn't change my ideas regularly, it would be about as unhealthy as not changing my undies regularly. I mean, for me being a feminist involves constantly thinking about my life and the life of others and the culture around me, and seeing it differently and thinking about it differently and feeling challenged.

In a similar fashion, Lorna described feminism as "emergent" and as "not a monolithic sort of theory." She also noted that as she had grown older she had become more aware of other forms of oppression, such as ageism.

Patricia also talked about the development of feminist ideas, which she suggested occurs "whether you're consciously aware of it or not." In her view, the experiences of daily life constantly shape one's worldview. Working with men throughout 1992 led Patricia to think about and to reevaluate her feminism in light of Sheila Jeffreys' analysis. As with Sharon, Jeffreys' ideas provided a stimulus to thought rather than a package to be uncritically adopted or rejected:

> I've been thinking about those sorts of things and where that places me in terms of my daily behavior . . . and whether it actually handicaps your feminism to get to like men. Whether it actually waters down your position . . . So I haven't really come to any conclusions about that, but I guess if we don't live in a dynamic world where we're changing each other and changing things all the time in relation to feminism and lots of other things then I don't see much point.

From the data presented above, we can see that the women in this study approached the feminist ideas they encountered through workshops, seminars, or written texts as active processors of meaning. Although they shared many life experiences as women, they each brought to the process of becoming feminist a unique set of life experiences based on personal biography and structural location. Therefore, each responded in her own way to particular feminist framings of issues. Frames that resonated with their own life experiences were accepted while others were questioned or rejected. Some embraced new ideas cautiously and resisted being overly influenced by women they admired. Others took a bolder, more confident, approach and sought out challenging viewpoints. Many reacted against rigid formulations of feminism. Feminist ideas were tested against lived experience and selectively appropriated accordingly. Combined with this basic skepticism was a widely held view that feminist discourse in general, and their own feminist consciousness specifically, should be constantly growing and changing. Thus, whether cautious or bold in their response, most welcomed the challenge of new ideas and the growth and change in their own understanding that resulted. Participating in a range of feminist events and organizations was seen as essential for gaining information and keeping one's feminism alive. New ideas were selected and reworked to suit individual needs. If the term socialization is to be used to refer to this reworking and adoption of feminist frames, it must be understood as an interactive process, whereby those being socialized are recognized as being actively involved in the framing process.

Negotiating Personal and Collective Identity

In Chapter 3, narrative approaches to movement identities were introduced with the discussion of biographical accounts of becoming feminist. In this section, I return to these ideas, and in particular, to the relationship between collective identity and personal identity in collective action. As Buechler points out, "people who participate in collective action do so only when such action resonates with both an individual and a collective identity that makes such action meaningful."[6] However, as with discussions of consciousness, there is a tendency in movements research to blur individual and cultural levels of analysis and to adopt definitions of collective identity that downplay individual agency.

Johnston, Laraña, and Gusfield suggest that although collective identity constantly changes throughout the life of a social movement, the difficulty of studying such a moving target has led researchers to employ the concept of collective identity as if it was fixed in time and space.[7] This approach is adopted by Debra Friedman and Doug McAdam. Consistent with the rational choice perspective of RMT, they define collective identity as "a shorthand designation announcing a status—a set of attitudes, commitments, and rules of behavior—that those who assume the identity can be expected to subscribe to."[8] In a similar manner to the framing and socialization approaches to collective consciousness, they see collective identities as produced and shaped by movement leaders then offered to individuals as selective incentives to motivate participation.

The mobilization of identity is also central to Taylor and Whittier's research into activism within a lesbian feminist community. Defining collective identity as "the shared definition of a group that derives from members' common interests, experiences, and solidarity," they develop a detailed model based on boundaries, consciousness, and negotiations for understanding the ongoing construction of collective identity.[9] According to this model, boundaries mark differences between activists and their opponents. They increase awareness of in-group commonality and out-group difference, thereby strengthening collective identity. In this formulation, as with Friedman and McAdam's approach, collective identity comes to resemble Durkheim's conscience collective—a social fact over and above the individual. While generally critical of the tendency to reify collective identity in this way, Johnston, et al, concede that there is a "grain of insight" in the Durkheimian position: "To share a collective identity means not only to have had a part in constituting it but also, in some instances, 'obeying' its normative proscriptions."[10]

Narrative approaches capture this dual nature of collective identity. The narratives constructed by social movements contest socially dominant discourses about who it is possible to be, thus creating alternative and oppositional identity resources through which individuals can construct personal identity. However, adopting such narratives as one's own can mean submitting oneself to a more-or-less rigidly defined collective identity. It also requires not only self-recognition within the discourse, but also recognition from others, and this is not always forthcoming.[11]

In the data presented below, it is evident that for many of the women in this study tensions arose in relation to in-group, out-group boundaries and to the sense of having to conform to collective identity. Tension revolved around a number of issues. First, tension existed between a desire for acceptance and recognition from the group versus a desire for personal autonomy. This was expressed in a variety of ways by a number of women. Some talked about a fear of being consumed by, or of submitting to, the group. Others mentioned rigidity within feminist groups, problems with labels, and the requirement to behave according to labels. A second theme revolved around feelings of inadequacy some women experienced in comparison to more educated and knowledgeable feminists. A third related theme concerned the problem of gaining recognition from other feminist women for one's self-definition as feminist. These themes were evident in interviews with long-term and strongly identified feminists as well as with those women who had more recently become involved in feminist groups. For some women, these tensions led to ambivalent feelings concerning participation and even to withdrawal from movement organizations or events.

"Sometimes I feel that I can't go against current thinking"

Catherine, whose involvement in feminism was fairly recent, described her feelings of distress during an exercise at the 1991 Winter Institute Workshop. She saw herself as having spent most of her life submitting to authority, and in particular to the authority of women, "I would just sit and say yes and no, and nothing else . . . Just polite things, and that's all." The long struggle to move beyond this way of being, "to get up and say what I really want," had left Catherine with an aversion to being told what to do. However, to her dismay, she found herself at the workshop in danger of submitting to outside authority once again:

> In that first session on the Saturday, I understood that the idea was to get some clue as to the diversity of representatives of feminism in the group, and how diverse feminism really was. That's what I understood Dale was saying, and yet when we got into our group I could see that I was in danger. For a moment—probably more than a moment—I sat there and I felt myself going into my old mode of withdrawal and I was terrified because I thought "I didn't come to

> this, to have a repeat performance of what I'd been doing for the last 40 years or more!" . . . I felt myself in great danger of submitting, as I'd done all my life, to women, to authority . . . going back to the old ways of being dominated by authority.

To submit to the authority of the more assertive members of the workshop group would, in Catherine's view, have negated the effort she had made to change previous destructive patterns of behavior. In this case, however, she did not submit or withdraw from the situation, but summoned the courage to express her opinion within the small group:

> It was a real turning point for me because I felt that my ideas were just as important as everyone else's, and yet I felt as though, at first, that they weren't going to be accepted. And then, when I made the decision to get right with it, and not withdraw, and somebody said to me "What do you think?" and I told them . . . It gave me great pleasure, because it was a real critical sort of point.

It was not only women who were new to feminism who struggled to assert themselves and express their views within feminist groups. Some women whose commitment to feminism spanned a number of years similarly talked about a tension between going along with the group and asserting themselves. Talking about her mixed feelings about attending the 1992 Winter Institute Workshop, Anne, a long-term and highly committed feminist, said:

> Sometimes I feel that I can't, you know, that it could be a problem with my lack of assertiveness—that I can't go against the current thinking . . . And that's probably another reason why I tend to say, "Well, will I go to this workshop or not?" because I might find it a bit oppressive.

Despite a long-term involvement, Anne found it difficult to express views contrary to the dominant opinion within feminist groups. Consequently, she tended in such situations to remain silent, a position she experienced as disempowering. The overall result was ambivalence about participating in feminist workshops.

Others expressed a similar ambivalence. Susan, another long-term feminist, also talked about her lack of comfort in group situations. She perceived a lack of tolerance for different opinions and a tendency to label people within feminist groups. In particular she felt nervous and insecure about expressing her views in situations such as the Winter Institute workshop where there were many women she did not know:

> There is not that freedom to really just express who you are and
> what you're about, because of all these terms, labels, rules, dah, dah,
> dah, dah, dah, dah. So that I withdraw a bit, but I withdraw into my
> arrogance, you know what I mean. I mean, "Yeah, well I'm okay!"
> (laugh) It's a protective barrier for me.

Susan preserved her sense of self by withdrawing, as she said, into her ar-
rogance, but she was concerned that other women whose voices may be
suppressed might withdraw to a less powerful position. Talking more generally about feminist groups, she reiterated her dislike of labels, expressing
the view that expecting people to fit within the boundaries defined by labels was destructive and elitist:

> It comes down to my whole feelings about the labeling of something
> . . . If you've got to wear that label to be accepted, to me that detracts
> from what the whole point of feminism is. I mean everybody's at
> different stages, so again it comes down to that you need that toler-
> ance, and it's the tolerance that helps people to learn and it helps
> people to educate each other and to experience ideas, and if you
> centralize too much that you have to be of a particular wavelength,
> or thought, or "degree of," you isolate the bulk of people from being
> part of it . . . To be that elitist excludes so many people and the
> whole point, in theory, for me, is that we should all be helping each
> other as women, no matter where you're at.

Julie also felt that acceptance within some feminist groups was contingent
upon going along with dominant views. In one group she found that "other
people were seeing me questioning too many things." Her response was also
to withdraw but, unlike Susan, not to a position of personal strength:

> I went through a period where I began to question whether I fitted
> any group . . . It's frustrating because it actually limits your own self
> confidence, and I felt the whole idea of women and feminism, in
> whatever guise it is, was strengthening women. And if you're actu-
> ally making people lose their confidence, it's not working.

Patricia, another strongly identified feminist, expressed a similar reluctance
about organized groups or events. In the initial interview, she explained her
lack of involvement in discussion or reading groups as follows:

> Well, I guess I'm almost a lapsed feminist, I think that I don't iden-
> tify with groups or groupings or that. I find that feminism has the
> difficulties of any other ideologies becoming intrusive and exclu-
> sive, and that's sometimes kept me separate from feminist groups

. . . in the recent past. But, in terms of my personal relationships and the way I relate to people, in work time and other places that I identify with, yes, I'm a feminist.

Lorna, a highly identified, long-term feminist talked about critically appraising and accepting feminist views selectively. She also described the long and somewhat difficult process of achieving sufficient self-confidence to reject powerfully argued perspectives. In the past, she had found it difficult to reconcile differences of opinion and had tended to question her own level of commitment rather than the ideas proffered by well-known feminists. Discussing Sheila Jeffreys' visit to Townsville in the follow-up interview, she said:

> It's always difficult for me to feel that I don't agree with what really strong committed feminists say. I think "Oh they must be right," you know, "I mustn't have just discovered the truth yet." So that's the way it's challenging for me, is to allow myself to believe that my opinions are okay, too, and that I don't have to agree with everything that is said. That, I suppose, I can absorb what I need to, into my way of thinking and that's okay . . . I used to try and believe everything. You know, I didn't know how to be a proper feminist (laugh). It's sort of like "If I think this, how can I call myself a feminist? Because that isn't what 'they' think." And it wasn't until I realized that there were all these streams, there were femin*isms*, and that if we did all have as our vision a transformed society in which there was an end to domination, then that seemed to be at least a common ground to meet with others who would have an opinion and would say "Well, yes, I can sit comfortably enough with that" or "No, I won't accept that."

Unlike others discussed above, Lorna did not withdraw from feminist groups, but continued to work on developing her own vision of a transformed society for women. It is interesting that Lorna points to her growing awareness of a diversity of feminisms as contributing to her increased self-confidence as a feminist. This ties in with the findings of the last chapter, where it was noted that higher levels of education were associated with stronger identification with feminism. It seems that those women who identified most strongly as feminist had greater access to the diversity of feminist thought, and, therefore, a diversity of potential narratives for defining the world and the self in feminist terms.

"It's been one group where I've felt less educated than the other women that are there"

Another theme that emerged from a number of interviews concerned feelings of inadequacy in terms of feminist knowledge. A couple of women who were new to feminism said they felt a need to read more feminist books and to be more knowledgeable about feminism before claiming the identity of feminist. The Winter Institute workshop inspired a number of women to buy or borrow feminist books. Rhonda and Liz borrowed books from the Townsville Women's Centre; Sandra bought one of the women's novels mentioned by Dale Spender at the workshop; Laura borrowed Spender's *Women of Ideas* from a friend, and Barbara and Catherine both asked their local libraries to order feminist books.[12]

For Laura, reading up on feminism was a response to feelings of inadequacy in relation to her lack of knowledge of feminist authors and texts. Laura described herself as a "closet feminist" when asked whether she called herself a feminist: "I don't know whether I am or not. I think I, I think I am, I think I'm a feminist and I think I was before I went but I'm a sort of a closet feminist (laugh) . . . I didn't know whether I measured up . . . so I didn't name myself as a feminist." Responding to the hesitancy in Laura's answer, I asked her about the idea of having to measure up, and what this meant to her:

> When I got back from the camp the first thing I did was to get a lend of a book from Betty on all the history of women because I didn't know anything about all these women who had done all these wonderful things and, sort of, that made me think, well you know, you can't be a feminist (laugh) if you don't know these things. And it sort of, it was overwhelming on the weekend, . . . and I sort of felt like, "Oh, I'm a feminist, but I don't know what sort of one!" . . . I just felt at the camp really inadequate in terms of my knowledge of feminism and that's made me more interested in finding out more about it.

Similarly, Nicole said she "felt like a little bit of a fraud" at the workshop because she did not share the level of knowledge of others there and because she "had no previous commitment to actively doing something."

Feeling inadequate compared to those who were more familiar with women's history, feminist theory, or feminist authors was, again, not restricted to those new to feminism. Emma first encountered feminism at university and had actively identified as a feminist for many years, yet she also talked about feeling less knowledgeable than other women in a feminist reading group to which she belonged. Because of this, she was reluctant to contribute to discussions:

It's been one group where I've felt—I don't know—less educated than the other women that are there . . . Like it's a bigger part of their life than what it is for me . . . So I guess I've been aware that they have a stronger background than I do, so I've tended to not say a lot. You know, that classic thing of thinking what I had to say wasn't that important.

Emma also talked about her continuing attempts to change "and actually participate a bit more" in this group.

"Some feminists would not consider me feminist enough"

There were numerous examples where women recognized that their self-definition as a feminist was not necessarily accepted by others and was open to challenge. Some described situations where they had actually been challenged. For others, there was a feeling that their self-definition could be challenged even if they had not actually experienced this themselves. Their concerns were similar to those above who felt inadequate around more knowledgeable women.

Jacqui recognized herself as a feminist but was not sure whether others would accept her self-definition, "I think I'm a feminist. I don't know for how long. It's a developing thing, I mean, I—some people may not call me a feminist because I'm not as far ahead as they are, or whatever, so it is a developing thing."

For Rachel, feminism means women gaining strength, being able to speak up and voice their feelings and opinions, and knowing how to look after themselves. On the basis of this definition she saw herself as a feminist; however, she recalled being told by another participant at the 1991 Winter Institute workshop that her definition of feminism was a weak one:

For me that's feminism. I haven't got it with me—a little piece—somebody wrote it, an author wrote it, and she said: "I don't really know what feminism is, but I know that whenever I express opinions that differentiate me from a doormat, people call me a feminist"[13] (laugh), and I really liked that because I felt that my husband saw me as a doormat, and various other people saw me as such a thing and whenever I did express opinions they seemed to be quite annoyed with me, they didn't like it at all . . . And so I really like that, but I think other women there had a much stronger view of feminism . . . Another woman there told me that was a very weak view of feminism, but I like that one.

Stella talked about confronting a similar attitude among feminist friends in Sydney with whom she stayed while attending a lesbian feminist conference.

From their more political perspective, Stella's self definition as a feminist was questioned.

Talking about issues of group belonging, and acceptance of different types of feminism (radical, socialist, revolutionary), Emma said she did not classify herself as a particular type of feminist anymore. In relation to her membership of a feminist discussion group she said, "I know I used to try to do that, and I know a lot of people still do, but it seems to work out okay." Classifying oneself as a particular type of feminist involves making a membership claim to a particular collective identity and Emma was clearly aware that such claims leave one open to judgment from others.

Another woman said she self-identified as a feminist and felt very strongly about feminist issues, but rarely called herself a feminist publicly. She recalled being questioned in some feminist groups about her manner of dress:

> I still get questioned in some groups about my appearance, because of the way I dress, and the fact I always wear pearls. It's you know, amongst my groups, there's a legend, you know, the only person who wears overalls and pearls. But, it's my—it's become almost me, but yeah, I have no doubt about my own beliefs.

She also expressed concern and impatience with women who make assessments and judge each other on their level of feminist consciousness, "I don't think anybody ever is the ultimate feminist, despite that some people think they may have reached that point. There is no such thing."

Ambivalence about defining oneself as feminist was expressed by a number of women and was as much about how other people related to them as about their own appraisal of their beliefs and actions. On the one hand, they were aware of the general social stigma attached to the label feminist, but, on the other, they were aware that labeling themselves feminist within feminist settings is a public statement of inclusion and belonging with which others may not always agree. Recognition from other feminists was necessary to the successful taking up of a feminist identity.

Multiple Identities

Closely related to the issues discussed above were tensions and contradictions arising from different life circumstances, and from the multiple ontological narratives through which the women in this study sought to define themselves and were defined by others. Multiple narratives, both dominant and oppositional, circulate within contemporary society, each attempting to name and constitute persons. Despite this, identity has often been theorized as unitary and integrated in a way that underestimates the tensions and struggle involved in forging identities. Calhoun argues: "As lived, identity is always project, not settled accomplishment" and this was certainly true for many of the women in this study.[14]

Participants were heterogeneous across a number of significant dimensions. The sample contained both lesbian and heterosexual women. Some interviewees were married or living in de facto relationships with men, some lived with female partners, and others were single and lived alone. Some were mothers, others were not. They ranged in age from early 20s to over 60. These characteristics are not simply demographic variables, however. They also have significant implications for personal identity. Narratives that define old women, young women, mothers, lesbians, married women, and single women are constructed by dominant institutions and by feminists. Consequently, many of the women in this study found themselves caught between sometimes contradictory and competing identities. Contradictions and tensions surrounding marriage, motherhood, and sexuality were the most significant.

Marriage and Motherhood

A common source of tension was a perceived incompatibility between marriage and motherhood, and being feminist. Colleen, for example, talked about this, "I struggle, because I'm married and I have children and I think it's easier for women to be feminists if they're single, without kids." The source of tension was twofold for Colleen. She felt torn between her husband's traditional expectations of her as a wife and mother and the expectations of other feminists who did not share her experiences of marriage and motherhood:

> Often I get the feeling that they [other feminists] see me, and think, "How can you be a feminist? You're married and you've got kids." I think, mm, I think a lot of people think "feminists" and "lesbians" together, but I think, I want to be married and I want to have a family, but I also want to be a feminist. I suppose other women would struggle with that, other women the same. It's hard for me, especially when I've got this fairly traditional kind of man.

The struggle is difficult because Colleen values and is committed to both her identity as a feminist and her identity as a wife and mother. Talking about her marital relationship, she said:

> Our biggest struggle I think is my growing, and my growth towards being feminist. It really upset the balance of our marriage a lot, but I'm not—that's okay for me. If he can't handle it, well that's his problem, he's got to. He's grown along with me to a degree, but he's

got to get used to that, because I think it's so important that I don't want to give it up—the feminist bit.

Jocelyn also talked about the difficulty of resolving similar contradictions. She talked about always being expected to be a conventional, working-class Australian woman. However, her personal journey had led to a strong identification and commitment to feminism:

> My philosophies and values are radical feminist even though I still do have this very conventional Australian mother and wife activity going on, so I'm still, I'm schizophrenic in that area . . . On one hand I've got this great kind of stubbornness and commitment to keeping the family together, but, on the other hand, I've got a great commitment to myself as a feminist as well; and at the moment I've got them both going side by side so it's okay.

Like Colleen, Jocelyn is caught in the middle. Her commitment to at least some aspects of traditional, hegemonic definitions of what a typical Australian working-class mother should be is not a blind commitment born out of a lack of awareness of alternatives. It is a stubborn commitment that persists in uneasy tension with an equally strong commitment to feminism.

When Janet decided to remarry in 1992, she reduced her contact and involvement with the women's center. She explained that her withdrawal was not the result of pressure from her new partner; rather it was her fear of being judged by other women that kept her away:

> When we got married this year, I wanted to invite some of the women from the women's center, . . . and I thought to myself "Now what will these women think at the women's center, if I tell them I'm getting married?" . . . I didn't want them to be judging me. I know it seems strange, but I was judged in my last marriage.

It is unlikely that the women at the center would have judged Janet, but her fear of this possibility had consequences for her behavior nonetheless.

In the early years of her involvement in feminism, Lorna "used to agonize over what was the proper feminist." In those days, tension between her commitment to marriage and motherhood and her commitment to feminism was a problem, "I really didn't know where I stood and how I could be the true feminist, and still do this, and be married and have these kids and love them, you know. (laugh) And boys especially; all those sorts of challenges were there."

Kathleen and Rose also talked about being mothers of sons, and how this influenced their feminism, particularly in relation to separatist ideologies. Kathleen noted a tension between what she saw as "high-flying ideas" about "women's land" and the reality of existing in a world with men, "We have male children, and my male children are as important to me as my females. So it's got to be all put together so that being a feminist doesn't mean that you've got to withdraw. I don't see that as the way." Rose also rejected separatism for similar reasons. In her search for personal change and movement toward alternative lifestyle politics and feminism, Rose chose not to adopt a separatist lifestyle primarily because of her commitment to motherhood, "I don't know what I'd have been if I wasn't the mother of four males . . . I never chose—I mean, I'd have probably been an absolute separatist feminist by about 1980 if I didn't have four sons. And I chose not to go the women only road."

Sexuality

Closely related to the tensions associated with the identities of wife, mother, and feminist were issues of sexual identity. Both heterosexual and lesbian women talked about the relationship between sexual and feminist identities. For the majority of those who identified as lesbian, these two aspects were merged. Typical comments were "I can't separate the two" and "I choose to be a lesbian because of my feminism." On the other hand, for heterosexual women, their feminist identity was often a source of tension within their personal relationships, while their identity as heterosexual was sometimes a problem for them as feminists.

Marie, for instance, said she had "always found it very difficult to reconcile [her] feminism with a relationship with a man." Doing so required "constantly managing an incongruity." The "maleness" of her partner's views and the legitimacy, rights, and privilege that he enjoyed as a male in a patriarchal society were a constant source of friction within the relationship. Her increasing commitment to feminism was bringing to the fore contradictions that she found uncomfortable and difficult to resolve:

> I get torn between believing that one way that you can assist women's rights and opportunities, and impose a woman's view, is by educating men too, and by breaking down the myths that only feminists—I mean, real feminism, you can only be a lesbian, or not be in a relationship with men, and those sort of myths that are perpetuated by men, there's a part of me that wants to retain this, so that I can constantly challenge it . . . The more that women are not in relationships with men, the easier it's going to be for them to perpetuate the stereotype.

Although Marie suggests that men perpetuate these myths, a number of women felt that the equation of feminism and lesbianism was also prevalent within feminism.[15] The feeling that, as a woman living in a heterosexual relationship one may be judged and evaluated by other feminists, was a concern for Carol. Prior to attending the Winter Institute workshop, she was not sure whether the group would accept her:

> I was curious about what level of dislike of men there would be, and I was probably a bit anxious about how I would be—I mean, I'm in a heterosexual relationship, and how that would be viewed, and all that sort of stuff. I was a bit curious about how accepted you'd be if you weren't, you know, living singly, or celibate or lesbian.

Another heterosexual feminist whose involvement in feminist groups had spanned several years suggested, "In the women's movement, my understanding is that if you're a heterosexual woman you're in a different category to what, I guess, what some people would see as the true lesbian feminist." In this formulation, heterosexual women may be recognized as feminist, but not as true feminists. Thus, this woman felt that she was "a bit of a wishy-washy feminist," a feeling that was reinforced by Sheila Jeffreys' visit.

Jeffreys' position was variously described by heterosexual women as "hard line," "almost missionary," "a bit over the top," "a bit black and white," "confronting," and "controversial," but also, and often by the same women, as "interesting," "stimulating," "absolutely amazing," and "powerful." Jeffreys herself was described as "brilliant," "extremely intelligent," "wonderful," "fascinating," and "inspiring." Emma found Jeffreys' ideas interesting but rejected "the idea that for us to be completely happy we have to be lesbians." Lorna, who was quoted earlier in relation to the difficult process of coming to terms with ideals of the "proper feminist" and the "truth," suggested:

> For me, I just have to accept that I just won't be able to think exactly like Sheila Jeffreys thinks about heterosexuality, you know . . . Maybe it's because I'm still very much a heterosexual, but it doesn't mean that I can't see some of what she's saying . . . I've been able to listen and say "That's an interesting analysis, but I don't know that it's for me."

Margaret acknowledged the value of being challenged, but felt angry and disappointed after hearing Jeffreys speak:

> I felt angry with her—I felt really fascinated by her speaking because I think that she is really extremely intelligent and I wasn't sort of horrified really by her ideas of separatism because I've heard that before and I can understand that's a viable option for some women, but I felt the night that she talked at *Gertrude's* it was almost like a

challenge to heterosexual women. Or, not even a challenge, it was saying "You're doing it wrong." You know, "I'm right, you're wrong!" There didn't seem to be any scope for "We can both be right, we do things differently." . . . I realized she perhaps wasn't as open minded as I had hoped she was.[16]

On the positive side, Jeffreys' views stimulated thought and discussion. Kathleen suggested that "people have to be like that to really raise consciousness." Lisa agreed:

I think it made a lot of people think, whether it was negative or positive the way people were thinking, certainly she made a lot of people think because she is a very controversial person. And I don't think that's bad, I think sometimes it's good to have someone who's very controversial because it makes people question where we are and what we're at, and what do these women mean to us. So I found it very interesting.

The concern expressed by some of the heterosexual women in this study that they are not fully accepted as feminists is not entirely in their own minds. Some lesbian feminists in this study expressed the view that heterosexual feminists were not as "advanced" as lesbian feminists. Some also felt that it was important to remain somewhat separate from heterosexual feminists. One woman suggested that she was "having less patience with heterosexual feminism," which she saw as peripheral to her "lifestyle and to where my life is heading." Following Sheila Jeffreys' visit, another suggested:

I've become stronger in my belief that it's necessary for me to spend more time with feminist lesbian women, so that's become a greater issue for me. Whereas in the past I was more inclined to think that it was fine for me to spend time with my heterosexual feminist friends.

She attributed this change to a strengthening feminist commitment over the past year and to a "growing awareness that being a lesbian is a political act." She described herself as previously having been a "wishy-washy," and "middle of the road" feminist. She now felt that it was important to spend more time with and to seek support and friendship with "women of a like mind."

In discussing her reasons for not attending the *Reclaim the Night* march in 1992, another clearly indicated her growing impatience with heterosexual feminist theories and strategies, and heterosexual feminists:

I've been involved in *Reclaim the Night* marches for 10 years or something, and I'm just pissed off that for 10 years women have been walking around saying "Look men, we don't want you to hit us any more," and I just find it really frustrating that the message hasn't gotten through, and I have to ask, Why hasn't it got through? And I think maybe, you know, the methods are wrong . . . While publicity is a good thing, it's not going to change male behavior. And until women completely withdraw their services from men, then male behavior isn't going to change. Why should it? So I don't think it's enough. I don't think it's enough to get a crowd of women to march once a year on a Saturday, with a couple of banners in a party-like atmosphere. Even though some important things are said in the speeches and some important media releases are given out. I don't think it's enough.

Although frustration at the lack of progress for women is understandable, its expression here comes close to blaming heterosexual women for male violence, rather than men.

Not surprisingly, lesbian women in this study received Sheila Jeffreys' ideas with fewer mixed feelings. For most, it provided a strong affirmation of self-identity. Her visit was described as "a real highlight" and her ideas as "stimulating," "interesting," "thought provoking," and "brilliant." The challenge she presented to heterosexual women was also welcomed. Judy said she "loved the way that she gave the feminist society of Townsville a serving for not supporting their lesbian sisters more openly." Similarly, Helen recalled:

I felt really, really, fantastically happy when Sheila Jeffreys said at Gertrude's, "For too long, heterosexual women had given lesbian women a hard time," because we'd remained invisible, even within feminism. I think having her say that made me feel more comfortable, because from my experience over the past 12 or so years, a lot of feminist action is done by dykes.

Negotiating Multiple Identities
Women dealt with and negotiated the tensions and contradictions of the multiple identities of feminist, wife, mother, and heterosexual woman in a variety of ways and with varying success. As noted above, the sources of pressure to prioritize one identity over others were also multiple: from husbands, children, and other feminists.[17]

Compartmentalizing—Keeping It Separate
Some women dealt with the tensions and contradictions of multiple identities by keeping different aspects of their lives and identities separate. In other words, they tended to compartmentalize their lives. Jocelyn coped

with the incongruity of expectations placed on her as a traditional working-class mother by maintaining this aspect of her identity separate from her feminist self. Interestingly, she justified this strategy to herself by redefining the problem on the basis of feminist understandings:

> One of the things that really is some comfort to me is that most patriarchal thinking is that things should be black or white. You've got to—you're supposed to know exactly what you're doing, you're supposed to be single minded, but that's very much a male way of thinking. Children have no problems with having a whole lot of unresolved things going on in their lives. They can compromise, . . . and I think women can do that very well, and I think I'm simply reflecting that as well.

By framing the tension inherent in multiple and competing identities in this way Jocelyn was able to maintain a coherent and positive sense of self. However, she also contemplated a possible future without men, "You don't ever know what could tip things either way. I mean I might end up so, so fully committed to feminism that I couldn't bear having a man in my life, which means getting rid of a husband and a son and retreating into some kind of separatist activities."

For Anne there was a sense in which others dictated the strategy of keeping a barrier or separation between her life as a member of a family and her life as a feminist. She saw it as understood within the feminist groups to which she belonged that this was the way it should be:

> I don't tend to have my feminist friends to my home . . . It's obvious that that's kept separate anyway. I think I became aware of that very early on, that the particular circle of feminist friends that you meet at the women's center here, that the socializing with them is always within their group and you don't include your spouse or any of your other friends. It's always that separate group . . . I guess it's always—it was made clear to me at the start, that part of being a feminist in this—attached to this particular women's center, is to not include spouses, or friends that perhaps weren't feminist.

This understanding went beyond not bringing outsiders along to meetings or into the women's center. It extended to not inviting feminist friends to her home, where the existence of another life and identity was obvious.

Marie also talked about keeping her feminism separate from her marriage and personal life, "I used to separate it a little bit, from other parts of who I was." Like Anne, she viewed this strategy as problematic and as imposed by others. Unlike Anne, however, she perceived the pressure to separate and compartmentalize her life and identities as originating with her husband:

> My husband, and I think men generally, really try to set that up, and try to say "Look, keep it separate. I don't care what you do outside, as long as you don't bring it into the relationship," which is an absolute. I mean that's a ridiculous, illogical statement, but I think it's because it takes so much energy to do both all the time, that it's almost like you subconsciously allow yourself to lapse and let things go by, in order to maintain some sort of feeling of harmony.

Marie found the incongruity of this situation increasingly uncomfortable and difficult to manage, and contemplated the possibility of a future without any men in her life, "I can conceivably imagine a future without men. And I couldn't have a few years ago, yeah. But they're too much hard work, and you just realize that they're just so much hard work (laugh)."

Forging Change through Assertion and Negotiation

A number of women found that compartmentalization was unsatisfactory as a strategy for dealing with competing pressures to prioritize one aspect of identity over another. They attempted to deal with multiple identities by asserting themselves both in personal relationships and within feminist groups, insisting on their right to forge their own hybrid, multiple identities and belongings. As noted earlier, Colleen's response to her husband's unease with her growing feminist identification was to expect him to take responsibility for his own feelings and to change and grow to accommodate her new sense of self. By the follow-up interview, she had, to some extent, resolved the tension in her marriage and between her identity as a mother and as a feminist. In addition to insisting on changes within her marriage, during 1992 she attempted to reconcile her identity as a mother with her developing feminism. One example of this was her decision to take her young daughters to a *Reclaim the Night* march. Their response was particularly significant for Colleen:

> For about two weeks later they kept chanting the chants that we were saying on the night. Here they were, playing with Barbies, and they were saying "Yes means yes, no means no!" It was wonderful, and we'd have a little chant together and it was really good. So I thought "that's wonderful, I'm really glad." I'm really glad. I suppose, before, feminism didn't fit well with me as a family, but it does now. It's fitting much better now. I can be a feminist, but I can also be a mother and a wife and that's fitting in better for me.

Colleen had also become more assertive in dealing with the expectations of other feminist women, taking on only those commitments that she felt able to squeeze into her busy life.

Although Sheila Jeffreys' visit created considerable anxiety, it also provided the impetus for a get-together of heterosexual women to discuss issues of relevance to them and to reevaluate and assert their own position as heterosexual women. Although one woman felt that it would have been preferable to address the issues in a mixed group of lesbian and heterosexual women—"there didn't seem to be any point in having a broken group of women"—others found it useful. For instance, one woman said, "I felt that was a very good dinner. I think the women who went to it all felt a sense of relief that we could talk about some of our concerns."

Although Margaret felt angry at being positioned as "wrong" when she heard Jeffreys speak, she also "fairly quickly realized what a great benefit it was because it made me look at what I was doing and clarify it and justify it." Thus, Margaret refused the negative positioning of her as a heterosexual feminist that was inherent in Jeffreys' analysis. She created for herself a positive outcome. She said, "I don't know if that was her intention? I don't really think that was her intention, but that was the outcome that it had for me, and it was successful."

For Margaret, achieving a level of assertiveness where she felt comfortable putting herself first was the result of a maturing process that had taken a number of years. This, she said, involved caring for herself, becoming "assertive in my own right," and working "very hard against pleasing people all the time, . . . including other women." Interestingly, she recognized a paradox in that through feminism women learn to be more assertive, but when this is exercised within feminist groups it can create tensions:

> It's probably by being involved in these sorts of areas that I've managed to become very assertive in my own right, which probably doesn't help the group itself sometimes . . . If everybody's making individual decisions about their own welfare, you're not going to get that really set up group that you want all the time . . . On the one hand, we're teaching ourselves all these things, but on the other hand, it does cause friction to an extent because you're less pliable within a group.

The tensions and contradictions associated with the construction of feminist subjectivity and the associated need to negotiate multiple identities elicited a range of negative emotions that were, in some cases, detrimental to continuing feminist involvement. Women felt unable to act assertively in feminist groups; they felt less educated than other feminists; they felt that they had to live up to other's definitions of feminism; and they felt torn between multiple identities. The source of these tensions and contradictions and the negative emotions they give rise to is primarily related to issues of identification and belonging. Identity narratives are often based on exclusively defined categories that suggest that to be a particular type of person forecloses the possibility of being some other type of person. On the other hand, knowledge was more easily negotiated and managed than feelings and identity. Ideas could be accepted or rejected, but feelings tended to intrude in ways that were unwanted, and a sense of belonging required not only self-identification, but also recognition from others.

Meaning and Identity: Social Facts or Social Constructions

The dual nature of collective identity and collective consciousness as both processes of social construction and constraining sets of beliefs, rules and expectations emerges clearly from the data presented in this chapter. A central issue is the consequent struggle and negotiation that occurs at the interface between collective and personal identity. Women strive to participate as agents in the constructive process at the collective level, but their participation is not a foregone conclusion.

Consciousness-raising (CR), as practiced by women in the early years of the Women's Liberation movement, provided a forum where women could meet as equals to discuss experiences and generate knowledge. Through CR women collectively created the public narratives of feminism and, in the process, created themselves as feminists. The women in this study, however, generally encountered feminist discourse through the already constructed public narratives of seminars, lectures, and written texts. As public narratives, feminist ideas were already codified and reified to a large extent. Encounters with these forms of feminist discourse were experienced as liberating when they provided the language through which to express long-held feelings, but there were also tensions. Many women found that aspects of their lived experience contradicted specific feminist stories made available to them. Some found it difficult to raise these issues within feminist groups. In such cases, collective beliefs were experienced as oppressive, as existing outside and above the individual as "social facts." This was evident throughout the data, but was most obvious in relation to Sheila Jeffreys' analysis of heterosexuality.

A number of movements scholars have noted the significance of group boundaries and boundary maintenance practices as central and necessary mechanisms in the construction of collective identity.[18] Boundaries enhance solidarity and help define who we are in contrast to who we are not. "Participants establish group boundaries through a symbolic system and by constructing an alternative culture or network that serves as a 'world apart' from the dominant society."[19] However, boundary maintenance, which is often based on fixed, unified definitions of identity, also generates intramovement disputes and factionalism. Barbara Ryan, in her study of the American women's movement, has argued that radical identities, based on rigid ideological divisions and boundaries, operated as demobilizing factors in the small group sector of the movement in the 1970s as "disputes over theory turned into disputes over who was the most feminist or who was the right kind of feminist."[20] This same pattern is evident in my data. When collective identity is encountered in crystallized form and boundaries are rigid, identity becomes a package to be accepted entirely. In this situation, an individual who is new to the movement may feel excluded for being who they are, and may withdraw from the movement before getting close enough to find out what the movement is really about and how it might relate to their life. Locked out of the constructive process, they may decide that the price of "insider" status is too high. The image of movements actively recruiting participants is thus thrown into question. In Chapter 3 I described a group of women whose biographical accounts of becoming feminist can be seen as a quest for personal change, but even women who are actively seeking transformative experiences can be put off by rigid boundaries that reinforce categorical rather than biographical subjectivity.

For all the evidence in this data of collective identity and consciousness existing as crystallized "social facts," it is also clear that their status as "fact" is constantly challenged. Women in this study did not passively adopt feminist consciousness or identity as unified packages. Instead, they asserted their right to autonomy and agency. They struggled to participate in an ongoing process of construction. They accepted, rejected, and mused over feminist ideas about the world, and they selectively adopted the ontological positions made available within existing feminist narratives. They acted as agents both when they chose to become more involved and when they chose to withdraw.

Most women who become involved in feminism have already rejected, or are in the process of rejecting, hegemonic, externally imposed definitions of femininity and womanhood. They are therefore wary of uncritically adopting a new identity presented as a unified package. They strive to forge their own multiple identities consistent with their own lived experience, drawing upon a range of public narratives including feminist ones. This was evident in the way women in this study talked about labels.[21] It was also evident in their responses to feminist texts and speakers.

I suggested earlier in this chapter that recognition, both self-recognition and recognition from others, is fundamental to identity. The data demonstrate that achieving this recognition is not unproblematic. Claims to the identity feminist were always open to challenge. This accords with Friedman and McAdam's analysis of collective identity as a selective incentive, as a status that is constructed and controlled by movement leaders and used as a reward that can be bestowed or withheld as required to motivate participation.[22] However, most of the women in this study valued the opportunity to participate as agents in the ongoing construction of collective identity more highly than they valued the right to claim access to a static, externally defined, identity.

The tensions the women reported in relation to identity claims were not primarily about impression management—as Hunt and Benford have theorized identity talk in the peace and justice movement—rather, they were about the struggle to achieve recognition at the same time as retaining a sense of agency in their own lives.[23] Simply to manage impressions and gain acceptance within the collectivity was insufficient. The women in this study expressed a desire to be recognized for who they were, in all their multiplicity. Thus, when the opportunity to contribute to the constructive process was limited, they tended to reduce involvement in feminist groups.

The data presented in this chapter indicate that the interpersonal context in which movement frames (narratives for knowing the world and knowing the self) are encountered, make it more or less easy to accept or reject them. When challenging ideas are encountered in a book, however persuasively written, the book can be put down, or read "against the grain," with little possibility of offending the author. Walking out halfway through a lecture is more difficult, especially for women who have learned the lessons of femininity well. Going against the grain in a workshop or small group setting is generally even more difficult. The tensions and contradictions involved in negotiating feminist consciousness and identity were most evident in small group contexts, explaining the reluctance of a number of moderately and highly identified feminists to join discussion or reading groups. The high association between education and feminist identification, noted in Chapter 3, may also be relevant here. In an educational setting it is possible to hear, read, and explore feminist ideas in an environment where one's identity as a feminist is not assumed and where it is (generally) accepted that ideas should be open to debate and discussion. It may also be that feminist collective identity is presented in a less crystallized and reified form in educational settings.

Among the women in this study, striving for agency and autonomy, and for an active role in the ongoing construction of collective and personal identity, was widespread. Interviewees possessed varying resources for achieving this. Some people have greater subjective resources to bring to the process of negotiation and construction of collective consciousness and collective identity. Jane Flax argues that subjectivity consists of multiple components including "temperament and orientations to the world; biological vulnerabilities and needs; capacities for abstract thought, work, and language; aggression; creativity; fantasy; meaning creation; and objectivity."[24] The unique combination of these components within particular individuals will influence their ability to participate in the construction, or, at least, the active interpretation, of collective identity. It will also influence their standing within groups and their power to define the boundaries of collective identity. Thus, while collective identity should not be viewed as a fixed and unitary social fact, clearly collective identity and collective consciousness are not as fluid and open to negotiation as some postmodern theorists suggest. The constant attempts to fix and reify feminist collective identity, and the varying resources and skills that individual women bring to the task of negotiation, mean that many women experience collective identity as a highly viscous fluid. Those who have greater subjective resources are likely to participate more fully in the process of construction and, therefore, to share a greater commitment to the collective identity. This is consistent with findings concerning feminist identification and education. Education enhances the ability for abstract thought, the ability to use language and create meaning. Consequently, those with higher education can more confidently contribute to the constructive process and challenge formulations of collective identity which do not fit their lived experience.

The process of becoming feminist has been presented here in terms of biographical narratives. Interviewees described becoming feminist as a story, with a beginning and an end, but not "the" end. They see the story continuing, and their feminist identity changing and growing into the future. The story also continues in this book, but shifts focus in the following chapter from interactions within feminist groups to the opposition and control women face as feminists in the wider society.

CHAPTER 5

Up against It:
Opposition and Control

If collective action is understood as being constructed through the framing of issues and the construction of collective and personal identity within movement networks, then it is also important to recognize that these processes occur within the limits of a broader environment that is not always receptive. The field within which collective action occurs contains both allies and opponents. As Melucci suggests, "Relationships with the outside—with competitors, allies, and adversaries—and especially the response of the political system and the apparatuses of social control define a field of opportunities and constraints within which the collective action takes shape."[1] Historically, women's mobilization has often encountered a politically hostile climate, meeting with resistance that at times has been violent. Thus, alongside "the study of feminist collective actions, the opposition of patriarchal forces to such demands must always be remembered."[2] For the women in this study, involvement in the women's movement and the process of becoming feminist occurred within a climate of opposition and control that operated at a number of levels and in a variety of sites. This chapter documents first the nature and extent of this opposition and control, second, interviewees responses to it, and third, the impact it had on them emotionally and in terms of continued involvement.

To date, interest in repression of collective action among movements scholars has focused primarily on the institutional level. The role of the state in opposing (and, sometimes, facilitating) social movements has received considerable attention.[3] For example, recent research into protest policing has examined national styles of policing and their effect on mobilization and repertoires of action. Such comparative research has led to the counterintuitive conclusion that harsh policing can aid mobilization by creating "a sense of injustice which increases the perceived risk of inaction."[4] Harsh repression can make people feel that they must act to do something about the situation. Another focus of research into opposition faced by movements at an institutional level has been the emergence and activities of countermovements.[5] These tend to operate in a similar manner to movements and to compete with them for resources and opportunities. They construct opposing frames in relation to issues publicized by movements and use similar strategies in their attempt to sway public opinion in their favor.[6]

Although Zald and McCarthy noted some time ago the wide variety of social control mechanisms, including economic pressure, that may be applied by private individuals and organizations to sanction those involved in social movement activities, little attention has been paid to these informal mechanisms or to opposition and attempts to curtail individual involvement more generally.[7] Nonetheless, the concept of biographical availability, "the absence of personal constraints that may increase the costs and risks of movement participation, such as full-time employment, marriage and family responsibilities," highlights the role significant others play in sustaining or hindering participation in social movements, and hints at social control mechanisms.[8]

The concept of biographical constraints has been used to explain erosion of social movement support and participation in a variety of contexts. In a study of support for the Dutch peace movement, Klandermans examined the reasons why some sympathizers failed to follow through on intentions to participate in major protest events. He concluded that the "turnabout was the result of a combination of factors, . . . the perception that one's environment did not support the movement; plus, initially, the expectation, and later, the experience, of negative reactions from significant others."[9] Similarly, McAdam found that younger applicants to the 1964 Mississippi Freedom Summer project were more likely to withdraw before the start of the project than older applicants. He attributed this to increased parental control that limited their availability for activism.[10] These examples demonstrate the usefulness of the concept of biographical constraints; however, it is important that analysis of such barriers takes into account structured social relationships. Parenthood, for instance, is not equally constraining for men and women since expectations of motherhood and fatherhood are unequal. Similarly, marriage is not equally constraining for men and women. Age and gender are not simple variables; therefore, in order to understand how biographical availability or biographical constraints might influence involvement, it is necessary to look behind the statuses of married, employed, and parent. Notably, an understanding of the barriers women face to movement involvement must take into account the construction of gender in institutions and interaction. For this we can turn to feminist analysis.[11]

A central theme of feminist writing has been the various forms of social control women are subjected to within patriarchal society. In the 1990s a number of authors pointed to an antifeminist backlash linked to the rise of the New Right, particularly in the United States. They described and analyzed patriarchal opposition to feminist mobilization on a broad, cultural, and political level.[12] Despite this work on the backlash, most feminist discussions of social control have focused on patriarchal control of women *per se*, rather than control directed specifically at feminist women. Male violence, and the role it plays in restricting and controlling women's lives, has been a particular focus of this work.[13] There has also been extensive examination of male-dominated institutions of social control—the legal, health, and welfare systems—and of informal control experienced by women in the course of their daily lives. In line with the "personal is political" concept, feminist writers have paid special attention to the informal mechanisms of social control that keep women in their place. As Edwards explains:

> The control of women . . . is exercised to a significant extent through informal mechanisms. It is more likely than is the case with men that particular individuals known to a woman—a male relative, family, close friends or community members—will take responsibility for her regulation and disciplining rather than officials in society.[14]

In relation to informal social control, feminists have drawn upon insights from the work of Foucault. Despite Foucault's own blindness to gender, a number of feminists have found his work on surveillance and disciplinary practices valuable in analyzing the processes by which gendered power relations are reproduced.[15] There are similarities here with Melucci's conceptualization of social movements and social control. Melucci suggests that in complex societies there is a "tendency to create capillary systems of behavior manipulation" whereby social control shifts its target "from the content of action to its languages, from the external regulation of behavior to interference in the cognitive and motivational preconditions for it."[16] These insights are particularly relevant to an examination of the opposition and control faced by feminists, since feminists personify the unruly, oppositional woman whose control is essential to the maintenance of patriarchal social relations.

Opposition to Feminist Involvement

Interviewees encountered opposition to feminist ideas and activities in a variety of settings including the immediate and extended family, the workplace, and in other nonmovement settings.

Immediate Family

Within the context of the family it was common, although not universal, for partners and children to react negatively to feminist involvement. Nineteen of the 45 women in the study were in relationships with men, either married or not, at the time of the 1991 Winter Institute Workshop. For most of these women, their involvement or interest in feminism caused some degree of tension in their relationships, ranging from mild questioning and dismissiveness, through occasional arguments, to major conflict. Six women had male partners who were highly antagonistic toward their feminist involvement and a further three mentioned ex-husbands who had expressed resentment and hostility in the past.

Disparaging or trivializing comments about the woman herself and feminists in general were common and centered around a number of areas including appearance (for example, hairy armpits and legs, clothing, lack of makeup), abnormal or weird behavior or ideas, being a bad wife or mother, and lesbianism. Typical of the comments made about appearance were the following: "He told me I looked absolutely revolting to him . . . I mean, I don't really think I look revolting whether I have makeup on or not"; "He teases me quite a bit—'there goes purple;'" and "He totally disapproves of all this; the unshaved arms and the unshaved legs and also the weird ideas . . . I don't think he approves of me at all, . . . I'm beyond the pale."

Reference to weird or abnormal ideas was common. Male partners who compared such ideas with "normal" conceptions of appropriate femininity made this accusation frequently. One woman's participation in feminist workshops was contrasted to the behavior of normal, "good" mothers. "There's a lot of pressure to stay and do what you should be doing. 'How come you're leaving?' You know, good mothers don't leave for the weekend!" Talking about her husband's reaction to her feminist tendencies another woman said, "You're not supposed to think like that, you know, you can't say that, that's not normal. That's an expression used a lot in our family, 'not normal.'" This woman's husband made disparaging comments about feminists in general in his attempt to dissuade her from becoming involved in feminist activities. "That was the idea that was tried to be painted in my mind—that I would just find a lot of disgruntled women who hated men."

It was not necessary for interviewees to act in overtly feminist ways, or to openly express feminist views, for their "deviancy" to be commented upon. "Inappropriate" displays of emotion or the absence of "correct" emotions were sufficient. One interviewee described her husband's complaint that she had lost her sense of humor since becoming involved in feminism. It was no longer possible for them to enjoy simple pleasures such as watching a movie together:

> He always says now that I've lost my sense of humor, which I'm sure a lot of men say about women that are still sort of angry about feminist stuff. I can't laugh at the same sort of things, I can't watch movies anymore, you know, I'd sooner not bother if there's one skerrick of sexism or if the women are portrayed badly, and I know that we just can't sit down and relax and watch any old tripe any more.

Arlie Hochschild suggests that the display of emotion performs a signal function, reflecting buried perspectives and providing clues to how a person might act.[17] In this case, failure to laugh at sexist movies indicated a perspective on the world that this woman's husband did not share. His response was to accuse her of having lost her sense of humor.

Of all the reports of disparaging comments and teasing from male partners, those related to lesbianism were the most frequent. Although some were supposedly said in jest, many were openly hostile. Talking about her partner's reaction to her attending the Winter Institute Weekend in 1992, one woman provided the following example: "A little bit different reaction than the year before . . . Still the similar comments said in jest, but probably with some truth behind it, things like 'oh, going up to your dykes weekend' and that sort of stuff." Others said, "He knew it was a feminist weekend, and made comments like 'oh you're going up with all your lesso mates' . . . and 'mumble, mumble, all your lesso mates will be up there, I know'" and, from another woman, "He doesn't even know about it, because I thought he'll only say 'oh, those stupid, useless feminists' you know, 'useless, lesbian shithouses' and that's the type of person he is." At its most extreme, one husband attempted to frighten his wife out of attending the 1991 Winter Institute workshop by suggesting that she would be raped by lesbians.

Emotional abuse and emotional withdrawal were also reported. One woman said, "He was violent to me verbally, but what he kept on doing for over a year was he kept on saying it was all my feminist phase." Another described her ex-husband's reaction to her attendance at social nights held at the local women's center, "I used to go to *Gertrude's* until that became such a battle that it was just not worth it, with Paul—he made it very hard . . . It was sort of a treat that I gave myself, but he'd go drinking until I came back . . . By the time I got home he was never a pleasant person." Another interviewee also talked about her husband's drinking as one of many forms of punishment he used against her; others included not eating and refusing to talk. Other women also experienced this type of moodiness and emotional withdrawal, on the part of male partners. The following passage relates to the period leading up to the 1992 workshop:

> I mentioned it a long time before, but then I didn't say anything until the beginning of the week. I said to him "I'm not here this weekend, I'm going to Crystal Creek again" and I think he didn't talk to me for about two days. And then he just withholds his support, and just as I'm leaving he said, "The car doesn't sound too good." He reminds me that I'm going off on a tangent that's unhealthy for the marriage.

Threats were also used, particularly as a means of dissuading wives from attending the Winter Institute workshop. In one case this involved threatening to end the marriage and in another, to harm the children:

> That was a threat perhaps that my husband uses. That if you do this, our marriage will be finished . . . I had the lecture bit, and then he said "Well that's it, that's the end of it, we'll sell the house and split up the money and that's it, you can go your way and be a feminist."

> And one time I remember he was really angry with me going away, and he scared me. I was sitting out in the car ready to go and he got a stick and slapped it on the fence and said "Right oh, you kids, get round the back!" and I went "oh" and I said to Sally "Oh, no, he's going to beat the kids."

Although this woman felt "quite sure" that her husband never would harm their children and that he was "putting on a little show, just to make [her] feel guilty," she nonetheless was placed under considerable pressure not to attend the workshop. This same husband, over a number of years, always demanded sex prior to and immediately after his wife's absence from home:

> When I first started going away for weekends he used to really crack up and I remember, I was thinking about this, this morning, he'd want to have sex before I left, and he'd want to have sex as soon as I got home. I don't know why that was, and he's not like that as much now, but there was this expectation that, you know, "If you're going to go away for three days, we'll have that quota for this week," you know, and it was like he had to arrange it for him.

Talking about how things had improved in this area, she added, "Before there would have been a big demand and big pressure and big belt and he would have gotten a bit aggressive, to scare me into doing what he wanted."

Fear of physical violence was behind the reluctance of another woman to become more involved in feminist activities. Separation from a violent male partner was not sufficient for her to overcome the fear he had instilled in her. "I sort of want to get involved more, but there's still, you know, a little bit of fear. Like the reaction that you're going to get another smack in the mouth."

Economic pressure was also significant for a number of women. These women said that they had to earn extra money and save up to pay for feminist activities. One woman worked a second job because income from her regular job was considered household income. Another said:

> I had to borrow some money, and I remember getting home with two dollars in my purse and feeling lousy, but that normally happens because every other weekend I've been away I've always got to do it. I've got to save—plan for it—and I'm always scratching, and I often borrow some money off someone, and I pay them back later.

At the milder end of the continuum there were a number of women who reported that their husbands or partners, although generally accepting their feminist involvement, were defensive, argumentative, or critical of feminist ideas. Others simply showed no interest in discussing issues or hearing about feminist activities. A typical comment was, "He's a fairly negative kind of person, when we do discuss something, his mode is to look for problems . . . and I have found that very destructive in the past."

In a number of cases, children, particularly those who were teenagers or young adults, reacted negatively to their mother's feminism. One woman talked about being ridiculed within the family, particularly by her husband and 15-year-old son. "Sometimes I feel like everyone expects me to do everything for them, and if I buck then I start to get it, I'm criticized." Talking about her large household, which contained young adult males, another said, "There's been lots of jokes, you know, about feminists and dykes and jokes like that."

Two women talked about their teenage sons' anger and defensiveness concerning feminism. One recalled, "When they were younger it was really very difficult, so it was hard for me. Extremely hard. There were times when I wished that I'd never, ever heard of it [feminism] (laugh). It really did create a lot of problems." Another woman explained how her young adult daughter had difficulty dealing with her mother's feminism and high public profile as a member of the Mackay Women's Health and Information Centre. She described the way in which her daughter would question her when she went out:

> My daughter is having a lot of difficulty coping with my feminism. She's asking things like—I might say I'm going out for tea tonight—

> "Well, who's going?" And I say "Oh, it's so and so, and so and so," a
> heap of women, and then she'll say "Well, what about so and so, is
> she bringing her husband?" And she's really intent on knowing if
> you have a husband, and you know, "Well, why isn't he going?" . . .
> She is struggling with it I think because she works at —— and I
> think she hears things like "Oh, those radical feminists, they're all a
> mob of gays, that's all they are" and I think she hears that and I think
> it really concerns her and worries her . . . If I'm going out it's "Oh,
> yeah, down to the women's center again," or "You're going out with
> a heap of women."

This type of quizzing from children concerning feminist activities was common. Again, the stereotype that all feminists are lesbians figured prominently, with a number of heterosexual women reporting that they were questioned about the presence of lesbians at the Winter Institute workshop.

Extended Family, Friends, and Acquaintances

Beyond the immediate family, opposition also came from extended family, friends, and acquaintances. In some cases this opposition involved overt and aggressive reactions, in others it was less direct. Defensive reactions were common when feminist opinions were voiced among members of the extended family. One woman was accused of being "one-eyed" and of engaging in "discriminatory thinking." Another described her mother's defensiveness that was related to sexuality as much as to feminism:

> She won't let it go, like if we argue about something she's very quick
> to say "Oh, that's just because you're a feminist," but she means that's
> because I'm a lesbian. I know that's what she means, but she uses the
> word feminist . . . She thinks that I should be less combative with
> the whole world, and she believes that I'm only like that because I'm
> a lesbian.

Another woman who began living with a male partner shortly before the follow-up interview, described the response of her extended family:

> My family think that I've finally settled down and that I'll be all right
> now because I've got a partner, a male partner, but then they find out
> that I'm still not going to marry him and that I'm still not going to
> have children and that I'm not going to take his name and I'm not,
> you know, all these things, so they still think "Oh my god, she isn't ever
> going to change, and she's still not going to shave her bloody legs."

Two women talked about receiving advice from their mothers, and one also from her sister, to tone down their feminism. One commented, "Because she [mother] thinks I'm lucky with Steve [husband] she thinks, you know, 'don't do anything to rock the boat,' 'don't do anything that might jeopardize it.'" It may be questioned whether it is appropriate to categorize this friendly advice from mothers and sisters as a form of opposition or social control. In these examples, the interviewees are not being ostracized, ridiculed, threatened, or verbally attacked. However, social control does not need to be overt or intended. Sociologists recognize the often-unintended consequences of all social behavior and, in the case of professional advice, the social control ramifications. For example, through their professional status and authority, "professionals like doctors and social workers, . . . in the course of handling the problems with which they are presented may come to exercise a more general influence over their clients' lives."[18] Similarly, Sandra Bartky points out that the discipline that enforces hegemonic femininity is not always overtly and obviously oppressive. Talking about the dieting advice women receive from both friends and strangers, she says:

> These intrusions are often softened by reference to the natural prettiness just waiting to emerge: "People have always said that I had a beautiful face and 'if you'd only lose weight you'd be really beautiful.'" Here, "people"—friends and casual acquaintances alike—act to reinforce prevailing standards of body size.[19]

When mothers and sisters provide friendly advice about not rocking the boat their actions may not be overtly coercive; however, their attempts to shape beliefs and actions operate to reinforce appropriate feminine behavior. In fact, it is likely to be effective in this pursuit precisely because it is not overt and coercive but is grounded in assumptions of love.

Friends and acquaintances were another significant source of opposition to feminist involvement. This often involved ridicule and teasing, particularly in the case of attendance at the Winter Institute workshop. Comments were made about "braburning" and "women going along to play in the bush." One woman was asked by her friend's husband whether there would be tanks guarding the entrance to the campsite (to keep out men). Another described her friends' reactions to her growing interest in feminism:

> I'd been going to those feminist workshops that I mentioned before . . . My friends knew that I was going to these workshops and they were just merciless with me about, "Oh, of course Judy can't come out this evening, she's got to go off with those bunch of wild women down at the women's center" and things like that. They're just stirring me, but they obviously thought I was wasting my time, and

they couldn't see what I was getting out of it . . . Then I started going to the series of lectures and things for the Winter Institute, so they really started to see me as going quite radical and over the edge. I was going too far. And the workshop was just that final step—I was going off to live with them.

Another recounted an incident that occurred with a male doctor friend in response to her attendance at the Winter Institute Weekend and her involvement in the Mackay Women's Health and Information Centre. She said:

I invited he and his girlfriend out for dinner and he brought out this book written a long time ago by this man—and he thought it was really funny, you know—and it had all these horrible things in it about what should be done with women that step out of line, and he was reading them out . . . He's fairly threatened, like a lot of GPs are, in this town, about the women's center, because they think it's going to be a women's health center which they will be excluded from.

Both male and female friends and acquaintances asked, incredulously, the purpose of spending a weekend with women and no men. Interviewees were asked, "What would you do together?" Such comments are consistent with Janice Raymond's observation that within patriarchal societies it is assumed that "women without men are women without company or companionship."[20] One lesbian feminist described the back-to-reality experience of visiting a married friend following one of the Winter Institute weekends:

I'd come off the boat and I went over to have a cup of tea with Margaret, and it was really hard for me, because Margaret had some friends there, so there were two couples. And the men were making little snide comments about—because they'd asked me where I'd been, and I said—and they made, it wasn't sort of nasty, but supercilious comments about women going off together, you know. And I felt really hostile towards them, but felt that I didn't feel comfortable about saying anything. But it was interesting that I felt, "Oh God, back into the real world straight away, and not even a half an hour break."

It was not only on the basis of attendance at specific feminist events that women faced teasing and attack as feminists. Being known as a feminist was sufficient cause for being questioned and "baited" at social gatherings. One woman felt that on some occasions she had been deliberately invited to social gatherings as the "entertainment" because of her feminist identity. "I think they all tend to know me as a feminist. Sometimes actually they try to goad me because of that. I have been invited to new friends' places and it seems to me that I've been invited specifically to be attacked in a way." A social evening at a hotel with friends was the setting for verbal attack described by another woman. Cast as a representative of feminism, she was held accountable for the perceived grievances of her attacker:

> I had this guy just really verbally attack me the other day, . . . and every time I tried to change the subject, he'd just bring it back to it . . . It started on politics and then we got on to women's rights and things like that, and this guy just felt that—well he was blaming feminism for his 26-year-old marriage breakdown. And that all these feminists had filled his wife's head with all this "crap." And that women were actually inferior to men.

The idea that feminism is a threat to heterosexual relationships and causes marital breakdown also arose in another interview. Talking about her friend's husband, one interviewee explained how he attempted to limit her influence on his wife:

> Her husband is very antifeminism and we have, he and I have trouble because he has asked her not to see me. He sees me, me and my ideas as very threatening, and I certainly don't meddle, or have never attempted to meddle in their relationship, it's just that she, you know, just comments on what I've said or what I'm doing or whatever, and he sees that as very threatening.

Workplace

Expressing feminist views at work or behaving in a manner that identified interviewees as feminists led to a range of negative reactions from colleagues and supervisors. Eighteen women (45 percent of those employed) described employment situations where they experienced ridicule, ostracism, or direct attempts to curtail their feminist activities.

One woman described the reaction she typically received when feminist issues arose at work, "Anything that I ever discuss, or hint about in terms of feminism is sort of met with a lot of skepticism and ridicule." Typically, the actions and comments of colleagues relied upon and perpetuated popular stereotypes concerning the appearance and characteristics of feminists. Labeling women as lesbians if they expressed feminist views was as common in the workplace as in the family and with friends. Similarly, being labeled a man-hater was common. The label feminist, in conjunction with adjectives such as radical, rabid, or militant, was sometimes used as a term of abuse itself. A religious sister in the Catholic Church was publicly labeled a "militant feminist" in a widely distributed diocesan document. She commented, "That label was put on me as a derogatory term in church circles." Another woman said she felt typecast when she began working for a family planning organization. "You know—'you've got hairy legs, therefore this means you're one of those, and that means that you don't like men, and you do this, and you do that' and they've got this whole picture ready built for you. It's all a bit much."

The focus on physical appearance, evident in this last passage, occurred throughout the data. A number of women described their colleagues' attention and reaction to their physical appearance. In these cases they felt singled out because they did not conform to dominant norms of feminine appearance. One said, "My two coworkers, they both think I'm a little bit strange because I have hairy legs and hairy armpits and I think it's quite alien to their knowledge." In the following passage, the intimidatory nature of the attention paid to the interviewee's physical appearance is clearly evident:

> There's this one fellow in there, . . . he just came up to me real close and said, "Oh, you're growing a beard are you?" And he always looks at my hairy legs really closely and stuff, and I just sort of, like, I always never smile at him and always give him really strong looks. He's horrible. Everyone else thinks he's really nice.

Another common form of ostracism within the workplace was to be picked out as the token feminist in a group or organization, and then to be subjected to tongue-in-cheek declarations of deference. The following scenario, which occurred in the context of a Workplace Health and Safety course was typical:

> And the fellow who led it, he set the scene, so his sexist remarks permeated through to the rest of us and I was appalled by it. And I stood up to him, and of course what was interesting about that—I mean, I'm old enough and big enough to be able to cope with that, but you know, you wouldn't do it if you were perhaps a young girl, because then you'd, well, I was subjected to ridicule. Jokes, like "Here she goes again, we'd better be careful what we say"; "That's what women are like, aren't they"; "You've got to watch them, you know" —that sort of thing.

Beyond the ridicule, labeling, and ostracism described above, some women faced institutional obstruction in the context of their employment. The religious sister mentioned earlier not only faced public ridicule within church circles, but also had funding for her position within a church-run adult education center withdrawn because the local priests were opposed to the work she was doing. Their action highlighted her lack of power as a woman within the Catholic Church:

Even though you think you're in a position that gives you some power—I mean, I thought I was here—in the end all they need to do is just cut off your funding and you're completely immobilized, you haven't got a job any more. And there's no consultation. They go through all the back doors and negate any kind of power that you might have . . . Because they don't control me, I don't do what they want me to do, then they just stop funding.

In a less dramatic way, another woman faced opposition to her feminist approach to work in a counseling agency. She described her boss (who was also a feminist) being "always onto me about not being too feminist," adding, "she's quite concerned about what our appearance is in the community." This concern extended to questioning the appropriateness of staff participating in a *Reclaim the Night* march where they would be seen as publicly supporting a women-only event. Thus, it was not only individuals who were kept in line by being labeled in a derogatory manner; organizations were also restricted in this way. In a generally conservative community it was thought necessary for the counseling agency not to gain a reputation as being staffed by feminists.

Nonmovement Organizations/Institutions and the General Community

Opposition was also encountered within nonmovement organizations and from various sections of the general community. While many of the women in this study came into contact with feminist discourse and networks through tertiary study, it was also common for them to experience opposition to their feminist perspective in this setting. One woman, who had introduced feminist ideas into an essay on stress, was advised by her psychology tutor not to read any more feminist literature while studying. Another described an incident in which she was singled out in a psychology class. "I was told, in front of forty students, that I had a psychological problem because I always talked about women's needs." Yet another encountered difficulties writing a feminist PhD thesis:

With my PhD being feminist, it was ——, a woman, who tried to stop me doing it. When I was converting from Masters to PhD which should have been a smooth and normal passage, and my two female supervisors said the work was good, and it was all going fine, and it should be all right, and she tried to stop me because I am a feminist basically, and she is very antifeminist.

A few women also talked about the difficulty of being openly feminist within church circles. Raising feminist issues in such settings was likely to elicit negative reactions. One lay member of the Catholic Church explained:

> The most hurtful one of course is the ostracizing. You know, and ridicule, and that sort of thing, because once you're isolated you have to then find other branches and other areas to get the point across . . . I would say that would be very widespread in the church for many women who have dared to say something that was a little bit controversial, say something that didn't fit the norm.

Throughout the interviews there were numerous examples of doctors acting individually or as a group to oppose feminist action, particularly in relation to women's health issues. Three mentioned opposition from the medical profession to feminist support for alternative birthing practices. One interviewee was involved in childbirth education and talked about there being a "constant battle with obstetricians." Another, who was involved in the home birth movement in Townsville and later in Cairns, explained that the home birth midwives—who held their meetings at the Cairns women's center—were "being harassed quite radically by the doctors." In Mackay, local doctors perceived the establishment of a women's health center as a threat. In response to this perceived threat, the reputation of the center was attacked in an attempt to reduce its influence:

> A lot of the GPs in this town were trying to do that. And one in particular, he was really trying to do that, because that was his way, he could make the women's center seem like it was just a radical bunch of women, and "don't take any notice of them." . . . He wrote a letter to a lot of the other doctors around, saying that one girl in particular, was a lesbian, you know, and she was too, but she was also a very loving and beautiful lady that was very much involved with the women's center. She's not there any more, but she really ah,—that was true—but it wasn't the whole thing. That was just something he was using to get his own way.

The reported response of the doctors in Mackay to the women's health center was typical of a general community opposition to anything associated with feminism. Throughout the interviews with women from Mackay there were references to the conservative and parochial nature of the town and the difficulty of raising feminist issues. One woman described the feminist movement in Mackay as a "secret society," with a "lot of closet feminists." Another described the general attitude of men in Mackay:

> They don't understand. They think it's something flippant and silly, or they think you're being silly. They don't really take you seriously.

And really a lot of women won't say how they feel, or what they're doing here in this town, because men—they know that men will think they're silly, you know, and really don't take them seriously.

The *Reclaim the Night* march in 1992 generated heated debate within the Mackay community. Many letters to the editors—both for and against—were published in the local newspaper. Women who participated were accused of being "anti-men" and against the family. Some found themselves having to justify their involvement to friends at parties. One woman decided at the last minute not to participate in the march because she feared repercussions. "One of the reasons I didn't was because of my job . . . I was at the path, but I did not actually walk in the march, no, and that was only for business reasons, because I just could not sacrifice my business and livelihood because of that." Of particular concern to a number of women was the policy of the local newspaper that insisted on publishing full names with letters to the editor. One explained, "That doesn't always happen in other towns. You're allowed to use a nom de plume or just put 'name withheld' and we've had instances of women being harassed after they've written a letter on a feminist theme or antipornography."

Within this hostile environment even feminist organizations such as the Mackay Women's Health and Information Centre and the Sexual Assault Committee were constrained with regard to presenting a feminist image. There appeared to be a general fear of the word feminism among women in the community. In some cases this extended to women who themselves were involved with feminist organizations:

Women are frightened still of the word feminism. Especially heterosexual women who think it's all about being anti-man, when it's not about being anti-man, it's about empowering women. But there's still that old ignorance attached to the word feminism. If you say you're a feminist, they automatically think, "oh, you're anti-man" which in fact is not true. Again, conservative Mackay . . . Even on the Sexual Assault committee that I'm on there's those of us who are very strong feminists, and the other half of the committee who still think it's a dirty word and we mustn't portray that in the community or people are not going to use the service. So it's that constant battle we have, even on the committee, and the whole founding of sexual assault services is a very strong feminist foundation. But there are half the committee members who are saying, "Please don't say you're a feminist because people won't access this service, because they'll think we're all a bunch of radical lesbian feminists."

This example highlights the way women have accepted the dominant masculine definition of feminism in this community. Similar pressure impacted upon the operation of the women's health center. Social evenings at the center were deliberately held on Thursday evenings—late shopping night—so that women would have an acceptable excuse for going out. The organization received widespread criticism, including a threat to their government funding, for including an advertisement for feminist t-shirts in their newsletter. Concern over this incident, and fears for the center's reputation in general, led to self-censorship of the newsletter. As one interviewee said, "Certain committee members get worried if we have too much of a feminist flavor."

For two women who came from a small central Queensland coal-mining town, the impossibility of anonymity was seen as a barrier to increased feminist activity. Members of the small feminist reading group were aware of plans for *Reclaim the Night* in Townsville and Mackay. They discussed doing something themselves:

> We talked about doing something and just thought no, it's really hard in a small town. But we should, we should stand up and be counted. We're just chickens I think, but we've all got to live here and have got, you know, boyfriends and spouses and stuff . . . We often find ourselves being questioned anyway in social situations, about our views. So to make it even that much more public—you can only handle so much. Sometimes you just want to go out and relax rather than having to defend your situation all the time.

Despite their intention of keeping a low profile, these women faced considerable publicity and community opposition when, in 1992, they obtained government funding through a Rural Women's Access program to stage a women's workshop in the central Queensland region. Before the women themselves were notified, the grant was publicly announced by the government minister, creating gossip and a backlash within the town and the local Shire Council. The women requested that the Council administer the grant money, in line with previous policy regarding community based self-help groups, but the prospect of money being spent on a feminist project was not well received:

> We applied to Council, thinking that they still had that policy and apparently it received the most negative reception at the Council meeting . . . One of our members is a female councilor, and she said she was just surprised at what happened at the meeting. They didn't want to have a bar of it at all . . . People said we should pay for it ourselves if we want to do consciousness-raising, that they believed it was the Labor government wasting money, that it was only for an elite, select few women in town and all that sort of stuff.

Women from Townsville were less likely to report a general antifeminist feeling in the community, although this is not to suggest that it did not exist. The first ever *Reclaim the Night* march in Mackay took place only a few weeks before the follow-up interviews, so the major public controversy generated by this event would have been fresh in the minds of the Mackay women. Since International Women's Day and *Reclaim the Night* marches had been held for a number of years in Townsville, they were generally less newsworthy.

Patterns of Opposition across the Data

Most of the women in this study (82 percent), faced some form of opposition to their feminist identity and involvement. This occurred in sites ranging from the intimacy of the immediate family to the impersonal level of the general community, and involved control strategies ranging from threats of physical violence to ridicule and ostracism.

Only one woman reported actual physical violence. This was from her husband and was associated with demands for sex prior to her absences from home. Another reported being afraid to become more involved in feminism because of past violence. Emotional violence, including drunkenness, moodiness, verbal abuse, and threats—primarily from male partners and ex-partners—was more common, but not widespread. Three women described this type of behavior from existing male partners, and a further three from ex-partners.

The economic dimension was also important. As Zald and McCarthy suggest, structured economic relationships provide crucial opportunities for social control in relation to movement activity.[21] In this data, such relationships existed within the family and the workplace and were the source of economically based pressure to limit feminist involvement. As described earlier, four women talked about either the difficulty of paying for feminist activities, or the guilt they experienced in using household income for this purpose. Economic dependence has long been viewed by feminists as central to women's lack of power within marriage. Even when women are in paid employment, many feel they have a lesser right than their husbands to personal spending money.[22] For some women in this study, it seems that expenditure incurred through movement activities is akin to spending on leisure, and therefore a luxury which must be justified. The relationship between employer and employee is also largely economic and the data contain one example where financial support through employment was withdrawn in response to the interviewee's feminist stance. Others were also clearly aware of the potential threat to their livelihoods posed by overt feminist allegiance.

Feminist ways of knowing were a target of opposition for some women. This took the form of persistent questioning of feminist ideas, particularly by family members. More common were emotionally based strategies of control. The most common strategy, reported across all sites, was verbal comments designed to reinforce hegemonic femininity. Included here is the labeling, teasing, joking, and intrusive questioning that interviewees were subjected to, but also the friendly advice described above. The use of ridicule and labeling as a way of dealing with women who engage in protest activity is widespread.[23] As Seager points out, regardless of the particular cause a woman is involved in, the techniques of control women activists face, and the labels placed on them, are usually based on sexist assumptions about appropriate female behavior. For women active in the environmental movement, being labeled an "hysterical housewife" or "angry housewife" is common.[24] When women are active as feminists, similar strategies are used, but with different labels.

The most obvious pattern in the ostracism and labeling interviewees reported was the prevalence of lesbian baiting. As is evident from the data already presented, this occurred across the board, in the family, with friends and colleagues, and from sections of the general community. The strategy of lesbian baiting—"use of the label 'lesbian' for any woman who dares to demand her rights or identify herself apart from men"[25]—has long been recognized by feminists as one of the ways in which patriarchal society attempts to divide and discredit the women's movement.[26] It is both disturbing and surprising to see how widespread this strategy still is, given the growing openness and acceptance of homosexuality in Australian society over the past twenty years. Kaplan provides a range of evidence indicating more open attitudes towards homosexuality in recent years, but this may be more relevant to the urban environment in large cities such as Sydney and Melbourne than to regional Australia.[27]

Ridicule based on appearance was also common. This focused primarily on body hair, but family members and work colleagues also commented upon clothing and lack of makeup. In the 1970s, women's liberationists challenged dominant norms of feminine appearance, rejecting practices such as wearing makeup, high heels and dresses, and shaving legs and underarms. According to feminist analyses, such practices reinforced the status of women as sex objects and as subordinate to men. More recent feminist work on the sociology of the body—while rejecting earlier portrayals of women as cultural dupes—is consistent with the view that feminine appearance norms reproduce male dominance and female subordination.[28] Furthermore, as Dellinger and Williams found in their research into appearance rules at work, such rules also reinforce norms of heterosexuality:

> In addition to marking women as healthy and well rested, makeup also marks women as heterosexual ... The experiences of both straight and lesbian women in this sample illustrate how a system of compulsory heterosexuality (Rich 1980) is maintained through workplace appearance norms.[29]

Drawing on feminist analyses, the rejection of practices such as shaving and wearing makeup presents a powerful symbolic challenge to male dominance. In response to this challenge feminists are ridiculed as unattractive.[30] The pressure feminists face to conform to feminine appearance has also been noted by Whittier.[31] In her study of long-term radical feminist activists in Columbus, Ohio, many recounted how in recent years they had moderated their looks by shaving and wearing make-up and dresses. Although some described this change as partly a reaction against rigid standards of appearance within feminist communities, others described it as a response to an increasingly hostile culture, where "conspicuous aspects of appearance that branded one as a feminist were most costly."[32] In the context of a widespread backlash against feminism these women chose to downplay their difference.

Another term of abuse commonly applied to feminists is man-hater.[33] In this study almost a quarter of interviewees mentioned variants of the term. Interestingly, most references were declarations that the interviewee was not a man-hater herself, or was wary of being labeled a man-hater, rather than accounts of being so labeled. It seems that the cultural potency of such labeling is so strong that it performs a social control function without needing to be uttered at an individual level.

Responding to Opposition

Interviewees adopted a number of strategies for dealing with reactions to their feminist involvement and identity. First, they exercised a form of self-restraint, whereby feminist views were kept in check in an attempt to manage the negative response of others and avoid conflict. This was a general strategy of avoidance, applied across the board. A related strategy was to distance themselves from a stigmatized feminist identity. A third strategy was confident self-assertion of feminist views and feminist identity. These strategies parallel those described in the previous chapter in relation to negotiating multiple identities.

Self-Restraint

Self-restraint involved being selective in talking about feminist ideas or beliefs and, in certain situations, refraining from expressing opinions. Approximately half the women in this study used it as a form of self-protection. One interviewee told me that feminism is a "closed topic" in her relationship; another admitted that she does not "say everything [she] thinks"; yet another that she had reservations about mentioning feminist activities at work "because it's met with ridicule, or you know that you're going to be talked about as soon as you leave the room." Others noted that people are easily threatened by feminism and it is not worth raising issues that could begin an argument. Some described situations in which, not always successfully, they attempted to change the topic of conversation when feminist issues arose.

One interviewee recalled, "Often discussions start where I make my views known, but, yeah I do a lot of weighing up about it—'Is it worth it this time to get into that discussion?'—and often opt not to." Another commented, "I've found it easier not to discuss material. I keep myself with a supportive group of people. I'm using my brain a bit. I just think it's fruitless, because people are different." Describing a situation in which she was talking with a feminist friend at a social gathering, another interviewee commented, "One of the men came and joined us. It was obvious he felt quite uncomfortable and a bit negative about it. We just made some kind of joke and changed to talking about sausages or something." This woman also talked about the risk of exposing feminist ideas to the critical appraisal of her partner and her decision, on a number of occasions, not to raise issues:

> My image of it is that I've just laid a new concrete floor, and I'm admiring how beautiful it is, and he comes across and marches across it with boots and stuffs it. So because that's happened in the past, sometimes I'm a bit reticent when I do feel particularly excited and sensitive and new about something. I don't want to expose it to that risk . . . That fear in me is still there, so I often just kind of let things slide a bit, and bring up things later, when I'm more confident or have had more time to think about it or have talked it over with other women friends.

In order to avoid her partner's defensive response in such situations, she suppressed her own excitement and kept her thoughts to herself.

The tendency to keep her feminism subdued within the family/household environment was commented upon by another interviewee, "I tend to be very quiet about it . . . My serious feminism wouldn't be up front in the family at all, except with my daughters. They respect it and they discuss it and believe it too, but they don't perhaps feel it as emotionally as I do." The interviews contained many similar examples. In each case, restraint was exercised as a way of managing the response of others to feminist identity and/or involvement.

Distancing

It was common for interviewees to make statements distancing themselves from other feminists who were described variously as extremist, militant, radical, or man-haters. Just over a quarter of the women made statements to this effect. Typical comments were "I'm not a radical feminist like some of the women, but I do believe in our rights, very much so"; "I'm not a really rabid feminist, but I'm definitely for women"; "I'm not a radical feminist, but I'm a feminist"; and "I'm not a man-hater." These comments are a variation of the familiar "I'm not a feminist, but . . . " refrain. They were made by women who did feminist things, attended feminist events, and joined feminist organizations, yet they distanced themselves from a stigmatized feminist identity which they defined as "other" to their version of feminism.

Bulbeck has also noted this phenomenon. She found it to be particularly related to the policing of acceptable femininity through lesbian baiting, noting "the association it conjures up: nice moderate women/feminists versus radical mannish lesbians/feminists."[34] In my data, both lesbian and heterosexual women used this strategy as a way of distancing themselves from the opposition and ridicule directed towards feminism. Not surprisingly, such statements were more common among those women who were newer to feminism and who had read less feminist literature. Some talked about becoming more comfortable with the label feminist, and more accepting of more radical or extreme feminists as they became more involved and more aware of diversity within feminism.

Self-Assertion

A less common, but still significant strategy for dealing with opposition to feminism was based on an assertive, confident expression of feminist views. This approach was used both in an attempt to educate others and as a strategy of self-defense. One interviewee talked about encountering "a lot of misplaced anger in some people," but rather than not express feminist views, her approach was to "work through" the anger before discussing issues. Although she considered the anger to be "misplaced," she nonetheless performed the emotion work required to defuse it, seeing her role as one of educator. The incident described earlier in this chapter in which an interviewee was subjected to ridicule while doing a Workplace Health and Safety course provides another example of an assertive response, albeit one that elicited further ridicule.

It was common for interviewees to talk with other nonfeminist women about feminist issues in informal settings such as parties or barbecues. On one such occasion, two or three men intruded on a conversation about a recent *Reclaim the Night* march, adding antagonistic comments. The interviewee concerned responded assertively to their taunts:

> One guy said, "You don't look like the type that would have gone to *Reclaim the Night*." . . . What they were saying is that the women who were going on the demonstration, really all they want is to have a good fuck. And I said to the men who were saying that, "Look I don't find that really funny because I have worked in the area where I've seen a lot of violation going on against women, and I think it's really important."

This assertive response allowed her to maintain a position of equality in the interaction.

In an analysis of the micropolitics of emotions, Candace Clark identified five strategies people use to "get and keep place in face-to-face interactions."[35] The assertive response described above can be understood as an example of a strategy that Clark calls controlling the balance of emotional energy. This strategy involves gaining place by "evoking another's anger, ridicule, or other negative emotions. In general, those who can elicit more emotion from others than they invest exercise control over the interaction."[36] Discussion of the march, whether intended or not, provoked the men's insults. By staying "cool" and responding assertively but not aggressively the interviewee gave no ground to her interlocutors and actually enhanced her own standing in the situation. It is interesting, however, that in this example the assertive response drew upon the authority of professional knowledge, rather than feminist understandings of the issues. This may tell us something about the power of professional discourses in relation to feminist discourse.

The situation described earlier, in which an interviewee found herself being verbally attacked as a representative of feminism, was also finally resolved through self-assertion. Being physically unable to remove herself, she tried several times to change the topic of conversation before finally defending herself assertively. "In the end I just said, 'Look we're from a different background and culture, I will discuss it with you but I will not be your point of anger.' . . . I was so upset when I got home, . . . I was just so angry . . . I thought 'I don't have to put up with that!'" Assertive responses of this type were far less common than self-restraint as a means of managing negative responses to feminism. Although the examples given tend to present the self-restraint and the assertive strategies as alternatives used by different women, some used both options at different times. As one woman said, she holds back when feeling "sensitive and new about something," but addresses issues assertively when feeling "more confident."

The strategies described so far were general responses to opposition. Given its prevalence, it is also important to discuss responses to the specific issue of lesbian baiting. How interviewees reacted to, and attempted to deal with, lesbian baiting varied. Breadth and depth of feminist knowledge influenced interviewees' responses, and lesbian and heterosexual women were affected differently. As one lesbian feminist put it:

> Lesbians who aren't "out" about their sexuality, I think that they suffer a great oppression even in the feminist movement, at times, because of the invisibility and because, you know, if mainstream society wants to criticize the women's movement they'll say "They're just a mob of hairy dykes" and so for heterosexual women that is a real issue. It's an issue for both, but in different ways, and for different reasons. And so for heterosexual women who see that as a criticism and something that might make them feel uncomfortable, they probably don't want to be grouped together with a mob of hairy dykes, but for hairy dykes who are proud to be hairy dykes, they probably get into a dilemma about well, this is seen as a criticism but it shouldn't be, and for hairy dykes who don't want to be seen as hairy dykes at all, it's another issue, because it sort of like makes you a bit schizophrenic, you know, because that's what you really are but you have to say you're not because you don't really want people to think you are because it might really affect the way you live.

As the above excerpt indicates, for lesbians who are not "out" lesbian baiting is a serious issue. Women in this situation may feel particularly vulnerable in relation to their employment. In addition to the woman quoted above, two women described their fear of being identified as lesbians at work. They both explained that this fear acted as a strong disincentive to expressing feminist views in that setting. One described the stress and feelings of powerlessness involved in not responding to sexist and homophobic jokes at work for fear of being dismissed if her sexual orientation became known to her employer. The other described how the 1991 Winter Institute Weekend helped her to overcome a similar reluctance to express feminist views:

> I am gay, and I used to think that they'd think "She's a lesbian," and I didn't want to be thought of like that, so I was often very quiet about saying feminist views because people immediately take it the wrong way anyway. And now I couldn't give a fuck. (laugh)
> Cheryl: The weekend made a difference there?
> Yeah, . . . I think what it was is that (pause) there were straight people, gay people, old people, young people, married people, single people, just women there. (pause) Yeah, somehow that made a difference . . . I feel like I can say my bit now about feminism.

Many of the heterosexual women in the study were confused about how to respond to lesbian baiting. Most had some awareness that simply asserting their own heterosexually or denying the presence of lesbians in the movement was problematic. In the earlier example of the doctor in Mackay who "outed" one of the women from the women's health center, the interviewee responded to the attack by asserting that the woman concerned was "a very loving and beautiful lady." Unaware of feminist analyses of lesbian baiting or of lesbian feminist theory, she was unable to respond more effectively. This type of response was typical of interviewees whose involvement in feminism was more recent and/or for those who were less familiar with feminist literature. It is significant that a few women changed their response to lesbian baiting as a result of discussion of the issue during the 1992 workshop. One said:

> It's made me a bit more open about being a feminist. I think having to face lesbianism made me think . . . Somebody said something that was really pertinent—I don't quite have the words now, but it sort of made me realize that we tend to defend feminism, and when it's put down as "a mob of lesbians" or something, and we then say "No, they're not all lesbians," you know, as though there's something wrong with that. And I think I realized the connotations of some statements, that I could dispense with. Now if someone said, "They're a mob of lesbians" I wouldn't feel that I had to defend it by saying it wasn't, as though there's something wrong with that. You're putting one thing down to lift up the other.

Another woman talked in the first interview about not understanding lesbianism and feeling threatened by it. Prior to the 1991 Winter Institute workshop she had rejected the label feminist because "if you call yourself a feminist, they'll think you're a lesbian." Nonetheless, she was motivated to attend the 1991 workshop out of a desire to learn and understand more about women's friendships. By the time of the follow-up interview, she had formed a close friendship with a lesbian couple from interstate, with whom she had been corresponding since meeting them at another feminist workshop. In this case it seems that lesbian baiting actually motivated her to examine her own views and to seek greater understanding.

The Effect of Opposition on Feminist Involvement

A significant question that arises from this material is the effect of opposition on individual involvement. On one level the opposition and attempts at social control experienced by the women in this study can be considered somewhat ineffective as a barrier to involvement. To begin with, it did not prevent them from participating in the Winter Institute workshop. Further, most of the women, including those who were new to feminism as well as the longer-term activists, continued throughout 1992 to participate in a range of feminist events and organizations despite any opposition they faced. They also acted in a myriad of ways to establish a feminist presence in daily life.[37] One woman even suggested that the impetus for her becoming involved may have been the supposed deviance of feminists:

> I probably had some preconceived ideas that they [feminists] were radical or divorced or something like that, or a little bit not normal. Which is probably why I got involved, because I thought, "If I'm not normal, I'd better become a feminist" (laugh). Now I realize that there isn't anybody who's normal, we're all not normal, and that's normal, isn't it?

This finding is consistent with previous research into social movements and repression. As noted earlier, repression often does not have the desired effect and may in fact facilitate mobilization by increasing the perceived risk of inaction.[38] Although previous findings relate specifically to state repression and official policing of protest, it may be that a similar dynamic operates at this less formal level. When women face ridicule and ostracism, and threats to their relationships and employment, this reinforces feminist understandings of oppressive social relations. The injustice frame of the movement is vindicated and the need to act is brought to the fore.

An important qualification, however, flows from the design of the study. Interviewees were selected for the study on the basis of their involvement in feminist collective action. These women have acted despite the various pressures to which they have been subjected. We cannot tell from this data how many have not. At least one interviewee commented concerning a friend's decision not to attend the Winter Institute workshop, "Any time she's dabbled in feminism over the years, it has gotten her deep in the shit at home." Further, although the women in this study reported little overt obstruction in terms of what they did, where they went, and how they spent their time, it cannot be concluded that the opposition they faced had no impact.

The opposition experienced by the women in this study was primarily directed at feminist identity rather than at consciousness or action. Participants were constantly defined by others and invited to define themselves in terms of negative images of feminists. They were ridiculed and ostracized for expressing feminist views or acting in other ways that identified them as belonging to the category feminist. Here, the role the media and countermovements play in constructing counterframes and negative definitions of movement issues and participants is significant. Movement opponents construct and disseminate opposing frames and negative public identities that circulate at a cultural level.[39] Pro-choice activists are defined as murderers, environmentalists as greenies, and feminists as man-haters, frigid, and ugly. These stigmatizing labels are picked up and deployed at the individual level to discourage women from claiming feminist identity.

Given the centrality of identity to collective action, we can speculate that a strategy that undermines feminist identity may well be more effective than more direct forms of obstruction. Attacking feminist identity requires less overt strategies than constraining or blocking feminist action. If a woman is directly prevented from taking part in a feminist event or gathering, the social control she faces is obvious and likely to be rejected. Attacks on identity, particularly when couched in the language of a game, are harder to name and harder to deflect. As Melucci has argued, in complex society social control targets motivational and cognitive structures to achieve behavior manipulation.[40] More overt forms of control only come into play when these forms of control break down. On this point, Tarrow's observation that strategies that depress preconditions for collective action are more effective than direct suppression is also pertinent.[41] Following Tilly, Tarrow sees organization as the main precondition for collective action. However, to the extent that identity is central to collective action, attacks on feminist identity and the sense of belonging to a collectivity of feminist women are highly significant. While feminist consciousness is clearly threatening to patriarchal social relations, on its own it does not imply active engagement in collective feminist struggle to the same extent as feminist identification does. "I'm not a feminist, but . . . " is a less threatening position to take than "I am a feminist, and . . . " No matter how many buts, or how feminist the buts are, the former phrase does not imply active engagement to the extent that the latter does.

The conflict between movements and their opponents variously resembles a debate, a game, or a battle.[42] At the individual level, much of the opposition described in this chapter looks like a game. Negative comments were usually made in jest. However, the game-like nature of these interactions obscures their potency in reinforcing hegemonic femininity and undermining feminist action. Furthermore, regardless of how the conflict between movements and their opponents is portrayed, it is true that "the game is never fair and the positions" of ruling groups and those who challenge them "are not those of parity."[43] The power to define situations and identities is not equally distributed. There is also the ever-present possibility that the game will turn nasty with battle lines drawn more clearly. This study clearly demonstrates the use of economic pressure to curtail feminist activity when less overt strategies are insufficient.

Applying the concept of biographical constraints, it is evident that individual life circumstances influenced the type and extent of constraints women faced. The single women in the study faced less opposition in the personal sphere than those with husbands and teenaged children, however some of them faced greater problems at work. Geographical location was also significant, with public feminist activism being associated with greater personal costs in smaller towns.

Apart from the question of whether opposition reduced involvement, there is the issue of how it impacted on well-being and sense of self. Although most of the women in this study adopted strategies designed to deflect negative evaluations, the opposition and control they faced in relation to their feminist involvement was not without negative consequences. In particular, ridicule and ostracism were deeply felt and often led to changed behavior, as described. Further, it was common for women to describe a state of emotional exhaustion and self-estrangement that flowed from the constant demand to monitor their own behavior and speech, and to actively assert themselves. They talked about the energy they expended in restraining themselves from expressing feminist views. One commented about the workshop, "It fired up my anger more, and . . . it's very difficult to contain that. It uses up a lot of energy of mine." Another described the frustration and stress that resulted from always being different.

Dana Crowley Jack suggests that when thoughts and emotions are suppressed and allowed to enter into relationships, the self they reflect is silenced.[44] This aspect of self-restraint was made very explicit by one woman when she talked about what she gained from attending the Winter Institute workshop:

> It really reinforced lots of things in me that I really felt that—sort of felt that they were becoming really personal to me because I was unable to communicate them to lots of people, because they were so obviously, you know, that sort of attitude people have towards angry feminists and such like, and I was sort of internalizing a lot of it.

Self-assertion also requires energy and is exhausting. This has been noted by movements researchers before. Turner and Killian have written about combat fatigue—"the wear and tear of participating in a continuing struggle."[45] Richard Kendrick has described peace activists "running out of gas" and needing "something to rekindle their enthusiasm."[46] In these cases, however, combat fatigue results from asserting a position against defined adversaries. In this study, opposition and the need for self-assertion operated at personal and institutional levels, in settings with family members, friends, and work colleagues.

CHAPTER 6
Participation in Feminist Events and Organizations

In this chapter and the next I turn to "doing," the final component in the fractal model of becoming and being feminist. In the field of social movements research, what constitutes participation in collective action is generally based on commonsense assumptions that view movement involvement in terms of participation in public protests and campaigns, and/or as membership of social movement organizations. For example, Klandermans lists giving money, signing a petition, taking part in a demonstration, sit-in or strike, doing voluntary work, or serving on a committee as examples of movement participation.[1] In line with the qualitative methods employed in this study, my alternative approach has been to define participation in terms used by interviewees. Therefore, in this and the next chapter I document the activities women in this study engaged in that, in their eyes, constituted feminist action. This included a range of action that was broader than, but also incorporated, common sense definitions of activism. In this chapter I begin by describing their participation in the type of activities usually associated with movement involvement, that is, in feminist movement events and organizations. This covers attendance at feminist workshops, seminars, and Women's Studies courses; membership in feminist reading and/or discussion groups; involvement through women's centers and women's services; attendance at protests, rallies, or marches; and participation in feminist social and cultural activities. In the following chapter, feminist action that occurs outside the organizational sphere is considered.

In addition to documenting participation in feminist events and organizations in this way, I explore in this chapter the meaning participation in these activities holds for the women concerned. Why do they engage in particular activities? What do they gain from participation in feminist events and organizations? Questions such as these have traditionally been addressed in the context of a mobilization problematic; that is, how do movement organizations and leaders motivate people to participate? As noted in Chapter 1, resource mobilization theory conceptualized movement participants as rational agents who engage in cost/benefit analyses before choosing to participate in movement events or join movement organizations. This conceptualization led to the often-discussed "free-rider" problem, introduced to the study of collective action by Mancur Olson. Olson proposed that rational actors would not participate in collective action unless they were offered individualized, selective incentives. When benefits are collective, but costs personal, rational individuals will choose to "free-ride," relying on the actions of others to gain collective benefits.[2] Recognition of the free-rider problem within RMT led to a focus on the strategies movement organizations adopt in order to achieve mobilization. These strategies were said to include the provision of "incentives, cost-reducing mechanisms or structures, and career benefits" for participants.[3]

The incorporation of rational choice theory, and the model of the rational actor this implies, has been a focal point of criticism of RMT. In particular, the applicability of Olson's utilitarian logic has been widely challenged. Fireman and Gamson dispute the necessity of selective incentives and cite solidarity and principle as more important mobilizing factors. Others have repeated and extended this critique, suggesting that successful movements overcome the free-rider problem by offering collective incentives such as group solidarity and commitment to moral purpose.[4] Ferree argues that the adoption of rational choice theory collapses internal and external motivators, reducing motivation to extrinsic rewards. It fails to take into account "value-rationality" in the Weberian sense and ignores the idea of identity.[5]

The way women in this study talked about their participation in feminist events and organizations clearly challenges the utilitarian logic of the free-rider problem. Themes that emerged from the data in relation to the meaning of involvement highlighted the intrinsic nature of the rewards of participation. Access to knowledge and information was a central theme. Feminist knowledge was sought out and valued as a source of personal empowerment. Participation in events and organizations also provided emotional and social support that was highly valued. Finally, participation was a means of affirming feminist identity. These themes that highlight the intertwined nature of knowing, feeling, belonging, and doing in the fractal model of movement involvement, are further elaborated and discussed below, following documentation of the extent and nature of participation in feminist events and organizations.

Workshops, Seminars, and Courses

Although participation in workshops, seminars, and courses is not generally included as a form of movement participation, women in this study frequently mentioned such activities as examples of feminist involvement. Prior to the 1991 workshop, a number of women were already familiar with the Winter Institute weekends, eighteen (40 percent) having attended at least one earlier workshop and eleven (24 percent) having attended two or more. Twenty-seven women (60 percent) attended for the first time in 1991. For some, the annual weekend workshop was looked forward to as a particularly exciting and enjoyable event, and they attended in 1991 as a matter of course. "Well, it was my third Winter Institute for women, so there was no chance that I was going to miss it."

Following established tradition, a Winter Institute weekend workshop took place again in August 1992. In general terms, the aims of the workshop were similar to 1991, although the format was slightly different. In place of a guest facilitator, the weekend's discussions and activities centered around recent feminist texts on the backlash. Small group work was based on the following texts: *Backlash: The Undeclared War Against American Women*, by Susan Faludi; *War Against Women* by Marilyn French; and *Anticlimax: A Feminist Perspective on the Sexual Revolution*, by Sheila Jeffreys. The workshop was advertised as:

> an opportunity for feminist women to get together to study the latest research and writing around the issue that has come to be called the "backlash" against the women's movement. We will ask questions like: Is there really a backlash? If so, where is it coming from? Do men care enough about women's struggle for equality and justice, or is the backlash coming from other women (on behalf of men)? What kind of response is called for? What is the future for feminism?[6]

During the first interview I asked each participant for her thoughts about attending the weekend workshop in the following year. Twenty-seven women (60 percent) indicated their intention to attend in 1992, some giving very positive and definite answers. For example, "I'll be there!" and "I'll be going, no matter what it is or where it is." A small number of women expressed a desire to attend in 1992, but indicated possible problems that could arise. "Yeah, I'd be very tempted, if it worked in with times and work."

The remaining women said they might attend, depending on a variety of factors such as who was facilitating the weekend, who else was going, and what issues were on the agenda. Although no one completely ruled out the possibility of attending in 1992, a small number were ambivalent and expressed some negativity. For example, "Well I guess once again it might depend on who will be there, but (sighing) I get a bit negative about it, but I'm not saying I won't go." Due to a variety of intervening factors, less than half (40 percent) of the 1991 participants carried through on their generally positive intentions and actually returned in 1992.

Apart from earlier Winter Institute Weekends, many of the interviewees had previously participated in other workshops, seminars, or lectures with feminist speakers. In the initial interviews, 36 women (80 percent) mentioned this type of activity. For some, their involvement began not long before the Winter Institute Weekend, while others had been attending workshops for a number of years. A useful distinction can be made between women who had been largely "consumers" of this type of activity and those who had been more actively involved in planning, organizing, and running such events.

Judy was one of those whose involvement prior to the 1991 Winter Institute workshop was both recent and limited. She first became involved earlier in the year through attending workshops held at the Townsville Women's Centre:

> I heard of a series of feminist workshops that were going to run at the women's center, and I found that through the newspaper, and from going to those workshops I heard from there about Dale Spender coming up and the Women's Winter Institute series of lectures.

Anna also attended a workshop at the Mackay Women's Health and Information Centre in March 1991, where she first heard about the Winter Institute Weekend.

Muriel had attended feminist seminars and lectures over a number of years, but beyond this her involvement in feminist activities was limited. In explaining how she came to attend the Winter Institute Weekend, Muriel described her prior participation while living in Brisbane:

> I had been quite used to attending things like that in Brisbane through the Federal Government's women's lobby . . . And there's just such a huge range of things going in Brisbane all the time with groups . . . The main ones I used to go to . . . would generally be, the lecture style thing that Dale would operate with, where she talked,

so there wasn't a lot of small group activity or things of that nature . . . A lot of those women were very strongly feminist and at times when the floor could speak, to either the panel or the individual speakers they would speak out very strongly about all kinds of things . . . Susan Ryan I know was a speaker one time.

Stella also described a history of participating in feminist workshops and conferences.

In contrast to the "consumers" of seminars, lectures, and workshops, a number of women had been actively involved in organizing and running such activities. Anne was involved in the establishment of the Townsville Women's Centre and talked about her role in planning and organizing women's events:

We were looking at establishing a women's center and we arranged a few women's conferences, which were very much feminist based and at that time I was out at the uni[versity] doing education and I was responsible for an education workshop at one of these conferences, discussing the education of women.

Carol and Liz, who live in a small central Queensland coal mining town, discussed their involvement in running courses and workshops for women in their local area:

It started off with an assertiveness course, collectively run, where we all did a bit, and Liz and I sort of coordinated and instigated it, but then we all did a bit. And then we had money that we thought we'd like to get someone down to talk to us, and that's when Betty came . . . We have her come and talk in the community, and I think each year that we've had her, we've had really quite a good response. We've had something like thirty women, I think, one night we had —and we even used the word feminism, it was Introducing Feminism, or something like that.

The opportunity for women to attend feminist events is perceived to be limited even in Townsville, but more so in places like Mackay, Rockhampton, and central Queensland. A number of those who had lived in Brisbane or other major cities talked about the lack of feminist activities in regional centers, highlighting the fact that involvement is shaped by the locality in which one lives.

Despite limited options, many of the women in the study took advantage of whatever opportunities were available in terms of feminist lectures, seminars, and workshops. For example, events such as the women's section of the Australian and New Zealand Association for the Advancement of

Science (ANZAAS) Conference, held in Townsville in 1987, were seen as significant highlights that were remembered for a long time. Three women specifically mentioned having attended the ANZAAS conference and hearing Dale Spender speak. Margaret said:

> One of the things that I really enjoyed . . . was ANZAAS, the women's section of the ANZAAS conference . . . I didn't go to everything, but I took a day off work and went to some of the talks that I particularly wanted to go to, and that actually was where I first heard Dale Spender speak, but there were some very interesting speakers at that with issues that were quite diverse of course.

For five women, an interest in learning and understanding more about women and feminism had taken them beyond the short workshop or occasional lecture, to more formal courses in the area of Women's Studies. Louise reported having done some courses in Women's Studies as part of a Bachelor of Arts degree. Helen completed a major in Women's Studies. Lorna, at the time of the first interview, was enrolled in master's level study that she described as "feminist oriented." Two others had attended Deakin University Women's Studies Summer Schools, and one was enrolled in Women's Studies as an external student.

During the follow-up interviews, 33 women (75 percent) reported having attended at least one feminist workshop, seminar, or conference in the period between interviews. Although this number is less than was the case for the initial interviews, it must be taken into account that in the earlier interview they were asked to recall *any* previous feminist involvement, so the time frame is quite different. Nonetheless, for a variety of reasons such as tight work or study schedules, lack of financial resources, and reduced contact with feminist networks, nine women (20 percent) reported reduced involvement in this type of activity. In contrast to the reduced activity of these women, seven others reported increased involvement in this area.

Throughout 1992, a number of feminist workshops, seminars, and conferences were held in Townsville, including the workshop and seminars presented by Sheila Jeffreys that were discussed in Chapter 4. Other activities included a course on Public Speaking for Feminists, a Weekend Feminist Festival titled *Celebrating Women's Knowledge*, and a Women's Health Forum. Feminist writer Sandra Shotlander conducted workshops and presented seminars while Writer in Residence at James Cook University. All of these were well attended by the Townsville-based women from this study. Less was available in Mackay, but a few women traveled to Townsville to attend some of these events.

Fifteen women attended at least one of the public lectures given by Sheila Jeffreys. Six participated in the public speaking course and 14 attended the Weekend Feminist Festival at which Valerie Walkerdine, Dale Spender, and Pam Gilbert spoke. Fourteen women took part in various health-related workshops or forums, including Women's Health Policy Forums held in Mackay and Townsville, an International Homebirth Conference held in Sydney, and a seminar on Women and Mental Health organized by the Brisbane Women's Health Center. Additional activities included a two-day workshop on lesbian ethics, a Women in Unions conference held in Brisbane, and a Feminist Spirituality workshop. In relation to Women's Studies courses, four women attended the Deakin Women's Studies Summer School held early in 1992. Three others continued to pursue studies commenced prior to the start of this research, and one began a Graduate Diploma in Women's Studies.

Reading and Discussion Groups

A further significant sphere of involvement that emerged from the initial interview data was that of feminist reading or discussion groups. The focus of these groups varied considerably, reflecting the diverse interests of participants. They ranged from general feminist discussion groups to groups dealing specifically with feminist literature, feminist theology, lesbian feminist politics, and ethics. While many of these reading/discussion groups were informally constituted, they can be described as movement organizations. As Kriesi points out, the "SMOs [social movement organizations] of new social movements in particular are quite informally structured and often do not have explicit membership criteria."[7] Therefore, participation in such groups can be considered as an example of movement involvement.

Fourteen women mentioned involvement in reading/discussion groups. This included a number who not only participated, but also were instrumental in establishing such groups. Sharon was involved in setting up a feminist collective in her workplace during the early 1980s:

> We started a group called the "felt collective," because it was a felt need, and that was a collective, which organized readings and performances and if any visiting feminist scholars came to Sydney we made sure they came and gave lectures at our department.

A particularly interesting example of a feminist reading group was one established in a small central Queensland coal-mining town. Two members of the group attended the 1991 workshop. Carol explained how the reading and discussion group evolved out of the assertiveness training course, discussed earlier:

> It's only in the last year that the reading group has started up. A few of us thought that we'd like to get together between times and read

more and learn more, and one woman in particular has got a lot of books and has done some Women's Studies units and things at university and she's probably been the longest exposed to feminism. She's got a whole pile of books and we would photocopy a chapter of a book and read it and then discuss it the next week. We've done stuff on the witches and midwives and compulsory heterosexuality and that sort of stuff, and it's been really interesting.

As noted earlier, the activities of this particular group moved beyond a simple reading/discussion group. Concerned not only to develop their own understanding of feminism, but also to spread the message to other women in their town, they organized public lectures and workshops. They also attempted to interest other women in feminist issues by setting up a display of feminist books in the local library during Feminist Book Fortnight:

We all combined our books and we got Women's Health in Rocky [Rockhampton] to send us out a few, and we bought some purple material and the librarian put it up in the library. The librarian was very curious about it all—was quite happy to do it. And we asked her to keep an eye on the books that people were interested in and to let us know what the comments were at the end of it. She said that she'd had quite a few inquiries about certain books that she was going to order now.

Although a low key activity, the book display was a means by which these women extended networks and spread information to a wider group of women in their community. It is a good example of "unobtrusive mobilization" as defined by Katzenstein and discussed in Chapter 3.[8]

Turning to the follow-up interviews, 21 women reported participating in feminist reading or discussion groups. For eight women, this was the first time they had ever been involved in this type of activity, and two joined new groups in 1992 after a few years break. As before, the focus of the groups varied. Muriel joined a support network for women in education, while Barbara joined one for women in the church. The group Barbara joined in Brisbane evolved over time from an informal get-together of friends to a slightly more formalized activity:

When I look back now, it was just that we had common difficulties that we started to meet and we felt the need for support, and we've just continued to meet . . . We come together to reflect on our own lives and because we're all women in the church . . . This whole thing, feminist issues, is always before us, because we're in such a male structured thing and we're all working towards familiarization, awareness raising, and that sort of thing . . . What we do is we come together, share our lives. We might have a meal, a bottle of wine, that sort of thing. And we share our reading. We always share the reading that we do. That's part of what we take to our groups.

In addition to those women who were members of formal or semi-formal reading or discussion groups, a number talked about the importance of having friends with whom they could discuss feminist issues and ideas.

A successful 1992 *Reclaim the Night* march in Mackay generated considerable momentum and led to the formation of a discussion group. At the time of the follow-up interviews, Jacqui and Stella were both involved in this group that was still in its early days and not yet clear about direction. A bond developed among the small group of women who organized *Reclaim the Night*:

> And that's formed a strong core for this other group that's now formed . . . We decided to have a follow-up, so as not to lose that energy. And just things that came up at the first meeting. We just sent around a book asking people to write down what their interests were, and then we had a little discussion about it afterwards.

Women's Centers and Services

A further area of involvement for many of the women in this study was related to women's centers and services. The development of women's centers or women's houses has been a central element of second wave feminism in Europe, the United States, and Australia.[9] In a study of participation in the Dutch women's movement, Briët et al. identified women's centers as significant movement organizations:

> Women's houses are gathering places for the women's movement. They are open only to women, and they provide space for all sorts of groups and activities . . . More than any other single activity, the women's houses are associated with the women's movement.[10]

Women's centers in Townsville, Mackay and Rockhampton figured frequently in relation to most areas of involvement discussed in this chapter. In the initial interview, most of the women in this study reported some prior contact with one of the centers mentioned above, or with a women's center in a previous place of residence. The extent of involvement varied considerably with a small number of women having contact with these centers as clients, while others were involved as members, as staff, or through serving on management collectives. For some, their involvement was quite recent, whereas others had been involved in the establishment of various centers and had a long-term commitment to them.

Six Townsville respondents were founding members of the Townsville Women's Centre. At the time of the initial interview, all six were still involved in some capacity: two were employed by the center, three were members of the management collective, and one was an ordinary member. A number of the Mackay women were also heavily involved in the Mackay Women's Health and Information Centre. At the time of the initial interview, four were members of the center's management group and one of these was also employed part-time at the center. Another six had attended workshops or other events held at the center. A further 24 women talked about being members, attending events and functions, or being on the mailing list of their local women's center, while not being involved at an organizational level. Rose was a member of the Rockhampton Women's Centre, and attended events that interested her:

> Oh yeah, I'm a member of that. I'm not on the committee. I go every time they have a guest speaker—the likes of Dale or things like that. They're having Jocelynne Scutt at the end of this month. Oh yeah, I go to those things, for sure.

Closely related to women's centers is involvement in women's services. Feminist women's services provide counseling and advice in a supportive, woman-centered environment. The "development of women's services is an important story of the everyday life and action of the women's movement," with work that is focused "on public education and action towards social change."[11] During the initial interviews, around one-third of the women mentioned having worked in women's services at some time on either a voluntary or paid basis. Six were, or had been, members of rape crisis collectives, five were involved in women's health services, one had been instrumental in establishing a women's legal service, and two had been involved in lesbian or gay telephone counseling services. In addition, a few women, from both Mackay and Townsville, had at some time received assistance and counseling from a feminist women's service.

Women's centers and services continued to provide an important avenue of feminist involvement for many of the women throughout 1992. Whether as ordinary members, as employees, or as members of management collectives/committees, 28 women (64 percent) maintained or began an association with at least one such organization. A small number of women were involved in new initiatives during 1992. A women's community health center was established in Townsville and a committee was formed to organize and fund-raise for a women's legal service. In Mackay, 1992 saw the development of a sexual abuse and rape crisis service. Women from the study were involved in all three ventures. The Townsville women who were involved in these initiatives during 1992 mostly had a long history of feminist involvement. In contrast, the two Mackay women who became involved in the development of the sexual abuse and rape crisis service had little previous experience of this type. Jacqui described some of the frustration involved in trying to establish a new service with an inexperienced committee/collective:

> I find it a little frustrating I suppose because we're all new, and we don't really have too many guidelines. It's not a committee following from last year's, we're actually setting up the service from scratch and just the practical things like finding premises and trying to buy fridges and carpets and doing it on a very limited budget, as well as setting up the service and promoting the service. So for me, personally, it's a bit frustrating that things aren't moving as quickly as I would like, but the service is in place and running well and it's only the premises that looks like a bit of a dog's breakfast.

Stella expressed similar concerns about the difficulties experienced by this group in attempting to operate according to feminist principles of collective decision making while still accomplishing tasks. Despite teething problems, at the time of the follow up interview the service was in operation and attempting to meet community needs. Jacqui again:

> We have one worker which isn't enough. She's at full capacity after two months of operation . . . We haven't even really made a public announcement that we're open because we just feel we can't provide any more—we have only one worker and she's at capacity.

Women's centers and services were central to movement involvement for the women in this study. They provided opportunities for participation in a range of activities, at various levels of commitment. These services represent significant movement organizations for the women of central and North Queensland.

Demonstrations, Rallies, Marches, and Campaigns

Demonstrations, rallies, marches, and campaigns are the traditional protest events of social movements. Although such events do not encompass the full range of feminist collective action, they have and still do play a significant role in the women's movement. Throughout the 1980s and into the 1990s International Women's Day (IWD) and *Reclaim the Night* continued to be observed and celebrated throughout Australia.

Both IWD and *Reclaim the Night* marches were important movement events for a number of women. Twelve (27 percent) mentioned having participated in at least one such event at some time prior to the 1991 Winter

Institute workshop, either in Townsville or a capital city such as Melbourne, Sydney, or Brisbane. International Women's Day marches were particularly popular. They have been held regularly in Townsville since 1984 and several women proudly recounted their part in these early marches:

> The "oldies" have been involved now since 1984, when we reclaimed International Women's Day marches in Townsville. That year we got, in this silly little *About Town* column, a paragraph something like "the old boiler hens straggling down the street" and that's what we were, there was about 20 or 30 of us if we were lucky. And the next year there might have been 10 or 15 of us, and a few more at the rally, but who wouldn't march. (Vicki)

Fewer respondents mentioned *Reclaim the Night* marches in the initial interviews; however, a number mentioned prior involvement in other marches and forms of protest. Two women had attended the Women's Peace Camp held at Cockburn Sound, Western Australia in December 1984, and others reported activities as varied as sticker raids and protests aimed at beauty contests.[12]

Due to the nonspecific nature of the questions asked, the figure for women who mentioned rallies and protest events in the initial interview underestimates the actual level of involvement in this type of activity. In the follow-up interviews, a further eight women (20 in all), indicated that they had participated in at least one feminist rally, march, or protest prior to attending the 1991 Winter Institute weekend. The level of involvement in this type of activity increased further during 1992, with 27 women (61 percent) reporting having participated in at least one such event in the previous 12 months.

Eleven women attended an IWD march and rally in Townsville during 1992, while two others marched in Brisbane or Sydney. Julie travels extensively with her work and attended an IWD march in Sydney and a *Reclaim the Night* march in Rockhampton, because she "happened to be there" on those occasions. Vicki also travels frequently, and managed to fit in two IWD marches, one in Townsville and one in Brisbane the following day. From a small number mentioning *Reclaim the Night* marches in the initial interviews, the number who participated in 1992 was very high (over half the women: 52 percent). This reflects the fact that in Mackay and Rockhampton, *Reclaim the Night* marches were held for the first time in 1992. For a number of women, this was their first experience of a feminist march or rally. In addition to involvement in IWD and *Reclaim the Night*, four women mentioned writing letters of protest to newspapers. One lesbian feminist mentioned attending the Gay Mardi Gras and an antiviolence rally in Sydney, events that she viewed as related to feminism. Another talked about taking part in "the women's contingent of the Labour Day march."

Social and Cultural Activities

Another aspect of involvement, evident in the initial interviews, was participation in social and cultural activities that are either focused on women or overtly feminist. Despite criticisms leveled at cultural feminism—that it represents an apolitical tendency within the women's movement—recent work points to the political significance and collective nature of women's culture.[13] Opportunities for participation in feminist social and cultural activities are limited in Townsville and Mackay, and virtually nonexistent in central Queensland. Despite this, 17 women (38 percent) mentioned this as an area of involvement in the initial interview.

In Townsville and Mackay, most of what is on offer is connected to the local women's centers. Each first Friday of the month, from the mid 1980s until 1996, the Townsville Women's Centre was transformed into *Gertrude's, A Salon for Women*. *Gertrude's* provided a venue for women to get together on a social basis and to celebrate women's talents and achievements. Over the years, many local women as well as interstate and international guests contributed to *Gertrude's*. For 12 women, attending and/or helping to organize *Gertrude's* was a significant aspect of their feminist involvement. Kerrie commented, "The major part of my life centers around feminism and women's activities and groups, . . . *Gertrude's* and things like that." Another group that operated out of the Townsville Women's Centre was the *Small Collective*, a collective that was established to promote women's music and "to bring prominent feminist singers such as Judy Small and Peggy Seeger to Townsville."[14] In the initial interviews only one woman mentioned attending a concert sponsored by the *Small Collective*, but in the follow-up interviews references to their productions were more common. Two Townsville women also mentioned attending theater nights at the women's center.

The Mackay Women's Health and Information Centre also initiated social events. One respondent mentioned their *Super, You Beaut!* nights that usually included a guest speaker and supper, and were held bimonthly. It is possible that, to a feminist who is familiar with the smorgasbord of women's cultural and social events available in Australia's capital cities (or in cities in the United States or Europe), these nights would be barely recognizable as feminist; however they did provide a space for women from a small conservative town to get together in a supportive, women-centered environment. In this sense they can be viewed, and were by this respondent, as feminist.

A number of women talked about attending feminist social and cultural activities in other cities. Prior to coming to live in Townsville, Monique had been involved in feminist broadcasting on community radio in Canberra. An extensive traveler, Rose had also participated in a variety of feminist cultural activities including women's dances.

By the time of the follow-up interviews, the proportion of women reporting involvement in feminist oriented cultural and social activities had increased substantially. Twenty-eight women (64 percent) participated in activities as varied as feminist film festivals, plays, art shows, music, women's dances, and a summer solstice party. *Gertrude's* retained its popularity during 1992, with over half the Townsville women attending at least once during the year. In addition, Townsville women attended concerts with feminist singers, women's movies and plays, art exhibitions, and women's dances. One woman attended a women's dance in Mackay. At the time of the interview, Rose was in the process of organizing a forthcoming women's music event:

> The same group of us, as I say, those activists who are also feminists, we're putting on a "Singing Up the Women" concert on 8th March here in "Rocky." One hundred tickets only, women only, and that would be the most radical thing that's ever happened to "Rocky." All local artists.

There was little opportunity to attend feminist social and cultural activities in Mackay and central Queensland, hence few of the women living in these areas were involved in this type of activity. Of the 12 respondents still living in Mackay at the time of the follow-up interview, only two had participated in Mackay-based activities. Another attended a Women's Film Night while visiting Sydney.

During 1992, a number of women moved to live in larger cities where they took advantage of the opportunity to participate in events and activities that were not previously available to them. Barbara and Carol both moved from country towns to live in Brisbane. In Brisbane, Barbara attended a women's art exhibition and Carol attended coffee mornings at a feminist bookshop. Rhonda, one of the Townsville women, moved to Sydney early in 1992. In Sydney she joined feminist and lesbian groups, and at the time of the follow-up interview was becoming more involved in feminist cultural activities, both formal and informal.

In summary, women in this study participated in a wide variety of events and organizations that they viewed as indicative of their involvement in the women's movement. They attended feminist workshops, joined discussion groups, worked to provide women's services and, for leisure, supported women's cultural events. In the remainder of this chapter I discuss the significance of this involvement.

Participation: Incentives and Outcomes

How do the women I interviewed view their involvement in feminist events and organizations? What do they gain from it? And what does this tell us about the processes of involvement in collective action in general? A number of themes emerged from the data in answer to these questions. As noted earlier, these can be grouped under the three headings of knowledge and personal empowerment, emotional and social support, and identity resources. I have listed these as separate themes in the discussion below; however, in practice they are often intertwined.

Knowledge and Personal Empowerment

An important outcome of participation in movement organizations and events for the majority of women in this study was access to knowledge and information that they considered valuable. When commenting about participation in various events and organizations, the importance of being exposed to new ideas, or of having previously held beliefs confirmed and affirmed, often arose. Terms such as "awareness," "knowledge," "information," and "ideas" were used frequently when talking about participation in various events and groups. Women talked about "moving forward" as a result of increased knowledge, and of feminist workshops providing "new insights and new ways of thinking." In total, 40 women (89 percent) mentioned gaining information and knowledge as a positive outcome of participation. Carmel suggested, "I've always been into grabbing any information I can about and on women." Others said, "It was just wonderful to go there and see someone with so much energy and so much power and lots of knowledge" and, "As far as facts and details about feminism, the theory side of it, I think it was really a very high score."

A number of women made reference to the significance, for them, of specific content. For example, "It hadn't occurred to me to be thinking of, you know, the information technology and the implications of that. And I was extremely interested in Valerie Walkerdine's input about the feeling-out-of-place notion, that 'classist' thing" (Lorna). As discussed in Chapter 4, a number of women expressed a conscious desire to continually increase their knowledge and understanding of feminist ideas.

Gaining knowledge was considered equally valuable by those women whose involvement and commitment spanned several years and by those who were relatively new to feminist ideas. For Vicki, a self-identified feminist for many years, there was a particular attraction to sometimes being the recipient rather than the provider of information. This was linked to her desire for continual development of feminist ideas. Talking about a range of workshops, seminars and conferences attended throughout 1992, she commented:

> I really love to be part of an audience sometimes and get information. I guess, often—and this is probably true for most feminists in Townsville—that we feel a bit that, like we do it, we organize it and therefore we don't necessarily get anything out of it in terms of new thoughts and new ways of looking at issues and stuff, so to have other women from other places come here, not to tell us how it should be done, but to just offer their way of thinking, their way of looking at things, I just find that an incredibly stimulating activity.

The importance of gaining knowledge and information was also apparent in negative comments made about some events. Talking about her experience of attending a two-day conference in Townsville during 1992, one of the Mackay women commented, "In one way I didn't feel as though I had a lot to take away with me. It was uplifting while I was there, but . . . I didn't gain much information that I could feed back." In attending the event in Townsville, she expected, and sought, to gain information that she could bring back to other women in Mackay. In Mackay, she suggested, "there's energy, but we lack information." Failure to realize this goal was a source of disappointment.

The popularity of workshops, seminars, and other educationally oriented activities reflects the value respondents placed on feminist knowledge. Overall, this type of event was the most frequently reported form of participation. The increase in the number of women who participated in reading and discussion groups during 1992—from 14 (31 percent) in the initial interviews to 21 (48 percent) in the follow-up—is also significant. Together, the data indicate a growing awareness among respondents of the centrality of knowledge to personal and political agency.

Knowledge has not figured in theoreticians' discussions of motivation for participation in collective action. As noted earlier, RMT-based accounts have tended to emphasize selective incentives such as material benefits or solidary and identity incentives.[15] Nonetheless, the importance of knowledge as an outcome and source of motivation for participation in movement events and organizations is clearly consistent with theoretical work on new social movements. NSMT views knowledge as a cultural resource produced and utilized by movements. As Melucci argues, knowledge "assumes a decisive role in rendering accessible a certain potential for action. And it can function as a multiplier of processes of change, because it gives the actors the responsibility for their choices."[16]

Many of the women in this study implicitly recognized the link between knowledge and action that Melucci writes about. They understood that knowledge, facts, and information are resources that they can utilize to achieve goals. Knowledge enhances their willingness to take action. As Kathleen commented, "Each time I do something like this it helps me, it clarifies my ideas and it helps me to be more willing to speak out about things." Sharon also remarked upon the personal power that flows from access to feminist knowledge:

> So that's power to facilitate, to assist, to encourage, to voice my own ideas, but without that meaning that we overrule other people. And obviously it's a personal issue . . . I have a whole lot of knowledge and power through my feminist reading.

As a cultural resource, knowledge is used by these women for self-empowerment and also to empower other women. They have an awareness that, as Melucci suggests, knowledge functions "as a multiplier of processes for change." Thus, in a range of settings they also acted to disseminate feminist knowledge. This aspect of feminist collective action is discussed in Chapter 7.

Emotional and Social Support

In addition to providing access to knowledge and information, participation in movement organizations and movement events contributed in many cases to feelings of solidarity and emotional support. Living as a feminist is not always easy. As discussed in Chapter 5, voicing feminist opinions or acting in ways that identified interviewees as feminist often resulted in antagonistic and defensive reactions from others. In a range of settings, the women in this study often found themselves in situations where their feminist identity set them apart as social outsiders. This comment from Sharon about her work environment typifies the emotional exhaustion that a number of women experienced:

> Sometimes I get very tired of that sense of—if I say what I really think . . . everybody moves back an inch or two in their chairs and looks really shocked and not quite sure where to go next. I feel like I think really differently, and that's a bit wearing . . . Sometimes I feel a bit tired of having that kind of role, but I can't help it. And sometimes it just happens without me thinking about it. I think I'm being quite normal and then everyone looks at me as though I've jumped off the deep end.

In this context, women in this study valued highly the solidarity and emotional recharge they received through participation in movement events.

Participation in protests or workshops with like-minded women served as a welcome relief from the emotion management required in nonfeminist settings. Women talked about having their views confirmed, clarified, and strengthened through involvement in feminist events, and of coming away from these nourished, replenished, renewed, and energized. Reflecting upon the weekend workshop, one woman said, "The whole weekend was such a positive experience. [It] was a replenishing of my values. If you want to put a feeling on it, it was like reenergizing and remotivating me." Another said she "felt lots of personal power" following the workshop, and yet another noted:

> Every time I go away for some serious feminist input like that, I do come away stronger. I never, ever doubt my feminist beliefs, but I get caught in life, and let some things go because it's easier to not pick up on some things, . . . but every time I go away on a feminist activity, I do come back stronger and with more energy to pick up on some of the fights that I haven't been engaged in for a while.

Rhonda described participating in a march as "an incredible feeling just being part of a group of people losing the feeling of being in a minority group, and having so much support around you." A number of women mentioned that in their daily lives, including employment, they felt isolated from other feminist women. They felt particularly in need of a periodical recharge, "a bit like a dose of medicine," as Margaret put it.

The emotional exhaustion described by interviewees and the boost received from participation in some events is consistent with Randall Collins' theory of emotions. For Collins, "emotional energy" refers to the long-term emotional tones produced through interaction in power and status rituals. Emotional energy exists on "a continuum, ranging from a high end of confidence, enthusiasm, good self-feelings; down through a middle range of lesser states, and to a low end of depression, lack of initiative, and negative self-feelings."[17] In power rituals, order givers gain emotional energy while those receiving orders lose it. Similarly, status enhancement increases emotional energy, while lack of status lowers it. The daily experience of suppressing feminist identity, or of not doing so and being perceived, therefore, as deviant and of lesser status, led to a state of low emotional energy for many of the women in this study. Collins further speculates that an individual's store of emotional energy is increased through the dramatic, positive, short-term emotions—enthusiasm and joy—that are generated through the successful enactment of interaction rituals. This may explain the reenergizing effect of participation in certain movement events. Aspects of some movement events become ritualistic and thus generate positive short-term emotions and increases in emotional energy.

Events like International Women's Day and *Reclaim the Night* marches are held annually on the same or similar dates throughout the western world. Slogans invented in one part of the country, or one part of the world, quickly spread to other regions where they are emblazoned on badges and posters and incorporated into chants. A famous slogan first used by Italian feminists—"Tremble, tremble, the witches are back"—has appeared on badges worn at *Reclaim the Night* marches in Townsville.[18] Similarly, chants such as "Yes means yes, no means no, however we dress, wherever we go!" are widespread. Thus, such events take on a ritualistic atmosphere that enhances solidarity and emotional connections.

This interpretation is consistent with recent scholarship on the role of emotion in collective action. Verta Taylor and Nancy Whittier, for example, have drawn attention to the way in which movements use ritual to achieve emotional framing.[19] "At demonstrations, marches, and cultural activities such as concerts, films, poetry readings, exhibitions, plays, conferences and music festivals, ritual evokes and channels women's emotions."[20] It may be that ritual creates a link between knowing and feeling that Harrington and Flint have argued is essential to the apprehension of efficacy.[21] Through participation in these events, consciousness and emotion are brought together: participants "know," they "feel," and they develop an awareness of the relationship between these two aspects of their selves.

Beyond these nationally and internationally observed feminist events, a level of shared culture had developed among those women in this study who frequently participated in local events. In particular, this was evident among those who had attended more than one Winter Institute weekend workshop. This was based on shared memories of earlier workshops, symbolism, and even language. One woman described a developing ritual among a group of women who had participated in the Winter Institute workshops over a number of years:

> It was a great topic around here for ages afterwards . . . Every time you'd see somebody that went there we'd just discuss how good it was . . . We came away with this kind of secret signal of—what was it?—we actually combined quite a lot, we had "athad, athad," which was a thing, which came out of a previous workshop, the first one we did, something in the middle, and then the last one was "snip, snip," because the thing that came out of this one was "votes for women, chastity for men" and so the "snip, snip" was the chastity part of it. So for a little while after we came back, every time we'd see each other we would go "athad athad, cackle cackle (which was a witchy activity that we'd been involved in) and then snip snip (which was the last Winter Institute)." So for a little while we went round with these signals that we'd all participated in and shared (laughing).

This ritualized form of greeting was based on one significant idea from each of the three previous workshops. The "athad, athad" segment refers to a piece of feminist writing about the socially constructed nature of language that was discussed at the first workshop:

> Vicki read a piece that a woman had written about the "athads," which was this part of the arm [pointed to part of her forearm], and it's a whole piece, which talks about the arm being complete and being round and so on, and it caught everybody's imagination, and so the whole rest of that weekend, every time we greeted each other we touched athads and then in a group we'd all go "athads, athads" so that was very much like the catchcry and so that group existed for a little while, "The Athads," which grew out of the first Winter Institute for Women.

Evidence of the shared culture that had developed between these women can also be seen in the term "camp groupy" that was applied to women who had attended a number of workshops.

The relationship between the dissipation of emotional energy through daily encounters with opponents, and the restoration of emotional energy through the rituals of formal feminist involvement, would tend to indicate that the value of events like *Reclaim the Night* and International Women's Day marches is not their direct effect on governments or those in power, but the solidarity and emotional energy that is generated through them. This is not to say that direct effects on institutions of power are not desired, only that they may not be the critical factor in sustaining collective action. For these women, carrying out the work of the movement through providing feminist women's services and support for women colleagues, friends, and acquaintances (all forms of feminist action described in the next chapter), required such periodical top-ups of emotional energy.

Before moving on to discuss the role participation in organizations and events plays in affirming feminist identity, it is necessary to note that while the shared culture that had developed between the "camp groupies" was experienced positively by many, there was a negative side to this aspect of participation. As discussed in Chapter 4, for some there was a fear of being stifled by the group. As Gamson has noted, there is often a fine line between social support and social pressure within social movement organizations.[22] Another negative aspect to this shared culture between long-term participants was its impact on new participants. The existence of an already strongly shared culture among some participants added to feelings of being "outsiders" for others. One woman, who attended the weekend workshop for the first time in 1991, talked about the difficulty of breaking into already existing cliques:

I had the sense that there was already a community formed and anyone who came in from outside was from outside and I got a—I suppose that hit me strongly on the Friday night—there was already a sort of a language going that anybody from outside couldn't join into, and that is exclusive. And I suppose any people that I reached out to was my own sort of initiating of it.

Affirmation of Identity

Finally, for many of the women in this study, participation in movement organizations and events was a means of affirming their sense of self and of making a statement about their identity as feminists. Talking about her increased involvement in feminist activities during 1992, Catherine commented, "I think it's to do with my own personal development. I've become more focused on *who I am* and where I'm going and all that sort of stuff, and I've become disciplined in what I really want to do and I go ahead and do it" (emphasis added). The distinction between "consumers" and "organizers" of feminist activities was seen as important to some women in terms of their identity as feminists. For these women, actively doing something to progress the movement is part of their definition of a feminist. This distinction is clear in Kerrie's understanding of her participation in a range of feminist activities and organizations:

> Those sorts of things are a way of acting feminism . . . It seems to me that private feminism is fine, but not enough, and that what sort of distinguishes private feminism from belonging to the women's movement, is the action and the activity that we initiate that attempts to move the cause forward in any way. And those sorts of things, . . . the organizations, the social activities, the conferences— all of those I see as a way of trying to act out feminist principles and in some ways spread the movement. They're a fairly integral part of my feminist philosophy.

The affirmation of identity was particularly significant in regard to participation in women's centers and services. Lorna suggested, "I think I'd find it very, very difficult to work somewhere where I couldn't express my feminist views, where I wasn't encouraged to do that." Sandra described her involvement with the Planning Collective for the Townsville Women's Community Health Centre and her later employment as a health worker at the center during 1992. At the time of the follow-up interview, she had lived in Townsville for 18 months, having come from Sydney where she left behind a supportive group of feminist friends. She said:

> It was really good to have something to do which I felt passionate about, because I think for the past year and a half I'd been sort of

> hanging around, and started off not really looking for a job, coming here not for my choice but from Ray's, and then getting a bit of work, but nothing that I had a real commitment to, so that started to change. It makes it feel more like a home.

The affirmation of self, through working in a feminist women's service, is evident in this quote. To feel passionately about one's work is the opposite of alienation. The alienated person feels that her work is separate from and not part of herself. In contrast, to feel passionately is to be in touch with the self. Dana Crowley Jack argues that the articulation of feelings supports our "being" in the world. To not give expression to feelings is to "silence the self," to deny one's identity.[23] For Sandra, working in a women's health center gave expression to her feelings and to her identity. Who she is was consistent with what she did. Significantly, it also made a difference to how she felt about living in Townsville by providing her with a sense of belonging within the wider community.

The desire to work in an explicitly feminist environment was expressed by two other women in the study. Judy talked about considering a complete career change from scientific work to women's services, while Sharon, an academic, hoped to switch to the discipline of Women's Studies:

> I guess one of the things I'm finding more and more is that I want it [feminism] to be incorporated into everything I do, and that's why I've applied for a job in Women's Studies, to lecture in that, so that my passion and concern about feminist issues can be my central part of my work, rather than . . . being a kind of side dish that I kind of mix in all the time, but it's not supposed to be the major focus.

Movement scholars have noted the significance of the activities people engage in for their sense of self. In Calhoun's words, "to engage in action is a process of living an identity that is always social . . . What one does defines who one is, both for others and especially for oneself."[24] The experiences of the women in this study support this position. Participating in feminist events such as marches and rallies, serving on the committee of a rape crisis service or the local women's center, or working in women's services were all ways of proclaiming and affirming feminist identity.

CHAPTER 7

Establishing Feminist Presence in Daily Life

The feminist activity described in the last chapter did not exhaust the limits of feminist collective action for the women in this study. When asked about their history of involvement in feminism, they mentioned a broad range of actions that fell outside the boundaries of movement organizations but that they saw as part of what being feminist meant to them. These actions that went beyond what would normally be considered forms of movement participation can be characterized as strategies for establishing feminist presence in daily life. The women talked about how they applied a feminist perspective, and attempted to bring about social change, in a range of contexts: through their employment and participation in nonmovement organizations (for example, churches, clubs, unions), in interactions with friends and families, and through choices concerning living arrangements, dress and even diet. Across these sites a range of strategies were employed in an attempt to bring about change consistent with feminist principles. Two strategies involved drawing upon feminist knowledge or discourses as a means of empowering the self, or other women, respectively. A third strategy involved directly challenging taken-for-granted understandings or actions in relation to gender and a fourth strategy was focused upon valuing and providing support for other women.

Dominant conceptualizations of social protest have in the past contributed to ignorance, misrepresentation and repression of women's collective action. According to West and Blumberg, "what is defined as 'politics' or 'political behavior' is historically linked to power conflicts and, at times, specifically to gender power struggles."[1] Due to an organizational bias within much social movements research, less publicly visible forms and outcomes of feminist collective action are often obscured. Resource mobilization theory, in particular has focused almost exclusively on organizationally based action.[2]

On the other hand, feminists theorists and researchers within the social movements field have rejected a public/private dichotomy, along with a range of other dualisms, and fought for the recognition of the political nature of personal life as articulated in the classic expression of second wave feminism—"the personal is political." Consistent with this position, Mary Fainsod Katzenstein has described and analyzed two forms of feminist politics that rely primarily on the spread of feminist consciousness.[3] The first, "unobtrusive mobilization," refers to the mobilization of women within core institutions of society—the military, the church, and educational institutions. These major social and political institutions are transformed from the inside in a process based on networks and a flow of information between women. In a later article, Katzenstein extends her work on unobtrusive mobilization through the concept of "discursive politics." Discursive politics is "the politics of meaning-making," and is language based. Through conversations, conferences, books, and newsletters, it challenges, reinterprets, and rewrites the discourses and practices of major societal institutions. According to Katzenstein, discursive politics can be contrasted to organizationally based "interest group politics" that pursue largely measurable goals such as legislative reform. Discursive politics can be seen as a form of informal consciousness-raising.

Carol McClurg Mueller also notes the significance of the spread of feminist collective consciousness. Her analysis of United States women's increased participation in conventional party politics during the 1970s demonstrates the central role played by a generalized shift in collective consciousness at that time. Most of the newly elected women were not members of feminist organizations nor did they receive significant resources or campaign funds from feminist organizations.[4] Thus, Mueller found that feminist consciousness was more significant than either increased resources or organizational support in explaining the rise of women in political office. This led her to conclude that the "development of a collective consciousness is itself a 'successful' social movement outcome."[5]

Consistent with Katzenstein's and Mueller's work, the material presented in this chapter highlights the fact that feminist collective action is much broader than participation in events and organizations. Many of the actions described below are actions taken individually, however, I argue that they can be viewed as a form of *collective* action because they are based on feminist consciousness, emotions, and collective identity. In presenting the evidence to support this contention, I have chosen to initially organize the data in terms of the setting in which action took place. I begin with action related to paid employment. This is followed by feminist action within nonfeminist organizations, then by action associated with living arrangements and lifestyle. After detailing this material, the strategies noted above that were applied across settings are further elaborated, drawing out implications for the study of social movements more generally.

Employment

Paid employment provided many opportunities for activism and for expressing feminist subjectivity. The case of women working in women's centers and services has already been considered in Chapter 6; in addition, another 13 women (29 percent) talked in the initial interviews about the incorporation of feminism into their paid work. With the more specific questions of the follow-up interview, 31 women (79 percent of those who were in paid employment) described some connection between their work and their feminist views. For some, the actual content of their work was amenable to feminist practice, for others the work itself was largely irrelevant to any obvious feminist analysis and their feminism was expressed in terms of workplace relationships.

Most of the employed women in this study worked in the welfare, health, or education fields, where opportunities to integrate a feminist perspective were common. Susan, for example, talked in the first interview about having worked within an Aboriginal community in central Australia, where she supported women's rights to appropriate health care:

> I've fought very hard within Aboriginal situations, fought the government bureaucracy on their attitudes to women and women's health and, especially in traditional communities, I worked very hard for women to have the right to their own birthing center, and there are women's values and traditions that go along with those that exclude men.

Similarly, Sandra saw many opportunities for incorporating a feminist approach into her work in the areas of health and education. In the initial interview she said:

> Feminism informs a lot of my work. I do one-to-one with clients at Family Planning, trying to empower women and enable them to make decisions in their own life. Also in teaching, to equip kids to critically question some of the sort of fairly patriarchal, hierarchical,

medical models, and try and make it a bit more real in people's lives, you know, the whole idea of empowering people to make decisions for themselves, with information from others where necessary.

Between the initial and follow up interviews, Sandra changed employment and in her new position as a health worker in a women's community health center, feminism was simply "part and parcel" of the work she did. As discussed in Chapter 6, Sandra considered this a particularly important move as it allowed her much greater opportunities to incorporate a feminist perspective in her work.

In contrast to Sandra's situation, a career move for Louise during 1992 led to decreased opportunities for incorporating a feminist approach. Having worked for some time in the area of women's health policy, in an office that had a decidedly feminist tone—"they'd all consider themselves feminist here"—early in 1992 she moved to a new management position in community health, where the environment was much less supportive, "It was quite a shock to my system because I was back working with men, and that was interesting because it was back with the sexist jokes and the 'put-downs' if you like." Despite the less conducive environment, Louise continued to employ a feminist perspective by supporting other women in the office and through her work with the nurses employed under her:

> I try to take my feminist views to work and I try never to leave a remark or anything go past. I still have things like "Women can do Anything" on the filing cabinet . . . There's a lot of young girls in the office and I've actually supported them individually. I remember one of the fellows sent round a rude cartoon, and she came round and said "I don't think that's at all funny" and I supported her with that. I said, "That's the way to go." I actually do a bit in my work with the nurses too, in that I think that it's important to tell them to take responsibility for themselves in all ways, and because most of the nurses are women, you know, it sort of comes through my treatment, the way I relate to people.

Michelle and Nicole also worked in the health industry, Michelle in community nursing and Nicole as a hospital nurse. Both viewed feminism as very relevant to their work situations. Michelle commented in the follow-up interview that all her colleagues were women, as were most of the clients her organization serves, "so it [feminism] is very, very relevant." In both the initial and follow up interviews, Nicole talked about adopting a feminist approach in relation to three main aspects of workplace relationships: with doctors, peers, and patients. In relation to doctors, this involved rejection of the traditionally subordinate position of nurses:

> First off, there's this typical "handmaiden to the doctors" attitude that a lot of the doctors have, and a lot of the nurses have as well, and also the public, and I don't fit into that at all . . . the image of nursing has changed. It's always changing, but it's changed dramatically, say, in the past 10 years. For example, the acute care center in a hospital, that is a place where nurses nurse and doctors come to help, . . . as do physiotherapists—they're adjunctive sort of therapies. Where nurses nurse, and most nurses are women—although there's big changes on there too—and they just don't see their role as the most important when people are in hospital, and *it is the most important* because they're there to be nursed.

The discourse of professionalism has gained strength in nursing with the move to university-based education. In the example above, Nicole draws upon this discourse as a resource for resisting the typical "handmaiden to the doctor" attitude. The dominant discourses surrounding nursing have not provided a way to deal with difficult interactions with patients, however, and it is in this area in particular that Nicole recognized the effect of her increased feminist consciousness. She described her changed approach to offensive comments made by male patients following the Winter Institute workshop:

> Pre Crystal Creek, if I was working on a male ward, with male patients, then often nurses are, whatever the word is, the men give them shit, as in sexual shit and I always recognized that before and did not react, but now I react, now I don't, no, now I *consciously* don't react (laugh), meaning—and I have actually—and it's really hard to do this when you're nursing someone—I have actually said to patients of mine, when they have made some sort of sexual whatever, or stupid comment, I've said things like, "My name is 'Nicole,' it is not 'sexy!'" Things like that. [Before] I didn't respond to it, . . . now I go that way and make an active effort to respond in a negative way which is what I think, rather than bolster their crappy little egos. But now, no holds barred.

Prior to the workshop, Nicole was clearly aware of, and offended by, male patients' attempts to sexualize her, but she had no way of dealing with it, other than to ignore it. Following the workshop, she drew upon feminist understandings to empower her to respond assertively.

Although sexual harassment from work colleagues has been recognized in the nursing literature, Jocalyn Lawler suggests that there has been a reluctance to label overtly sexual behavior from patients as sexual harassment.[6] Those who have written about the problem have tended to trivialize the issues by referring euphemistically to "seductive behavior." Lawler identifies two possible explanations for this reluctance, the second of which is particularly relevant to Nicole's situation. First, is the fear on the part of nurses that discussing such issues may tarnish their image, and second, the role of the ethic of care within nursing:

> Nurses have not systematically challenged the professional (religious) notion that one must be able to care, irrespective of the patient, the patients' behavior, or the circumstances. To challenge the care ethic would be heretical, yet this ethic contributes to a practice environment in which sexual harassment is not openly and officially discussed, although everyone knows it occurs.[7]

Nicole's difficulty in dealing with harassing patients can be attributed partly to this ethic of care within nursing. After describing how she reacted following the workshop, she said:

> And that's really hard to do because you're there, supposed to be caring for these people and somehow juggling, letting them have heaps of independence and nurturing and being nice and everything else, you know, you're supposed to do everything you can to—and that becomes a bit of a problem.

A parallel can be seen between this example and Valerie Walkerdine's research in which preschool boys harassed their teacher who was rendered powerless to act because of her investment in "progressive" discourses of child development.[8] Both of these examples occur in situations where male power is compromised, either because the males are children or because they are patients. By sexualizing the women in these situations, male power is restored. What is important about Nicole's changed approach is that it was her newly acquired feminist understanding that provided a counter to the traditional feminine "ethic of care." Through feminist discourse Nicole saw the sexual harassment for what it was—an attempt to restore gendered power relationships—and responded accordingly. Thus, established gendered patterns of interaction were challenged and transformed through informal methods.

The final aspect of Nicole's adoption of a feminist approach to work was in relationships with peers. She talked about providing positive reinforcement of peers as a way of expressing feminism through work, "I positively stroke, as in positively reinforce my peers . . . and that's where I class myself as a bit of a feminist at work."

Women employed in education also incorporated a feminist approach in their work. Both Kathleen and Muriel talked about working with young women in educational institutions in an effort to empower them and "raise their consciousness about feminist issues" (Kathleen). Muriel commented:

> I'd like to get involved with women more, and also to look around
> in the school and do something for our girls in the school. Girls are
> victimized in this community, without a doubt. We've only been
> back at school a fortnight and there's already been another sexual
> abuse case, where the father of the child is involved, so I think there
> is enormous work to be done there, just in education.

In the follow-up interview Muriel talked about positive steps she had taken
during 1992 to encourage and support girls to be more outspoken in the
school and not to allow boys to dominate school committees and organizations such as the student council. She described a leadership program for
year 12 students in which she tried "to get girls thinking about how they can
support each other and feel secure in what they're doing and know they've
got a voice, and are able to speak out and take control."

Barbara and Stella were both involved in adult education at the time of
the initial interview. Stella described running personal development groups
for women at the local TAFE (Tertiary and Further Education) college as
her "way of contributing to the cause of feminism." As a member of a religious order, Barbara worked in adult education within a Christian organization. Within this conservative organization she applied a Christian
feminist framework to the types of activities she organized and to workplace relationships:

> I suppose the area that I've really taken up has been Christian fem-
> inism, and to bring about change within the church. Things like in-
> clusive language and women, and that kind of thing . . . I've
> probably always had a bias towards working with women before,
> but I would now say I work with women's groups, and I don't have
> any hassle about having groups that don't include men . . . For ex-
> ample, this Women's Wisdom workshop, I will invite certain
> women, there will be no men. I mean, they may know about it, but
> I wouldn't invite them, and if they ask to come, I will say "no," and I
> won't shake on it, whereas I would have perhaps once, I would have
> felt the need to be more inclusive.

In a similar manner to Nicole's rejection of the "handmaiden to the doctor"
attitude, Barbara challenged the traditional subservient relationship between women and men in the church. She refused to provide a purely supportive role to the men in her organization and encouraged other women
to follow her example:

> One of the things that I say to the women here, when I see them run-
> ning after Peter, I say to them, "You don't have to clean up men's
> mess all the time," you know. "Why are you picking up Peter's mess

all the time? Allow him—make him take responsibility for his actions." . . . But I certainly don't put myself in a position where I'm
subservient to Peter. And I think I use that example of encouraging
Hazel, when Hazel said to Peter, "This is the information you need
for a meeting next Monday." It was midweek, and he said, "Oh, give
it to me on Monday" and she looked at me and she said, "I'm giving
it to you now." And he came back and said, "Let me know, remind
me on Monday," and she said, "No! I'm giving it to you now, what
you do with it is your business!" So I'm encouraging them to do that
kind of stuff.

This is very powerful action. In this situation Barbara questioned centuries
of tradition and incited another woman to follow her example. It is not
surprising that, as discussed in Chapter 5, attempts were made to curb her
activities and influence within the organization.

It was largely the conflict that arose over Barbara's feminist approach to
her work in adult education that eventuated in her taking up new employment as a hospital chaplain early in 1992. Her feminist orientation was,
however, carried through into the new position where she continued to
support other women, both clients and coworkers, and to fight for recognition of women's roles within the organization and more generally within
the Catholic Church. Talking about the role of chaplains she commented:

Part of my job here is education of other chaplains and so all the
time I'm bringing this issue into it—of inclusion—of our chaplains
taking their rightful place. And our women very often stand back
and allow the males to make the decisions and allow them much
more room than they should have, with regard to taking over and all
that sort of thing . . . The women are intimidated, so they stand
back and don't take their rightful place. And so it's honoring our position and calling that force in women here—our women chaplains.

Another aspect of Barbara's feminist approach is her mode of working with
clients. She has found that many women, particularly those who are very ill,
prefer to speak with a woman chaplain, and she has fought for a division of
labor that facilitates this:

Particularly where women are really sick and, for example, women
who have cancer, women who have gynecological problems in the
women's hospital. I speak out all the time, that women should be the
ones that go there.
. . . The women just continually say, "Thank God *you've* come, I
feel free to be able to talk to you." . . . When male chaplains go to
these people, often they talk about the tradition and things out

there. When we talk to women, it's their own personal issues that they really bring forth, and how they're affected by them; their health issues, their family issues, their relationships, and personal growth areas. Their own feminine spirituality. That sort of thing.

Most of the large proportion of interviewees who worked in the welfare field operated from a feminist perspective. Colleen, for instance, talked in both the initial and the follow-up interviews about taking a feminist approach in relationships counseling, "What I do with a lot of clients in my work is to teach them skills—well, I support women. First of all, I support women who are in bad situations and I empower women by giving them more information about themselves, about society, and changes that society's made."

Counseling, providing information or advice, or group work of some kind was a component of the work done by at least six other women in the study. Many described the way they worked using terminology such as "empowerment" or "supporting" and "valuing" women. For example, one woman suggested that although feminism was not central to her work as a dietitian, her feminist views influenced the way she interacted with and advised clients:

> Well you can look at things like body image and I guess I think more about the way that I try to be with people. My work is about getting people and motivating or convincing them sometimes that they need to make some changes with their lifestyle or their eating patterns, but I try to do it fairly gently and not in a way that you'd call authoritarian or really pushy . . . If sometimes a woman says something that might be a negative type comment about herself, then I'll just try to get her to talk about that and hopefully change it into something more positive rather than putting herself down so much.

This approach to working with clients draws upon a feminist analysis of the social and cultural basis of the low self-esteem many women experience in relation to body image. It is also based on a commitment to valuing and supporting women.

A number of respondents worked in human services administration or management where they were not involved on a one-to-one basis with clients. Nonetheless, whether working in aged care, disability services, or youth services, they also talked about fighting for women's rights and working for social justice more generally. Marie, for instance, expressed in very strong terms the importance to her of fighting injustice through her work:

> The major agenda for me in work is social justice, that's what drives me. Every job, every decision that I make, that is fundamental to what I do, and the greatest social injustice is the injustice against women. So they are so tied that I can't separate them. I can't separate them, so it drives every decision that I make. It's about how best to position myself so that I can further increase social justice, and a major target for that is women. That's the core of it all.

During the study period two women worked part-time as research assistants conducting oral history interviews. Both talked about making a particular effort to highlight women's stories. The project, in one case, was a commissioned history of the coal-mining industry and, even here, a feminist perspective was brought to bear. The focus on women's lives was welcomed by respondents, "I came across a very positive response when women, who generally thought they had no history, realized they did, and were quick to act upon it and enliven the research with their feedback."

Most of the examples covered so far relate to situations in which it was possible to integrate a feminist perspective with the actual content of the work. In some employment situations this was not the case. There is no peculiarly feminist way to peel potatoes, type a letter, or prepare the books if you are employed as a cook's assistant, a secretary, or an accountant. Despite this, respondents who worked in these types of occupations still brought their feminism to work through a "politics of everyday resistance."

At the time of the initial interview, Rhonda was working as a personnel manager at a meat works. Within this macho setting she took the opportunity to engage in informal feminist activism. Following the Winter Institute workshop, she specifically made feminist reading material available in her office, and encouraged other women in her workplace to assert themselves:

> The girls at work used to always come out and—my office always has books or magazines around—now if they borrow a book, it's normally one of the feminist books from the library. I won't keep anything else there for them to read . . . So that's what the girls at work have been reading.

In addition to providing "subversive" reading material, Rhonda found herself speaking out at work, challenging assumptions and disrupting taken-for-granted understandings of gender:

> (laugh) It was sort of a drastic change in, just on speaking out on a lot of things, and sort of, having a few little facts and figures to back up my arguments, you know, and a few little answers like, oh it came up one day, "Oh I'll have to ask my husband to baby-sit," and I turned round and asked this woman how many times he'd ever

asked her to baby-sit, you know, and just little things you'd heard on the weekend. She turned around and said, "no, he never has, yeah, actually" (laugh) and got her right going.

By pointing out the anomaly in this situation, where the woman feels she has to ask her husband to baby-sit, but he is not required to reciprocate, Rhonda questioned the assumption that child care is women's work and that men have a stronger claim to independent leisure time.

Janet also reported an incident that involved encouraging a coworker to stand up for her rights. In this case, in relation to a sexual harassment case:

> She was just very stressed out. She was even getting scared about going home. She thought if I go home he's going to turn up there, and I came out and said, "Do something about it!" I didn't tell her why or what I'd been through, I just said, "Do something about it." Because she was just terrified. And it wasn't long after that, that it was all brought up.

Three women talked about being in positions of authority where they were able to influence the tone of their work environment by proscribing sexist, homophobic, or racist remarks. For example, one commented:

> I use some of what I believe to be my feminist principles and feminist philosophy in terms of office management. We have unstated and stated rules about nonsexist language, nonracist language, and attitudes towards women, attitudes towards domestic violence and child abuse. All of those sorts of areas, and it's very well known what my background is, that I'm a feminist and I don't stand for those kind of things.

Although not in the fortunate position of being "boss of the office," another woman who worked as a secretary within a large bureaucracy still insisted on being treated with respect and addressed in a manner she found acceptable. Her feminist views provided the force behind this insistence, "I do try to live it [feminism] all the time."

A final, and more overt example of activism coinciding with employment was that of Rose, who produced screen-printed t-shirts, stationery, and stickers that incorporated "women-positive images." Through self-employment Rose created a situation where she could earn a living in a manner consistent with her political principles.

What emerged from many of the interviews, and is highlighted in this last example, was the importance attached to working in positions that were compatible with or at least not in conflict with feminist values. For those women working in feminist women's services or in other human service organizations that, at least in principle, support social justice goals, this was attainable if sometimes difficult. Others achieved congruence between their values and their work life through self-employment. For a small number, however, conflict existed between their feminist values and their employment, creating anxiety and a desire to seek alternative employment.

Nonmovement Organizations

A number of women mentioned the relevance of feminism to a variety of groups and associations to which they belonged. They recounted bringing to bear a feminist perspective in a range of organizations including trade unions, voluntary community service associations, advisory committees, clubs, and churches. Such organizations provided a further avenue for unobtrusive activism. Examples of feminist action taken within this context included setting up a women's network within a union, promoting women's sport, involvement in childbirth education, and the expression of feminist views in church settings.

During 1992, Anne initiated a Public Sector Women's Network following a union conference:

> The idea came up at this conference, because women traditionally, I believe, see unions as male-dominated organizations that they are reluctant to join. The idea of a network was considered to be a really good alternative for women in an informal way to get together and perhaps to discuss issues that related to their particular working lives and the problems that they encounter. And also to get guest speakers in, and I guess in that way somehow tap into the public sector union structure.

Anne's action in initiating the Public Sector Women's Network can be seen as part of an ongoing struggle to make unions more responsive to the needs of women workers. From its inception, the Australian union movement served men's interests and reinforced gender divisions within the Australian workforce. Since the 1970s, feminists have attempted to bring about change in this area.[9]

Turning to another area of community involvement, four women were members of advisory or management committees for community or government organizations including a community legal service and the Queensland Museum Association. Often as a minority voice, they provided feminist input into decisions. Sarah and Emma, who were both members of advisory committees established to improve the position of women in sport, provide a useful illustration.

From a background in the fitness industry, Sarah became a volunteer community member of the local Division of Sport and Recreation Area Committee. In the weeks prior to the first interview she initiated, and helped to organize, a Women's Sports Forum in Mackay. Sarah described the opening of the forum and her introductory talk:

> [I had] a report of a forum that was held in Canberra and there was some really good information . . . A study was taken in 1988 of six major television stations down South. Women had 1.3 percent coverage, men had 56 point something, mixed sport had 30 something, and animals in sport had 2.1 percent! So I thought, "Oh, this is some good information," so I went through and got lots of information out of this book. Then I thought from my feminist point, I put across the notion that women needed to support women to empower women, irrespective of what sporting activity they were in, what recreational pursuit, and I kept on repeating that to them. And at the end of the night, one of the older women said, "Now, what were those words of wisdom you said?" (laugh) I mean, I've got them from other feminist things that I've been to.

A Women's Sport and Recreation Advancement Committee was formed following the forum and in the follow-up interview Sarah talked about her continued involvement throughout 1992.

Between the initial and the follow up interviews, Emma also became involved in the promotion of women in sport through membership on a similar committee. At one meeting she put the issue of media coverage of women's sport on the agenda:

> One of the things I've been pissed off about is the way they report women in the media. There was something in the paper today about a woman who's an athlete, she's 30 years old and she's got two kids, and it said something about "Mother does well," the heading—and you think "Oh!"
>
> At the first meeting I went to, a couple of weeks ago I actually brought up that as an issue that I'd like to do something with, but they sort of said, "Well, actually the *Bulletin*'s got a really good name in terms of comparison to other newspapers, it actually does quite well in terms of reporting women's sport." But I just sort of said "Well, they might do quite well, but do we want to just leave it at that?" Other people agreed that they didn't like the way they were reporting it, but I don't know what we can do about it. But I thought I'd keep cutting things out and get a collection.

Again in this example, Emma applied a specifically feminist analysis to the issue of women in sport. She was critical of the media positioning of women in traditional feminine roles and brought this analysis to the attention of fellow committee members. Although the attempt to put this issue on the agenda was only partially successful, she decided to continue collecting examples that would strengthen her argument at a later meeting.

Further areas where feminist perspectives were incorporated were childbirth education and advocacy, telephone counseling, marriage education, youth work, and family planning workshops. In the initial interview, Michelle talked about her involvement in childbirth education, and the constant battle with male obstetricians over women's birthing rights. Over time, Michelle had come to understand childbirth education in feminist terms, as a challenge to the male-dominated medical establishment, and as a way of supporting women:

> When I was involved with childbirth education . . . there was a constant battle with obstetricians, you know, trying to get them to realize that it was okay for a woman to squat or get up on all fours or walk for most of her labor or, you know, and to get them to feel that it was okay for them to follow their own instincts . . . In those days I wouldn't have even thought about it as a feminist issue, or an independent thing. It was just trying to get the obstetrician, the male obstetrician to see that they had taken this from us, and taken it from us as midwives too, . . . that basic thing of women being with women when they gave birth, and supporting them.

This example illustrates receptiveness to the sociological critique of medical dominance within the nursing profession.[10] It also highlights a growing awareness of feminist analyses of gendered power relations and their impact on women's health. Emerging out of second wave feminism, the women's health movement formulated women's health care as a political problem.[11] Through a process of diffusion, what were considered radical ideas about male medical dominance, and the importance of empowering women in childbirth, have spread to a wider audience. Alex's involvement in a home-birth support group draws even more directly on a feminist analysis of male dominance in the area of health. Describing her involvement in feminist groups and activities in the initial interview she said:

> Well the main thing that I've been involved in, in Townsville, . . . has been the home-birth support group, which has been working through the women's center . . . I've spent quite a bit of time organizing newsletters and information about home births and alternative medical things . . . That's been the main thing that I've put energy into . . . To me that's a feminist thing, because I sort of see that the medical system's a real patriarchal expression, and I think that it's really healthy for women to experience decision making

about their own bodies. So I feel really strongly about women feeling strong in their choices about what happens to their bodies, and having the information and knowledge to act on that, so they can make those choices.

During 1992, Alex gave birth to her second child at home. In her follow-up interview she described her continuing involvement in the home-birth movement. Again she stressed the centrality of feminism, and her opposition to medical dominance, as the basis of her decision to have a home birth.

Another example of action in the area of women's health rights was the work Liz undertook in providing information and support for young women. Having trained with The Family Planning Association as a community educator, Liz organized informal family planning workshops for young women in a town where this type of service was not readily available. Unlike other counseling services available in the town, Liz covered all options including abortion, and assisted young women with making appointments:

> I keep it as low key as possible, because in a small community—I mean, some people know I do it, and others don't, but word of mouth sneaks around, and I don't think the women and the young women discuss that so much with their husbands or boyfriends. And often it's the mothers that come to me and say, "Look, so and so's pregnant, can we come and have a talk to you? But don't tell the father." So they come out and I help them decide what they're going to do from there. It only happens infrequently, about four or five a year, but I still think, you know, at least there's somebody here that can do that on the ground for them.

Liz provided a range of information to empower young women to make decisions for themselves. Her approach was similar to that of women employed in the welfare sector and to Alex's involvement in the home-birth support group. Another way in which Liz supported and attempted to provide options for young single women was through her involvement in a youth housing organization, "So that they have another choice, rather than moving in with a miner, or getting pregnant to get a house."

Other examples of the influence of feminist values on voluntary community service include Louise incorporating discussion of domestic violence into marriage preparation classes, and Kathleen, as a volunteer crisis counselor, continuing to refer women to the local women's center despite opposition, "They much prefer us to send people to [counseling agency] whereas I always listen to the story and decide . . . They have the idea that the women's center's going to say to them 'Leave your husband, go and be a lesbian, do this, do that,' and that's just utter garbage."

Three women, in addition to Barbara, mentioned feminist activity within the church. Laurie was interested in feminist theology, subscribed to *Women Church*, and had attended seminars on Women in the Australian Church. Similarly, Tracy saw no separation between her faith and her feminist views. In practice, this meant bringing "lashings of feminism into every aspect of people's lives that I touch." She encouraged women to see birth control as a choice, and at church gatherings challenged taken-for-granted assumptions about women's roles and responsibilities by "refusing to wash up" and by "making smart-arsed comments when they're not expected." In this way, Tracy felt that she often got "the feminist point of view across."

As a final example of action that attempts to bring about change in non-movement organizations, Toni challenged the education system over the issues of violence in sport and sexism in school readers. Talking about her children's school she said:

> I like to think I take my feminist principles with me outside . . . I have had several arguments with coaches on the field who have urged my male children to go for blood . . . I've been to the school on occasions over sexist school books, and I've made scenes there, and I've written to the education department about books I think should be withdrawn. I've had some success too. I've had a couple of books taken out of the school readers.

Living Arrangements and Lifestyle

A defining feature of second-wave feminism has been the insistence on viewing the personal as political. Personal relationships, household living arrangements, friendships, and even aspects of lifestyle such as dress and diet have been analyzed from a feminist perspective. These areas of daily life provided another avenue for feminist action for many of the women in this study. For some, action in these areas was an ongoing and integral part of their lives, something they had been aware of for years. For others it was more recent, and in some cases had been inspired by the feminist input provided by the Winter Institute workshop itself.

Jo VanEvery suggests that feminist theoretical analyses of marriage and the family have led in practice to two alternative approaches: first, an attempt to improve women's position within marriage and second, a rejection of marriage.[12] The first approach relies on strategies that increase women's economic and social independence, the second "is evident in campaigns around sexual violence and wife battering" and tends towards strategies that involve alternative living arrangements, refusal to marry, and political lesbianism.[13] Both approaches were evident in the choices made by women in this study concerning relationships, household composition, and living arrangements.

Of the 45 women in this study, 17 (38 percent) were living with a male partner at the time of the first interview. Eleven lived alone, seven were living as single parents with their children and the rest lived in shared households or with a female partner. One woman spent weekends with her husband, but during the week lived in a unit on her own. Between interviews, 18 women changed their living arrangements.[14] The number living with male partners increased by six and another six moved into women-only households, including at least two who began living with a lesbian partner.[15] Four moved from living alone to living in a variety of shared arrangements, while three commenced living alone. Two had retired fathers come to live with them and one went from living alone on weekdays to living full-time with her husband.[16] What is more important than the percentages living in different household arrangements, is the fact that a number of women suggested that their living arrangements, whether living with a male or not, reflected their feminist values.

In the initial interviews, Alex and Monique both expressed the view that they simply lived a feminist lifestyle, and that feminism affected most areas of their lives. Alex, for example, talked about living with women when she first left home at 17 to go to university, "I just found myself living with a group of women, like older women and becoming really involved, just because it just seemed to be right for me. Because of the sort of woman I am." Similarly, Monique talked about feminism becoming a "subliminal" aspect of her life:

> Throughout that time my friends were all lesbian feminists and so our activities were always centered on those politics. We just talked it all the time. So, in the early days we did, and then you know, it came to a level where it was kind of subliminal, it was always there and always understood.

In the follow-up interview Rhonda talked about moving toward a more separatist lifestyle since moving to live in Sydney, and Stella, Judy, Patricia, and Helen all mentioned the link between lesbianism, feminism, and their living arrangements and lifestyle. For instance, Stella suggested:

> Because I've got three daughters and for the last seven or eight years been a lesbian, I have really only involved myself with women. It's been an all female house for so long, and always with feminist values

in place. And there hasn't been a struggle with men in the house . . .
It's sort of just part of the whole plan and that's that.

Marie described feminism as "an absolute, everyday part of every commu-
nication that I have, with everyone at every level, all the time." At the time
of the initial interview she was sharing a house with her brother, but when,
in 1992, she moved to live in Sydney, she made a deliberate decision to
move into a shared house with another woman.

It was not only women who were living without men in their lives who
said they lived feminism on a daily basis however. Most of the partnered
heterosexual women also attempted to apply feminist principles in their
personal lives. In her study of nonsexist living arrangements, VanEvery
identified a variety of strategies employed by heterosexual women in their
rejection of, or attempts to transform, the institutions of marriage and
family. These included cohabiting without marriage, retaining one's own
name in marriage, not wearing rings, living apart, and not revealing one's
married status.[17] Women in this study described similar strategies.

Emma talked about her long-distance relationship and the importance
of maintaining autonomy and control, "John and I have a long-distance relationship, but it's important to me that I have equal, or at least a strong
sense of control over what's happening in that relationship." In a similar
vein, Vicki sought to maintain independence in her relationship, which between the initial and follow-up interviews had shifted from a live-apart to
live-in arrangement. Despite this change, she described her continued rejection of marriage and motherhood and the ideology surrounding them,
"I'm still not going to marry him . . . I'm still not going to have children
and . . . I'm not going to take his name."

Although Janet married her partner in 1992, she continued to reject assumptions of sexual availability in marriage and assumptions surrounding
the ideology of motherhood. She expressed her views very strongly in relation to the first of these, "As I said to my husband, I said 'Don't ever force
me to do anything, like sexually. If I don't feel like sex I don't feel like sex,'
and I said, 'Don't force me! Don't ever!' He knows my views, he knows that
if I say 'no,' that's it." In relation to the second, she felt less sure of her position. Feminist analyses of the family have pointed out that prevailing ideology requires women, as wives, to "bear and rear children for the head of
household."[18] It was this requirement that was behind Janet's ambivalence
towards motherhood. She feared the loss of independence that would come
with motherhood but was aware that her new husband was "hoping for
children." In her struggle to reconcile her own feelings with her husband's
feelings and expectations, her desire to make this decision for herself, without any pressure, was legitimized within a feminist framework.

A general assertion of rights and independence within relationships arose in a number of other interviews. In the initial interview Rachel recounted her resolve, following the Winter Institute Workshop, to assert her rights within marriage, "Each thing like that reinforces the feeling, a feeling that I have as much right to do what I want as my husband does . . . I'm going to exert whatever power I have to maintain a clear position of equality in the home." Her determination to be treated equally was put in even stronger terms by the time of the follow-up interview:

> I guess in the home I'm being very assertive about myself and wishing to be considered as an equal partner and not as a lesser person, and I've had to make that clear because I have been involved in what they're calling a cycle of domestic violence. I haven't personally had any physical violence, mine has been emotional . . . For me, I've been working very hard at establishing the fact that I'm somebody in my own right, and equal.

Sharon also mentioned the family as a site of feminist activism in the initial interview, "Oh, and of course the personal front (laughter). I fight a lot of feminist battles every day about, you know, how things are done and all that kind of stuff." Both Colleen and Sarah reported in the follow-up interview that they had recently been standing up for their rights more assertively despite some opposition from within the family. Sarah said:

> I don't stand for any put-downs . . . I say, "I find that statement inappropriate," "I'm not willing to put up with that sort of behavior," "I don't see any reason why we should be together." . . . Really making some pretty heavy statements . . . I'm definitely not being passive. (Sarah)

It is important to emphasize that these women see their increasing assertiveness as, at least to some extent, a result of their growing involvement in feminism. This is not individualized resistance, but resistance that is made possible through the resource of feminist discourse.

The influence of feminist values and beliefs on respondents' approaches to marriage and family was evident in two further areas: first, the rejection of a traditional division of labor within the family and second, their approach to parenting. It is more than 25 years since Pat Mainardi, inspired by the women's liberation movement, wrote a paper on the politics of housework and her husband made the infamous comment, "*Housework? Oh my god how trivial can you get. A paper on housework.*"[19] And yet the battles surrounding domestic labor are still being fought daily. Despite a widespread rhetoric of gender equality in Australia, domestic labor is still highly segregated by gender and women still spend far more time doing housework than do men.[20] Housework—who does it and the social relations through which it is organized—arose as an important theme in VanEvery's study of antisexist living arrangements. VanEvery argued that rejection of an unequal division of labor within the household indicates a rejection of the role/identity of "wife" and a challenge to the assumption "that anyone has the right to the services of a wife."[21] A similar rejection of traditional assumptions concerning domestic labor is evident in my data.

A number of women considered the division of domestic labor to be a feminist issue within their relationships. For example, Margaret talked about a continual feminist analysis of roles within marriage, including the division of labor and "expectations of what we do for each other and why we do it." Vicki was also aware of the gender issues surrounding domestic labor, and the tendency for relationships that start out as equal to slip into gendered patterns. She was adamant that her approach to these issues stems directly from her feminist beliefs:

> And I certainly relate with my partner totally as a feminist, and he has absolutely no doubts whatsoever that that's how I am and who I am and how we will relate, on that basis. That's how we argue, [about who does chores and who organizes them] on that basis. I have to remind him that they need to be done, or organize the time that they will be done or organize something so that something can happen . . . They are gender issues. I don't let things go because I have a feminist awareness and an understanding of what often happens in relationships so while we are two adults who are sharing a house, I am not, as the organizer, going to organize another adult. Now, most of that is because I am not, as the woman who is a feminist, going to organize the man. So there is a very strong gender issue about how we relate in our relationship.

For Liz, achieving a fair distribution of domestic labor involved a high degree of conflict and required a determined effort on her part. At the time of the initial interview her partner was not contributing and arguments over domestic labor were common. Liz continued to challenge her partner's expectations and by the follow-up interview the situation had improved somewhat:

> He's doing half the housework. He slips occasionally and then we have a discussion about it, so he's actually picked up on that point because we've had a few discussions about it. Yeah, he can see that it's probably not fair just because I'm born a female that I do all the washing and the washing up and clean up.

For Beverly, an equitable division of labor meant that all members of the household, including both male and female children, shared the necessary chores. Talking about the relevance of feminism to family life, she said, "Division of labor is the obvious one—who does what and why. 'Why? Because it's not my job, it's our job, it's our house.' . . . All my kids, female and male, at 14 get a laundry basket and do their own laundry." This example highlights a further way in which interviewees incorporated a feminist approach into family life. A number of women talked about the way they attempted to raise their children to be independent, assertive, and aware of gender issues. This meant similar expectations of chores from sons and daughters, discussions with sons about how they relate to women, providing daughters with strong role models, and encouraging them to be assertive.

A number of women talked about the ways in which their own awareness of gender issues influenced their children's attitudes and beliefs. For example, Kathleen suggested, "Well I think they are quite influential, and they have a good influence, on my son in particular. I think he's benefited by the fact that I'm more assertive about how I think women ought to be treated and where men can make changes." Jacqui, whose children were much younger, similarly felt that her feminist views influenced her children:

> I think greatly, I mean all the children, even Anthony who's only five, has got some idea of what feminism is. He'll say things like "That's sexist," or something. Without always understanding completely what it's about. So the whole family has a feminist awareness, and that would be pretty true in the extended family as well.

Jacqui also recounted an incident in which she overheard her 10-year-old son arguing with friends over the issue of men not being allowed to join the *Reclaim the Night* march. He explained to the other children that if men were allowed to march, the media would concentrate on them and ignore the women.

Talking specifically about daughters, a number of women mentioned the importance of encouraging assertiveness and self-esteem. In the follow-up interview, Kate talked about a change in the way she related to her daughters since attending the first Winter Institute workshop in 1991. In particular, she has encouraged her teenage daughters to stand up to their father:

> It's influenced me with my daughters, particularly the one at home, because in some instances where I would have just said, "Look, don't argue, it's not worth it," I find no, I'm not going to say that. I want

her to express her ideas, and I'm not going to try to shut her up for peace.

Including daughters in feminist events such as International Women's Day and *Reclaim the Night* marches was another means by which feminist values influenced parenting. As noted in Chapter 4, this was particularly significant for Colleen. At three, Sharon's daughter is too young to comprehend feminist issues, but Sharon also feels that her feminist beliefs have a positive influence:

> For me it's working quite well in the sense that she does seem to have a good strong sense of who she is, and one afternoon she was out on the verandah and she just made up a song—"I'm a big woman," and she was running around singing that over and over to herself. And I just thought, for me that is a really positive, practical expression of feminist thought in her life. I don't think, before I was three, anyone had ever given me the sense that "I'm a big strong woman" who's got power and the right to do what I want.

Relationships with members of the extended family were also often subject to a feminist analysis and action. When Julie's sister, who had three sons, gave birth to a baby daughter, Julie sent her flowers and a card that said, "A feminist at last." Vicki described not allowing her siblings or their spouses to hit their children in her presence. She also refused to talk to one brother-in-law because of the way he behaves towards his wife. Christmas present shopping was another avenue to bring feminist principles to bear on family relationships:

> I was just even thinking at this time of year about Christmas present shopping. My Christmas present shopping is based on feminist principles, just in terms of nonviolent toys, nonsexist toys, or presents for girls and boys, preferably things that are going to have a double effect, like buying things from World Vision and Community Aid Abroad.

This example demonstrates the enormous expansion of opportunities for activism when informal action is acknowledged as collective action. Describing the opening up of possibilities for resistance that accompanies a growing feminist consciousness, feminist philosopher Sandra Bartky reflects on Christmas present shopping in a similar manner:

> In a lighthearted mood, I embark upon a Christmas shopping expedition, only to have it turn, as if independent from my will, into

an occasion for striking a blow against sexism. On holiday from political struggle and even from political principle, I have abandoned myself to the richly sensuous albeit repellently bourgeois atmosphere of Marshall Field's. I wander about the toy department, looking at chemistry sets and miniature ironing boards. Then, unbidden, the following thought flashes into my head: What if, just this once, I send a doll to my nephew and an erector set to my niece?[22]

Another arena for feminist action involves interactions and relationships beyond the family/household or the organizational contexts discussed earlier. Relationships and encounters with friends, and even with strangers, were defined within a feminist framework. An orientation toward valuing and supporting women, discussed earlier in the context of workplace relationships and community organizations, was applied to a broad range of relationships by a number of women. This general stance involved explicitly supporting women artists, singers and poets, buying women's books, choosing to deal with a woman real estate agent when buying a house, making an effort to notice and pay attention to women, and generally supporting women friends. Stella recounted an incident, after the 1991 workshop, in which she made a determined effort to direct her attention to a woman:

> I live in a little country beach area, where we've got our local Post Office couple—and I wanted to check something with the Post Office, follow something through. And a husband and wife run it, and I went in and I directed most, I purposely went in and directed my question to her. He was sitting right over the other side of the Post Office at his desk. I hadn't even finished my sentence, he had jumped up out of his chair, and came over, and took over the conversation, and she didn't say a word. And I hadn't even directed anything at him, because, it was her that I was chatting to. And I was surprised, and I kept referring to her in the conversation, but she did not say a word. She physically withdrew from the whole thing—I watched it, yes, he took over like—"She can't answer any of these questions! Here I am!"—and *stunned*! But I'm doing that a lot more. If there's a man and a woman I will focus on the woman rather than the man in the discussion, and generally it's very empowering for me, but I think generally men really don't know what to do with you, because they're used to the interaction. And I must have done it before.

Barbara described how her growing awareness of feminist issues and commitment to supporting women led to the decision to open her home to women in need, thereby providing a "safe space" for women, "I really have made a determined effort to have a safe place for women in my home, and I'm very conscious about that, and there's not very much time when I don't have women staying there." Throughout 1992 she continued to offer this form of support to other women, "Women come and stay and freely be themselves, and be creative in that. I probably encourage and share any women's art that I have, and women's music. I share that with other women."

In some cases supporting women involved specific attempts to empower them through providing information or engaging in a form of informal consciousness-raising. For Liz this meant telling her friends about the ideas that came up on the weekend, in particular ideas about using humor to get a feminist message across, and about paying more attention to women. In a similar manner, following the 1991 weekend, Rhonda encouraged women friends to break out of old patterns of behavior with men:

> I'd explained the colors, and everything I could remember about the weekend. I talked about it, especially to, you know, some of the women that I've been hanging around, that I think are used and abused, and they let men walk all over them and I've sort of been encouraging them to—I don't care—be rude to men, ignore them (laugh), anything. So, it's quite funny I suppose, but it's good, it feels good so I'll keep doing it.

Another aspect of lifestyle that was raised by two interviewees as integral to their feminist politics was the choice of vegetarianism. Both Toni and Monique described coming to the conclusion that the domination of animals and eating of meat were feminist issues. Monique said she had once thought that animal liberation and vegetarianism were separate issues—ones that distracted women from strictly woman-identified issues. Later she came to view vegetarianism as crucial to feminism, believing that feminists should be vegetarians. Toni expressed similar views, "I read a great book on the sexual politics of meat, and I was already a vegetarian when I read this . . . It's given me a conviction I didn't have before . . . It's sharpened my attitudes towards meat eating and dovetailed them to my feminism, so those two aspects of my politics have married."

Finally, many of the women in this study consciously adopted cultural symbols associated with feminism. As Gamson suggests, collective identity "is manifested through the language of symbols by which it is publicly expressed. We know a collective identity through the cultural icons and artifacts displayed by those who embrace it."[23] Women in this study demonstrated their investment in feminism through symbols such as buying purple clothing and t-shirts printed with feminist slogans. In a variety of ways they promoted "feminist" colors of purple, green, and white. Seven women in the initial interviews explicitly mentioned adopting the color purple as a symbolic expression of feminism, and a few made a point of wearing purple to the interview. The significance of feminist colors emerged again in the follow-up interviews, with five women mentioning actions ranging from buying a purple backpack to choosing a purple, green, and white theme for furnishing a new office.

Strategies for Change

As noted in the introduction to this chapter, four distinct strategies for bringing about feminist change emerged from the interview data. The first strategy involves using feminist knowledge for personal empowerment. Closely related to this is a strategy of using feminist knowledge to empower other women. The third strategy involves directly challenging taken-for-granted understandings or actions, while the focus of the fourth strategy is on valuing and providing emotional and social support for other women. These four strategies were evident across settings and, as with other themes and categories developed in this book, they are not mutually exclusive. Many of the actions described above are relevant to more than one strategy.

Using Feminist Knowledge for Personal Empowerment

As discussed in Chapter 6, an important motivation for participation in feminist organizations or events was access to feminist knowledge and information. The accounts in this chapter indicate why this was the case. Many of the examples of action described above involved women utilizing feminist knowledge as a resource for personal empowerment. Feminist ideas were drawn upon by women to empower themselves at work, in personal relationships, and in interactions with organizations and institutions. Nicole drew upon feminist understandings to help her deal with sexual harassment from male patients. For Alex, feminist understandings of the medical profession, and its treatment of women, provided the force behind her choice of a home birth. For a number of women feminist ideas provided support for challenging the ideology of marriage and family life, including assumptions about sexual availability, motherhood, and the division of labor within families.

Using Feminist Knowledge to Empower Other Women

Knowledge was not only central to personal empowerment, but also was the basis of feminist action aimed at empowering other women.

Throughout the study there were many examples of women disseminating knowledge and information as a deliberate strategy for change. Spreading feminist ideas at home, among friends, at work, and in the community was viewed by these women as a form of feminist action. They talked specifically about attending feminist workshops, courses, and seminars with the purpose of gaining information and knowledge that they could pass on to other women, thus creating ripples of change that spread in ever widening circles. Specific actions ranged from informal consciousness-raising among groups of friends and acquaintances, to running a leadership program for high school aged girls. Whether it was in the context of counseling work, family planning sessions, or running marriage education classes, the common thread in this strategy was a focus on providing alternative ways of thinking about and acting in the world. By providing a range of information, these women saw themselves as enhancing options and choices available to women and girls.

Challenging Gendered Assumptions and Ways of Acting

The actions included in this category directly challenge taken-for-granted gendered ideas and/or ways of acting. This involved strategies based on language and symbols—Katzenstein's discursive politics—as well as forms of behavior that directly challenged hegemonic understandings. Barbara referred to God as "She," and incited work colleagues to challenge male privilege in the workplace. Rose printed t-shirts with "women-positive" designs, Emma questioned media images of sports women, and Toni challenged sexism in school books. Others challenged the ideologies of marriage and motherhood through comments and actions. Political lesbianism was a clear example of this strategy but heterosexual women also challenged hegemonic lifestyles. Vicki and Emma chose to conduct long-distance relationships with male partners rather than risk their careers by moving. Women insisted on sharing domestic labor within the household and those who were mothers attempted to raise their children in unconventional and nongendered ways.

Supporting and Valuing Women

Supporting and valuing other women was the fourth theme to emerge from the data as a strategy for establishing feminist presence in daily life. This support was both formal and informal. On a formal level, many women talked about organizing or participating in projects designed to provide support and encouragement to other women. Muriel's leadership course for young women in the school where she taught is one example. Sarah's Women's Sports Forum and Anne's Public Sector Women's Network are others. On an informal level, they provided emotional and practical support for women colleagues and friends, for women in their extended families, and women within their general communities. Janet encouraged a colleague to pursue a sexual harassment case. Liz assisted women who needed to access family planning services, and also helped provide housing for young women. Through attending women's cultural productions and buying women's books and artwork, women in this study demonstrated the value they placed on women. They also demonstrated this by directing their attention to women in conversations, by seeking out women's stories when conducting oral history research, and in the way they raised their daughters. This action, of course, is similar to the support many women provide to sisters, mothers, daughters, friends, and colleagues. What distinguishes this as feminist collective action, however, is that it is consciously labeled as such by participants. The support and valuing of other women is specifically linked to feminist ways of knowing and feminist identification.

The actions and strategies described in this chapter underscore the necessity to move beyond narrow definitions of movement involvement, mobilization, and recruitment to activism. As noted earlier, Mueller has argued that feminist consciousness is both an outcome of successful feminist mobilization and a resource for further mobilization.[24] The data in this chapter provide support for this proposition and reaffirm the importance of consciousness within feminist discussions of women's movements. Although women often participated in feminist organizations and events prior to developing feminist consciousness, the action described here was based on this. It was also based on feminist emotions and feminist identity, both of which can equally be viewed as both outcomes of and resources for mobilization.

This study also extends Katzenstein's work on unobtrusive mobilization and on feminist discursive politics.[25] Unobtrusive mobilization not only occurs within major institutions such as the church, the military, and education, but also within local community groups and through formal and informal means. The challenge to hegemonic discourses and practices to which Katzenstein's "discursive politics" refers, occurs both through language and through nonlinguistic actions.

Consistent with recent discussions of emotion and collective action, the link between emotion and culture is also highlighted. The strategy of valuing and providing support for other women demonstrates the significance of these issues in the study of collective action. Although participants had different levels of familiarity with the radical feminist literature that introduced concepts such as the woman-identified woman, the influence of this discourse is evident in their actions, and in the way they talked about supporting and encouraging other women. Symbolic expressions of collective identity are also highlighted. As Taylor and Rupp suggest, symbols are central to the politicization of daily life. Through "feminist t-shirts, jewelry (especially labryses), books, music, and bumper stickers . . . women can adorn and surround themselves with their politics."[26] Women in this study connected with feminist women's culture in this way, indicating to themselves and others where their political loyalties lay.

The actions described in this chapter all challenged patriarchal symbols, values, and relations of power in various ways. And although most were undertaken individually, I believe they should be viewed as a form of collective action. This is not "resistance" as conceptualized in poststructuralist theory, but political action based on collective feminist consciousness, emotions, and identity. The actions taken by these women in the workplace, in community organizations, in their families, and with friends all form part of a powerful force for social change that is fundamentally collective and goes beyond individual resistance and organizationally-based activism.

Finally, an important point to make in relation to the strategies described here is the symbiotic relationship that exists between participation in feminist events and organizations, and feminist action taken in daily life. In Chapter 6 the incentives and outcomes associated with participation in events and organizations were addressed. Knowledge and personal empowerment; social and emotional support; and affirmation of identity were found to be significant outcomes and sources of motivation for participation. The material presented here shows how these outcomes can, in turn, generate further action. These women established feminist presence in daily life by drawing upon and deploying the cognitive, emotional, and identity resources they gained from participation in events and organizations. Through formal and informal actions, they spread feminist ideas and practices throughout the social fabric.

CHAPTER **8**

Conclusion:
Stepping Out of Line

I set out in this book to explore the process of becoming and being feminist, of women stepping out of line in relation to patriarchal patterns of social relations and creating new ways of being in the world. In the experiences recounted here, we have seen women stepping out of line in terms of how they view the world and themselves, how they feel, who they identify with, and what they do. Despite the opposition they faced as feminists, instead of repeating the popular phrase "I'm not a feminist, but . . . ," most of the women in this study had arrived at a point in their lives where they could say "I *am* a feminist, *and* . . . " In attempting to reach some understanding of how this process of personal transformation occurred and of the context in which it occurred, I have developed a fractal model of feminist subjectivity based on four intertwined components—knowing (consciousness), feeling (emotions), belonging (identity), and doing (action). In sum, becoming involved in feminist collective action combines oppositional ways of knowing, feeling, belonging, and doing within an environment that is constituted by both opportunities and barriers. This model builds upon, but also extends, existing social movements and feminist approaches, and highlights the complexity of the process of becoming and being feminist.

The nonlinear nature of the fractal model distinguishes it from other prominent models of movement involvement and recruitment within the social movements field. Such models tend to view social movements as relatively static and homogeneous, and to define involvement in terms of membership of movement organizations. They view recruitment as a linear process, usually positing attitude alignment as the starting point and organizational membership or participation in organizationally based activities as the end point of the process. Contrary to this, the findings of this study indicate that there is no necessity for change in consciousness or beliefs to occur prior to participation in movement events. The personal transformation involved in becoming and being feminist can be initiated through change in any one of the four dimensions of subjectivity in the model. Participation in movement events (doing) preceded, and led to, changes in knowing for some women. The starting point for others was their emotional response to certain life events. Still others reported experiencing a sense of "being feminist" that extended back into childhood, while "doing feminism" came later and was dependent on access to networks and opportunities. In this way, the fractal model is more fluid and dynamic, allowing for the multiple influences, and twists and turns, in the biographical narratives of feminist subjectivity.

As this study has shown, the process of becoming and being feminist does not occur in a vacuum but in an environment that constantly produces and reinforces hegemonic ways of articulating experience, formulating understanding and taking action. By documenting and analyzing this environment of opposition and control, this study makes a further contribution to the field of social movements research. Movements theorists recognize that collective action occurs within environments that are often not receptive to movement action. They conceptualize the field within which movement activity occurs as containing both allies and opponents. However, attention to allies and opponents and to the structured nature of the field has focused primarily on institutional actors such as countermovements and agents of the state (police, government agencies, and so forth). Consequently, the effects of opposition and social control have largely been measured in terms of their impact on movements at a macro level, rather than on individuals. Furthermore, where opposition to involvement at the individual level has been addressed, it has not been theorized in terms of structured social relations.

The concept of biographical constraints alludes to the exercise of social control at the individual level, yet it still fails to help understand the structured nature of opposition at the individual level. Further, it only recognizes constraints in relation to participation in specific events. In Klandermans' model, for example, barriers to participation (in which he includes opposition from significant others) only enter the picture as the last step in the mobilization process.[1] As this book has shown, however, the struggles or conflict that define a movement are as much at work at the individual level as at the organizational or institutional level. Opposition is formal and informal, institutional and noninstitutional, and targets not only movement organizations but also individuals who form the movement. At the individual level, opposition does not only target feminist action, but also targets feminist consciousness, emotions, and identity. Importantly, this opposition draws upon and reinforces existing structures of patriarchal power.

A further major conclusion to be drawn from this study is that women are active agents in the process of becoming feminist and being involved in feminism. The women in this study were not moved as mere pawns by structural forces, nor were they manipulated dupes of a conversion process engineered by clever movement leaders. In contrast to such passive and mindless images, women were active agents who sought out resources through which to construct their lives. For some, becoming feminist was part of an active search for change and alternative ways of being in the world. The possibility of seeing feminist subjectivity as socially constructed and yet not socially determined is most obvious in these examples. These women sought out situations and engaged in actions that would provide the cognitive, emotional, and identity resources necessary for personal and social transformation. Even those women who "fell into feminism" had to actively work to turn happenstance into a choice they felt they could and wanted to live with.

Agency is evident in the way in which participants negotiated personal and collective identity and the tensions between autonomy and belonging in feminist groups. It was also apparent in the strategies they developed to deal with multiple identities. Even though movement events reinforced feminist identification in a process that resembles what Snow and his colleagues call frame amplification, this way of making sense of experience was something women actively sought, and not simply an orchestrated strategy to which they were subjected.[2] Most importantly, the book shows that when women encountered feminist ideas and collective identity in reified, crystallized forms, they did not simply accept such knowledge passively. When feminist narratives resonated with lived experience they were accepted, but when contradictions and tensions arose, these women questioned the ideas put to them and insisted on being part of the ongoing construction of a fluid and changing collective identity.

The women I interviewed for this study are neither the irrational, psychologically disturbed selves of collective behavior theory, nor the rational, calculating selves of resource mobilization theory. They did not step out of line in relation to patriarchal patterns simply to step into line in relation to feminist collective beliefs and identities. Although they responded emotionally to gender-based grievances, this response led them to a search for knowledge that went beyond blind acceptance of "generalized beliefs." It also went beyond a self-interested calculation of costs and benefits. Seeking knowledge resources, they accessed feminist collective action frames through workshops, seminars, courses, and the written texts of the women's movement. In a bottom-up process, and in interaction with others, they reworked ideas into personal beliefs and identities. Importantly, they also reshaped the movement through this process, challenging static and homogeneous images of "the" feminist women's movement, as represented by institutionalized movement organizations.

What are the broader implications of this study and the fractal model for other social movements? Is the model in some way specific to contemporary feminism or does it have wider applicability to other movements? Although it is not new in any historical sense, feminism is one of the movements that inspired the development of NSMT, and it is to this theory that I return in arguing that feminism as a social movement faces special opportunities but also distinctive challenges in relation to the construction of collective identity and activism.

Alongside the focus on culture and the construction of collective identity, NSMT reintroduced a concern with macro-level analysis of social movements. Scholars associated with NSMT view new movements as having emerged as a result of major structural change. In particular, they argue that material production is less central today than it was in industrial society, while the production of knowledge and the manipulation of symbols have come to the fore. Industrial societies, according to Touraine, "were able to transform 'means of production' to invent mechanical devices and systems of organization, but our society invents technologies to produce symbolic goods, languages, information."[3] This change is reflected in a shift in the economic base of most western democracies from manufacturing industries to service industries. With the growth of service industries and the emphasis on a knowledge-based economy has come pressure for a more educated workforce. As Melucci argues, postindustrial societies cannot survive unless the individuals within them share a capacity for autonomous action. Such systems must produce resources for individualization, for self-realization, and for the building of identities.[4] It could be argued that women have been at the forefront of these changes and feminist subjectivity as it appears in the stories of the women in this book reflects this.

One of the most significant changes for women in Australia and other western democracies over recent decades has been the dramatic movement of women into the paid labor force. This shift has been particularly pronounced for married women. In the mid-1960s approximately one-third of married Australian women were in the paid workforce; by the early 1990s more than half were.[5] Similar changes have occurred in the United States and Europe. Feminism, as a movement, has facilitated women's increased entry into education and the paid workforce. However, feminism can also be seen as, in part, a consequence of postindustrial society and the movement of women into an expanding segment of the labor market. In Australia, the United States, and Europe, women are largely employed within the service sector. Thus, women are the new knowledge workers who, as Melucci puts it, are capable of autonomous action. It is not surprising, then, that the women's movement, should be at the forefront in terms of new movement subjectivities.

Women are increasingly well placed to engage in the reflexive project of socially constructing movements and movement-related subjectivities. With higher levels of education and workforce participation, women have developed capacities for abstract thought, language, and meaning creation. Many of the women in this study exemplify this shift in the position women now occupy in postindustrial society. As a group they are highly educated with just over half holding degrees or equivalent and a further 13 percent having completed certificate or diploma qualifications. As noted in Chapter 3, higher education was the single most common context in which these women first encountered feminist ideas. Their relatively high level of education was also reflected in their employment status, with almost 90 percent in paid employment. Most worked in occupations and industries associated with a knowledge economy. Seventy-two percent were in community services and a further 15 percent in public administration.

The macro-level changes associated with the shift from industrial to postindustrial society also pose special challenges to feminism as a movement. As this book has shown, patriarchal structures of social control are alive and well, and although women bring increased resources to the struggle, they must create new subjectivities within a hostile environment. As I argued earlier, in contemporary society they face opposition that targets beliefs, identities, and motivations in insidious ways that are often difficult to name and are emotionally wearing. Creating a strong collective identity is also made more difficult as women exercise increased autonomy. They not only challenge patriarchal social relations, but also become less pliable in relation to institutionalized manifestations of the movement. Their increased autonomy makes women less willing to accept any ready made belief systems, emotional responses, identities, and modes of activism as defined by mainstream society or by movement leaders or spokespersons.

Macro-level changes associated with the shift from industrial to postindustrial society have implications for all social movements. As NSM theorists have argued, however, these changes are likely to have different implications depending on the distinctive histories and identities various movements offer. Postindustrial society has brought about increased opportunities for the development of new subjectivities for those who have access to education and employment, but for other segments of the population it has led to fragmentation and marginalization. Writing about young people's struggles for subjectivity, for example, McDonald points to "sections of the population who fail to mobilize their subjectivity, who fail to become 'entrepreneurs of the self'."[6] The fractal model may be less relevant to movements based on segments of the population, such as working-class youth, whose experiences of contemporary society provide fewer, or different, resources for constructing subjectivity.

Turning to reflect on the contribution this study makes to feminist theory, it is clear that there can be no return to a simple click model of becoming and being feminist. Any model in which all women are viewed as being similarly oppressed, and in which raised consciousness is the key to automatic identification with a homogeneous group of feminist activists who together represent a singular feminist movement, is far too simplistic. As Iris Marion Young argues, deconstruction of the categories "gender" and "women" has made such a uniform view of what experience is and where it leads impossible.[7] As noted early in this book, fears that the deconstructionist project undermines the possibility of a feminist politics cannot be ignored. Nonetheless, the movements perspective utilized in this study, along with the empirical findings, I believe, offer a way forward in this debate.

Where feminist theorists have often agonized over the consequences for feminist politics of the recognition of the constructed rather than the essentialist nature of the feminist "we," movement scholars have made the construction of collective identity the subject of investigation. As Melucci argues, collective action "is not a unitary empirical phenomenon, and the unity, if it exists, should be considered as a result rather than a starting point, a fact to be explained."[8] When researchers examine movements such as environmentalism or the peace movement, the lack of an essential category as the basis of collective identity is not viewed as problematic. It is taken for granted that solidarity and the "we" of the environmental movement are socially constructed. From a social movement perspective, it should not be viewed as any more of a problem that feminist collective identity is also socially constructed and not based on an essentialist understanding of the category "women." Nonetheless, this formulation runs the risk of creating a feminism that is arbitrary. As Young asks, "On what basis do those who come together to create such a politics, do so?" She asserts that we need "some conception of women as a group prior to the formation of self-conscious feminist politics, as designating a certain set of relations or positions that motivate the particular politics of feminism."[9]

Young's response to this dilemma builds on Sartre's concept of seriality. Sartre makes a distinction between groups and series as different levels of social collectivity. Members of a series are "unified passively by the objects around which their actions are oriented or by the objectified results of the material effects of the actions of others."[10] While members of a series might be aware that others are similarly positioned and constrained by the material milieu, identity is not defined by membership in the series. There is no mutual recognition and members are isolated from each other.[11] In contrast, members of a group recognize each other and themselves as being part of a group that is unified and that undertakes common projects. The relationship between series and groups is of central importance. "Self-conscious groups arise from and on the basis of serialized existence, as a reaction to it and an active reversal of its anonymous and isolating conditions."[12] For Young, gender can be conceptualized in this way as a series. Feminist politics depends not on the assumption of an automatic identification between women on this basis, but at least on the possibility that in some contexts and at some times, women will and do form self-conscious collectives or groups. The contribution this book makes is to develop a model of how this occurs, of how women move from being members of a series based on gender to being members of a collectivity as feminists.

The stories presented throughout this book illustrate the process of becoming and being feminist in terms of the four intertwined components—knowing, feeling, belonging, and doing—identified in the fractal model. The central role of consciousness, that is, of knowing the world and knowing the self in specifically feminist ways, emerges from these stories. Although feminist ideas were encountered in different settings and at different life stages, most of the women interviewed for this study came to accept a set of beliefs that define women's problems in structural terms as a gendered form of social injustice. However, as we have seen, specific feminist ideas were interrogated, measured against lived experience, and accepted provisionally in an ongoing process of meaning construction.

Feelings or emotions were also significant to the development of feminist subjectivity. For many, feelings of dissatisfaction, shame, and depression, associated with being women in a patriarchal world, prompted a search for alternative ways of knowing and being. These feelings provided the impetus for a shift from serialized existence in relation to gender, to a more self-conscious sense of group belonging based on gender consciousness. This sense of group belonging, or feminist identification did not, however, flow automatically either from these feelings or from a shift in gender consciousness. Women may constitute a series based on gender, but individual women also experience serialized existence in relation to a range of other positions such as age, sexuality, ethnicity, or motherhood. Each of these can similarly form the basis of self-conscious group identification. This was reflected in the tensions, contradictions, and negotiations surrounding multiple identities as these women struggled to find a place where they could be all the different things that they were. The two-sided nature of identification—that to belong one must identify with, as well as be accepted by others as belonging to, the collectivity—was also evident. Finally, becoming and being feminist involves doing feminist type things. Again, through the experiences of the women in this study, we see that this feminist action is intertwined with knowing, feeling, and belonging. Informal feminist activism was based on feminist knowledge and emotions and in turn aimed to spread feminist consciousness to a wider audience. Participation in organizationally based feminist events was often associated with a quest for feminist knowledge, but also provided solidarity, emotional support, and affirmation of feminist identification.

The opposition and social control the women in this study faced in relation to feminist involvement also has implications for the process of transformation from serialized existence to the "we" of feminist subjectivity. Much of the opposition they encountered targeted feminist identification rather than feminist action, highlighting the political significance of women self-consciously identifying as a collective. However, although this "soft repression" led to a certain amount of self-restraint and distancing from other feminists, overall, it reinforced feminist understandings of gender injustice and group identification.[13]

Consistent with Melucci's analysis of collective identity, the experiences narrated in this book demonstrate that feminist collective consciousness, identity, solidarity, and unity are painstakingly negotiated and constructed as women come to see themselves as part of a feminist "we." Feminist subjectivity is not presumed, but neither is it entirely arbitrary. As Young argues, the feminist "we" relates to the serialized experience of gender, but is not an automatic consequence of it. Returning to the dilemma posed by postmodern feminism, Young summarizes the position taken by Judith Butler, that "[f]eminist discourse and practice should become and remain open, its totality permanently deferred."[14] It is my contention that despite attempts by some feminists to define, fix, and reify feminist collective consciousness and collective identity, the totality of feminism *is* permanently deferred as negotiation and construction of feminist subjectivity and feminist movement continues to occur. This is the case not only for feminist theorists, but also for the many women within grassroots feminist groups who are not trained in theory and who do not generally write about feminism. This should not be viewed as a problem. The human participants who create movements require them to be this way.

In summary, becoming and being feminist is a process of construction in which women create themselves as feminist subjects while simultaneously creating the movement along the four dimensions of knowing, feeling, belonging, and doing. This constructive process occurs within an environment that is structured along gender lines and is often hostile. As with the beautiful and intricate fractal images created by computers, there is no one starting point to this process and there is no single end point to the story of becoming feminist. Attempts to freeze the process of construction and to solidify collective identity are ultimately futile. When collective identity solidifies, movement is no longer an appropriate term. We need to envision feminism as the *movement* of women (in all their diversity), rather than as the *women's movement*. Pictured in this way, change, development, growth, and fluidity are fundamental to feminist politics. When consciousness, emotions, identity, and strategies become fixed and static we can no longer talk of *movement* at either the collective or individual level.

Endnotes

Introduction

1. This anecdote was told to me by my daughter, a Bachelor of Arts student at the University of Queensland. The episode took place in a tutorial early in 2002.
2. Judy Horacek, *Unrequited Love.*
3. For a discussion of the "I'm not a feminist, but . . ." phenomenon, see Rosemary Pringle, *Secretaries Talk: Sexuality, Power and Work*; Christine Griffin, "'I'm Not a Women's Libber, but . . .': Feminism, Consciousness and Identity;" Anne Summers, *Damned Whores and God's Police*, Updated ed.; Amrita Basu, ed., with assistance from C. Elizabeth McGrory, *The Challenge of Local Feminisms: Women's Movements in Global Perspective*; Kathy Bail, ed., *D.I.Y. Feminism.*
4. This article was reproduced in the special collectors issue of *Ms. Magazine* in Spring 2002 to celebrate the magazine's thirtieth anniversary.
5. Jane O'Reilly, "Click! The Housewife's Moment of Truth (1972)," 5.
6. Sonia Johnson, *From Housewife to Heretic*, 106–107, 111.
7. Dale Spender, "What Is Feminism? A Personal Answer."
8. The book I found on the prawn trawler was *Masculine/Feminine: Readings in Sexual Mythology and the Liberation of Women*, edited by Betty and Theodore Roszak. Some years later I loaned the book to another woman who accidentally left it on a train. Although the content would now be dated, I like to think that it is still circulating around, being left behind and picked up by women on trains, buses, and in waiting rooms.
9. Townsville is a tropical city situated in the northern region of the state of Queensland, Australia. With a population of 130,000, it is the largest Queensland city after the capital, Brisbane, which is located 1,500 kilometers to the south.
10. The workshop continued a tradition initiated by a small group of Townsville women in the mid-1980s. This group of feminist friends began holding an annual weekend retreat where they discussed feminist issues and concerns in an environment of mutual support. In 1989, the weekend retreat was incorporated into the Winter Institute for Women, an annual program of feminist seminars, workshops, and cultural events. Prominent feminists were invited to facilitate the weekend workshops and participation was extended to a broad range of women outside the original group.

11. The interview schedule contained no specific questions about sexuality; therefore, it cannot be assumed that the remaining women were all exclusively heterosexual. My belief at the time of the study was that the open nature of the interview questions would allow women to raise sexuality as an issue if they chose to do so, and that it was more in keeping with feminist principles to allow them to make that decision. In a number of interviews, this did occur, leading to interesting and useful discussions of how respondents viewed the relationship between sexuality and feminism. However, in at least one case, discussion following the interview indicated that the lack of explicit questions about sexuality was viewed as a silence, indicative of the marginalization of lesbians.

12. Feminist researchers have utilized the full gamut of research methods, but a preference for qualitative methods is widespread because such methods give voice to women's concerns, maintain the complexity of real social relations, and provide the opportunity for unanticipated issues to be discussed. For discussion of these issues, see Sandra Harding, ed., *Feminism and Methodology*; Maria Mies, "Women's Research or Feminist Research? The Debate Surrounding Feminist Science and Methodology." Qualitative methods are also common in social movements research, where researchers have been interested in questions of meaning, identity, and process, rather than the "factual" outcomes of collective action. See David A. Snow, E. Burke Rochford Jr., Steven K. Worden, and Robert D. Benford, "Frame Alignment Processes, Micromobilization, and Movement Participation," 464–81; Alberto Melucci, *Nomads of the Present: Social Movements and Individual Needs in Contemporary Society*; Paolo R. Donati, "Political Discourse Analysis;" Hank Johnston, Enrique Laraña, and Joseph R. Gusfield, "Identities, Grievances, and New Social Movements."

13. By the time of the follow-up interviews, a number of women had moved, some interstate and one overseas. I was able to contact and interview all but one of these women, resulting in a total of 44 follow-up interviews.

14. Before being appointed to the Australian Senate in 1983, Margaret Reynolds was a local councilor and was active in the feminist, peace, and Aboriginal rights movements. She founded the Townsville branch of *Save Our Sons* during the Vietnam War era and was a member of the *Women's Electoral Lobby*. In her 16 years as a senator, she maintained a close relationship with women's groups in north Queensland and provided a feminist voice in the Australian Parliament. Margaret Reynolds retired from the parliament in 1999.

Chapter 1

1. Anthony Giddens, *New Rules of Sociological Method: A Positive Critique of Interpretive Sociologies*.

2. Alberto Melucci, in a discussion of research methodology in relation to social movements, labels these two positions identification and distance. Distance equates with a positivist stance and the notion of objectivity and is limited. But identification is also limited, since it is based on "the illusion of the power to destroy the gap between reflection and action." Alberto Melucci, "Liberation or Meaning? Social Movements, Culture and Democracy," 54. Neither in his view allow us to come to terms with the ongoing constructiveness of social action. One stands unreflexively outside the process, claiming to provide an objective account of "truth" and "reality;" the other stands unreflexively inside it, risking a confusion of research with political activism. Melucci, *Nomads of the Present*, 239. Verta Taylor, *Rock-a-by Baby: Feminism, Self-Help, and Postpartum Depression*, 16, 166, puts forward a similar argument about the way in which social movements theory can usefully shed light on the women's movement from a perspective outside the movement and thereby enhance existing approaches to gender change.

3. Sandra Bartky, *Femininity and Domination*.

4. Hester Eisenstein, *Contemporary Feminist Thought*, 35.

5. For example, Barbara Susan, a participant in the New York-based Redstockings group, described the process of consciousness-raising as "a way of analyzing political problems that is relevant to us as women. Our method is not abstract. Each woman talks about herself and her own feelings and experiences . . . We direct our talk to one particular question at a time in order to formulate an analysis based on our real experiences and so that any generalizations we might come to will be based on fact." Barbara Susan, "About My Consciousness Raising," 238–39.

6. Two among a number of books from the 1980s that addressed these issues were Juliet Mitchell and Ann Oakley, eds. *What is Feminism?* and Denise Riley, *Am I That Name? Feminism and the Category "Women" in History*.

7. Nickie Charles, "Feminist Practices: Identity, Difference, Power," 4–5.

8. See Chris Weedon, *Feminist Practice and Poststructuralist Theory*; Bronwyn Davies and Rom Harré, "Positioning: The Discursive Production of Selves;" Patricia T. Clough, "On the Brink of Deconstructing Sociology: Critical Reading of Dorothy Smith's Standpoint Epistemology."

9. See Tania Modleski, *Feminism Without Women: Culture and Criticism in a "Postfeminist" Age*; Sylvia Walby, "Post-Post-Modernism? Theorizing Social Complexity;" Ailbhe Smyth, "A (Political) Postcard from a Peripheral Pre-Postmodern State (of Mind) or How Alliteration and Parentheses Can Knock You Down Dead in Women's Studies;" Susan Bordo, "Postmodern Subjects, Postmodern Bodies;" Kalpana Ram, "Too 'Traditional' Once Again: Some Poststructuralists on the Aspirations of the Immigrant/Third World Female Subject;" Somer Brodribb, *Nothing Mat(t)ers: A Feminist Critique of Postmodernism*; Dorothy Smith, "High Noon in Textland: A Critique of Clough;" Pauline Johnson, *Feminism as Radical Humanism*.

10. Brodribb, *Nothing Mat(t)ers*, 144.

11. Iris Marion Young, "Gender as Seriality: Thinking About Women as a Social Collective".

12. See Dorothy Smith, "High Noon in Textland;" Pauline Johnson, "Does Postmodern Feminism Have a Future?"

13. See, for example, Beverly Thiele, "Vanishing Acts in Social and Political Thought: Tricks of the Trade;" Elizabeth A. Grosz, "The In(ter)vention of Feminist Knowledges," 96; Valerie Walkerdine and Helen Lucey, *Democracy in the Kitchen: Regulating Mothers and Socialising Daughters*, 200; Nancy Jay, "Gender and Dichotomy;" Bronwyn Davies, *Shards of Glass: Children Reading and Writing Beyond Gendered Identities*, 95–96; and, specifically in relation to social movements theory, Myra Marx Ferree, "The Political Context of Rationality: Rational Choice Theory and Resource Mobilization;" Verta Taylor, "Watching for Vibes: Bringing Emotions into the Study of Feminist Organizations."

14. Neil J. Smelser, *Theory of Collective Behavior*.

15. Verta Taylor and Leila J. Rupp, "Researching the Women's Movement: We Make Our Own History, but Not Just as We Please;" Alan Scott, *Ideology and the New Social Movements*.

16. Leila J. Rupp and Verta Taylor, *Survival in the Doldrums: The American Women's Rights Movement, 1945–1960*.

17. John D. McCarthy and Mayer N. Zald, "Resource Mobilization and Social Movements: A Partial Theory."

18. Doug McAdam, "Micromobilization Contexts and Recruitment to Activism."

19. J. Craig Jenkins, "Resource Mobilization Theory and the Study of Social Movements;" McCarthy and Zald, "Resource Mobilization."

20. Ferree, "Political Context;" Steven M. Buechler, "Beyond Resource Mobilization? Emerging Trends in Social Movement Theory."

21. Steven M. Buechler, *Social Movements in Advanced Capitalism: The Political Economy and Cultural Construction of Social Activism*.

22. Ibid.

23. David Snow, Louis A. Zurcher Jr., and Sheldon Ekland-Olson, "Social Networks and Social Movements: A Microstructural Approach to Differential Recruitment."

24. Snow et al., "Frame Alignment Processes," 464.

25. David A. Snow and Robert D. Benford, "Ideology, Frame Resonance, and Participant Mobilization;" William A. Gamson, "Constructing Social Protest."

26. See Jean L. Cohen, "Strategy or Identity: New Theoretical Paradigms and Contemporary Social Movements;" John A. Hannigan, "Alain Touraine, Manuel Castells and Social Movement Theory: A Critical Appraisal." Cohen labels the approach I refer to as new social movements theory, the identity-oriented paradigm, and Hannigan talks about the French School of movement theory. I view these as synonymous. Scholars associated with the approach include Habermas, Touraine, Castells, Melucci, and Offe.

27. Alberto Melucci, "The Symbolic Challenge of Contemporary Movements."

28. See Jürgen Habermas, "New Social Movements;" Alain Touraine, *The Voice and the Eye: An Analysis of Social Movements*; Alain Touraine, "An Introduction to the Study of Social Movements;" Melucci, "Symbolic Challenge;" Melucci, *Nomads of the Present*; Alberto Melucci, "The Process of Collective Identity;" Claus Offe, "Challenging the Boundaries of Institutional Politics: Social Movements Since the 1960s." For an overview of new social movements theory, see Steven M. Buechler, "New Social Movement Theories."

29. See, for example, Verta Taylor and Nancy Whittier, "Collective Identity in Social Movement Communities: Lesbian Feminist Mobilization;" Barbara Ryan, *Feminism and the Women's Movement: Dynamics of Change in Social Movement Ideology and Activism*; David S. Meyer and Nancy Whittier, "Social Movement Spillover;" Myra Marx Ferree, "'The Time of Chaos Was the Best:' Feminist Mobilization and Demobilization in East Germany."

30. Melucci, "The Process," 52.

31. For a concise and clear introduction to fractal geometry and the history of fractals in mathematics, see Ron Eglash, *African Fractals: Modern Computing and Indigenous Design*.

32. A third major feature of fractals is that they exhibit fractional dimensions. This is probably the most difficult feature of fractals to grasp. We are used to thinking in terms of one-dimensional lines, two-dimensional planes, and three-dimensional space. Fractals have fractional dimensions such as 1.5 or 3.68. Sierpinski's triangle, a famous fractal shape devised by Polish mathematician Waclaw Sierpinski in 1915, has a dimension somewhere between one and two. In fractal geometry, the fractional dimension is a measure of the texture of a shape or object. To say that human subjectivity has a fractional dimension may be pushing the metaphor too far; however, the complexity of subjectivity certainly makes it difficult to imagine it within the confines of three-dimensional space.

33. Jane Flax, *Disputed Subjects: Essays on Psychoanalysis, Politics and Philosophy*, 93.

34. Taylor, *Rock-a-by Baby*. See also Bartky, *Femininity and Domination*; and Skye Fraser, "Reclaiming Our Power, Using Our Anger: Working in the Field of Sexual Violence."

35. Wendy Simonds, "Feminism on the Job: Confronting Opposition in Abortion Work," found that the anger abortion workers felt towards antiabortion activists was related to their empathy for the women they help. Many feminist groups and organizations also promote female bonding based on empathy between women. This is particularly evident within lesbian feminism and is signified by the use of the term "sisterhood" and the concept of a "lesbian continuum," as coined by Adrienne Rich to describe woman-identified women. See Adrienne Rich, "Compulsory Heterosexuality and Lesbian Existence."

36. For a discussion of the concept of "outlaw emotions," see Alison M. Jaggar, "Love and Knowledge: Emotion in Feminist Epistemology."

37. Collective identity is not the same as the social-psychological concept of social identity that too often treats identity as static and unitary. See Verta Taylor and Nancy Whittier, "Analytical Approaches to Social Movement Culture: The Culture of the Women's Movement."

38. Linear models of recruitment to social movements usually treat participation as a dependent variable. See, for example, Bert Klandermans and Dirk Oegema, "Potentials, Networks, Motivations, and Barriers: Steps Towards Participation in Social Movements;" Martien Briët, Bert Klandermans, and Frederike Kroon, "How Women Become Involved in the Women's Movement of the Netherlands;" J. Richard Kendrick Jr., "Meaning and Participation: Perspectives of Peace Movement Participants;" and Bert Klandermans, *The Social Psychology of Protest*, for linear models that posit attitude alignment as the first step and participation as the end point in a process of recruitment. Johnston et al., "Identities, Grievances," 17, have argued that, in practice "doing (appropriate movement-related behaviors) and being (identity) are inextricably linked." However, they have not adequately theorized the link, probably because as they see it, it is inextricable. See also Taylor and Whittier, "Collective Identity."

Chapter 2

1. Barbara Caine, "International Links."

2. Caine, "International Links."

3. In Australia, the Commonwealth Franchise Act of 1902 established a uniform federal franchise for adult British subjects but excluded Asians, Africans, and Australian Aborigines. Women in the United States finally gained the right to vote in 1920 and British women in 1928. Lisa Tuttle. *Encylcopedia.*

4. Joy Damousi, "Marching to Different Drums: Women's Mobilisations 1914–1939."

5. Caine, "International Links."

6. Verity Burgmann, *Power and Protest: Movements for Change in Australian Society*, 110.

7. Marian Sawer and Marian Simms, *A Woman's Place: Women and Politics in Australian Society*; Burgmann, *Power and Protest.*

8. Katy Reade, "'Struggling to Be Heard:' Tensions Between Different Voices in the Australian Women's Liberation Movement in the 1970s and 1980s," 202.

9. Ibid, 204.

10. See Ann Curthoys, "Australian Feminism Since 1970;" Sawer and Simms, *A Woman's Place*; Reade, "Struggling to Be Heard."

11. Gisela Kaplan, *The Meagre Harvest: The Australian Women's Movement 1950s–1990s*, 32–33.

12. Jan Mercer, "Part 1 The History of the Women's Electoral Lobby."

13. Belinda Probert, "Women's Working Lives."

14. Ann Curthoys, "Doing It for Themselves: The Women's Movement Since 1970," 429.

15. Kaplan, *Meagre Harvest.*

16. Tuttle, *Encyclopedia.*

17. Wendy Weeks, ed., *Women Working Together: Lessons from Feminist Women's Services.*

18. Ibid.

19. Summers, *Damned Whores.*

20. Dorothy Broom, *Damned If We Do: Contradictions in Women's Health Care.*

21. Burgmann, *Power and Protest*, 115.

22. Curthoys, "Doing It for Themselves;" Kaplan, *Meagre Harvest.*

23. Anne Summers, "Where's the Women's Movement Moving To?"

24. Broom, *Damned If We Do*, 96–97.

25. Anna Yeatman, "Women and the State," 190.

26. Hester Eisenstein, *Gender Shock: Practising Feminism on Two Continents*; Kaplan, *Meagre Harvest*; Yeatman, "Women and the State."

27. Quoted in Marian Sawer and Abigail Groves, *Working from Inside: Twenty Years of the Office of the Status of Women.*

28. Kaplan, *Meagre Harvest.*

29. Leeds Revolutionary Feminist Group, "Political Lesbianism: The Case Against Heterosexuality," 5, 7.

30. Bobbi Sykes, "Black Women in Australia: A History."

31. See, for example, Pat O'Shane, "Is There Any Relevance in the Women's Movement for Aboriginal Women?", 31–34; Eve Fesl, "Eve Fesl;" Jackie Huggins, "A Contemporary View of Aboriginal Women's Relationship to the White Women's Movement."

32. Kaplan, *Meagre Harvest.*

33. Jude Irwin, "The Empty Promise of Multiculturalism for Women," 111.

34. Chilla Bulbeck, *Living Feminism: The Impact of the Women's Movement on Three Generations of Australian Women*, 6.

35. Zelda D'Aprano, *Zelda*, 331–32.

36. Quoted in Sawer and Groves, *Working from Inside.*

37. D'Aprano, *Zelda*, 332.

38. Diane Menghetti, *The Red North: The Popular Front in North Queensland.*

39. Burgmann, *Power and Protest*; Kaplan, *Meagre Harvest.*

40. Margaret Reynolds, interviewed by author, Townsville, Queensland. 21 July 1997.

41. Ibid.

42. Coralie McLean, "Townsville Women's Centre."

43. The Townsville Women's Centre is operated by the North Queensland Combined Women's Services (NQCWS) Incorporated.

44. In a review article on the concept of social movements, Mario Diani argues that agreement on this point is evident across a range of theoretical schools in the field of movement studies. Based on the identification of "elements, that are common to the different 'schools,'" Diani defines "social movements as consisting of networks of informal interaction between

a plurality of individuals, groups and/or organizations, engaged in a political and/or cultural conflict, on the basis of a shared collective identity." Mario Diani, "The concept of social movement," 3.

Chapter 3

1. McAdam, "Micromobilization Contexts," 134–5.
2. See W. Gamson, "Constructing Social Protest;" Ferree "Time of Chaos;" Melucci, "The Process."
3. See Snow, Zurcher, and Ekland-Olson, "Social Networks;" Alberto Melucci, "Getting Involved: Identity and Mobilization in Social Movements," 329–48; Melucci, *Nomads of the Present*.
4. McAdam, "Micromobilization Contexts," 32.
5. Meyer and Whittier, "Social Movement Spillover," 277–98.
6. Mary Fainsod Katzenstein, "Feminism Within American Institutions: Unobtrusive Mobilization in the 1980s;" Mary Fainsod Katzenstein, "Discursive Politics and Feminist Activism in the Catholic Church."
7. For an account of the media-created insult of "bra burner" applied to feminists following the misreporting of a Miss America protest held in 1968, see Tuttle, *Encyclopedia*. See also Susan Faludi, *Backlash: The Undeclared War Against Women* and Bulbeck, *Living Feminism*, 143.
8. It may be that today the Internet is providing this type of link; however, my guess is that it is unlikely to be sufficient on its own without face-to-face interaction with other feminists.
9. For a discussion of feminist critiques of women's self-help, see Taylor, *Rock-a-by Baby*, 7–8.
10. Verta Taylor's research on postpartum depression self-help groups also found that, far from depoliticizing participants, these groups in fact encouraged political action. Taylor, *Rock-a-by Baby*, 146.
11. Snow et al., "Frame Alignment Processes."
12. Sally Kennedy, *Faith and Feminism*, 108.
13. Katzenstein, "Discursive Politics," 41.
14. Of the nine women who were classified as low on identification and commitment to feminism prior to attending the 1991 workshop, eight became more committed or involved throughout 1991. Their accounts of becoming feminist are included here, along with the 36 women who initially identified with feminism to a moderate or high degree.
15. Psychologists have established that individuals often reinterpret past events when recalling them in order to reduce cognitive dissonance or increase social desirability. Clearly, this type of reinterpretation plays a part in the accounts of becoming feminist presented here; however, this does not invalidate the stories. Indeed, the argument I present in this book is precisely that the process of becoming feminist involves interpretation and reinterpretation of experiences and feelings in terms of feminist frames. Nonetheless, I would argue that real biographical differences of significance to the process of becoming feminist are evident in the stories, and that these should not be ignored or discounted on the basis that interview accounts cannot be taken as purely factual reports.
16. For biographical or narrative approaches to movement identities, see Craig Calhoun, "The Problem of Identity in Collective Action;" Scott A. Hunt and Robert D. Benford, "Identity Talk in the Peace and Justice Movement;" Francesca Polletta, "'It Was Like a Fever . . .' Narrative and Identity in Social Protest." The difficulties conventional social psychology has in dealing with the issues raised by a social constructionist approach have been addressed within that discipline by proponents of discursive psychology, rhetorical psychology, and narrative identity. These related approaches underscore the centrality of language in social interaction and conceptualize identity discursively. See Derek Edwards and Jonathan Potter, *Discursive Psychology*; Michael Billig, "Rhetorical Psychology, Ideological Thinking, and Imagining Nationhood;" Morny Joy, "Feminism and the Self."
17. Polletta, "Like a Fever," 141.
18. See Margaret R. Somers and Gloria D. Gibson, "Reclaiming the Epistemological 'Other': Narrative and the Social Constitution of Identity;" Carol A. Heimer, "Cases and Biographies: An Essay on Routinization and the Nature of Comparison."

19. In 1973 the "Aquarius Festival" was held in Nimbin, a small rural town in northeastern New South Wales, Australia. Nimbin became, and remains, a major center for people seeking countercultural and alternative lifestyles. The *Women's Weekly* is a mainstream women's magazine.
20. Interviewees were placed into categories of high, medium, and low identification as feminists largely on the basis of their answers to the question of whether they called themselves a feminist or whether they identified as a feminist. To check the veracity of these classifications, they were qualitatively cross-tabulated with data on participation, using the NUD*IST Matrix function. This showed a high level of consistency between self-identification and reported participation in feminist organizations and events.
21. Johnson, *Feminism as Radical Humanism*, 123.
22. Arlie Russell Hochschild, *The Managed Heart: Commercialization of Human Feeling*, 30–31.
23. Myra Marx Ferree and Frederick D. Miller, "Mobilization and Meaning: Toward an Integration of Social Psychological and Resource Perspectives on Social Movements;" Snow and Benford, "Ideology, Frame Resonance."
24. See Gamson and Klandermans for discussion of collective action frames as injustice frames that imply causality and attribute blame to external forces. William A. Gamson, *Talking Politics*; W. Gamson, "Constructing Social Protest;" Klandermans, *Social Psychology of Protest*, 17.
25. Jane Flax, *Disputed Subjects*, 108.

Chapter 4

1. See Melucci, "Liberation or Meaning?"
2. William A. Gamson, "The Social Psychology of Collective Action," 67.
3. See Snow and Benford, "Ideology, Frame Resonance;" Snow et al., "Frame Alignment Processes."
4. Taylor and Whittier, "Collective Identity in Social Movement Communities," 114.
5. Bronwyn Davies, "Education for Sexism: A Theoretical Analysis of the Sex/Gender Bias in Education," 3.
6. Buechler, "Beyond Resource Mobilization?" 228.
7. Johnston, Laraña and Gusfield, "Identities, Grievances, and New Social Movements."
8. Debra Friedman and Doug McAdam, "Collective Identity and Activism: Networks, Choices and the Life of a Social Movement," 157.
9. Taylor and Whittier, "Collective Identity in Social Movement Communities," 105.
10. Johnston, Laraña and Gusfield, "Identities, Grievances," 16.
11. For discussion of the importance of self-recognition and recognition from others to the construction of personal identity, see Craig Calhoun, *Social Theory and the Politics of Identity*, 20, and Melucci, "The Process of Collective Identity," 47.
12. Dale Spender, *Women of Ideas and What Men Have Done to Them*.
13. The original source of this statement was British Feminist Rebecca West, writing in *The Clarion*, in 1913.
14. Calhoun, *Social Theory*, 24, 27.
15. The way in which lesbian baiting is used to control women and counter the influence of feminist ideas is covered in Chapter 5.
16. *Gertrude's*, named after Gertrude Stein, was a regular social and cultural evening for women held monthly at the Townsville Women's Centre.
17. Chapter 5 explores the opposition and social control women experienced from sources outside the women's movement, including husbands, children, extended family members, and employers.
18. Taylor and Whittier, "Collective Identity in Social Movement Communities;" Nancy Whittier, *Feminist Generations: The Persistence of the Radical Women's Movement*; Joshua Gamson, "Messages of Exclusion: Gender, Movements and Symbolic Boundaries."
19. Nancy Whittier, *Feminist Generations*.
20. Ryan, *Feminism and the Women's Movement*, 61. For another account of boundary maintenance and intra-movement disputes see J. Gamson, "Messages of Exclusion," 178–199.

21. Distancing from labels, as a response to the stigmatization of feminist identity is discussed in Chapter 5.
22. Friedman and McAdam, "Collective Identity and Activism," 157.
23. Hunt and Benford, "Identity Talk," 488–517.
24. Jane Flax, *Disputed Subjects*, 106.

Chapter 5

1. Alberto Melucci, *Challenging Codes: Collective Action in the Information Age*, 4. Donatella della Porta and Mario Diani, *Social Movements: An Introduction*, 207–213, present a similar view of social movements existing within a field constituted by alliance structures and opposition structures. Alliance structures consist of supportive political actors who provide movements with resources and opportunities, while opposition structures are defined as political actors who are against the movement. These work to erode resources and political opportunities available to movements.
2. Kay Saunders and Raymond Evans, eds. *Gender Relations in Australia: Domination and Negotiation*, 319.
3. See, for example, Gary T. Marx, "External Efforts to Damage or Facilitate Social Movements: Some Patterns, Explanations, Outcomes and Complications;" Sidney Tarrow, *Power in Movement: Social Movements, Collective Action and Politics*, 92–95; Melucci, *Challenging Codes*, 302–303; Donatella della Porta, "Social Movements and the State: Thoughts On the Policing of Protest;" della Porta and Diani, *Social Movements: An Introduction*.
4. della Porta and Diani, *Social Movements: An Introduction*, 211.
5. See for example, Tahi L. Mottl, "The Analysis of Countermovements;" Erin Steuter, "Women Against Feminism: An Examination of Feminist Social Movements and Anti-Feminist Countermovements;" David S. Meyer, and Suzanne Staggenborg "Movements, Countermovements, and the Structure of Political Opportunity."
6. Julian McAllister Groves, "Learning to Feel: The Neglected Sociology of Social Movements" shows how opponents of animal rights attempt to frame the issue of scientific experimentation on animals in terms of the tragedy of human suffering, portraying animal rights activists as uncaring in their opposition to experimentation that might lead to cures for debilitating diseases. Similarly, pro-choice and antiabortion activists compete on a symbolic level to frame issues surrounding abortion.
7. Mayer N. Zald, and John D. McCarthy, ed. *The Dynamics of Social Movements: Resource Mobilization, Social Control, and Tactics*, 240.
8. Doug McAdam, "Recruitment to High-Risk Activism: The Case of Freedom Summer;" Dirk Oegema and Bert Klandermans, "Why Social Movement Sympathizers Don't Participate: Erosion and Nonconversion of Support;" Doug McAdam, "Gender As a Mediator of Activist Experience: The Case of Freedom Summer."
9. Klandermans, *Social Psychology of Protest*, 86.
10. McAdam, "Recruitment to High-Risk Activism," 84.
11. McAdam, "Gender As a Mediator," addressed the mediating effect of gender on participation in the Freedom Summer project and found that female applicants faced greater barriers to their involvement than male applicants.
12. See, for example, Judith Stacey, "Are Feminists Afraid to Leave Home? The Challenge of Conservative Pro-Family Feminism;" Faludi, *Backlash*; Manuel Castells, *The Power of Identity*, 179.
13. See, for example, Carol Smart and Barry Smart, eds., *Women, Sexuality and Social Control*; Jalna Hanmer and Mary Maynard, eds., *Women, Violence and Social Control*; Marianne Hester, *Lewd Women & Wicked Witches: A Study of the Dynamics of Male Domination*.
14. Anne R. Edwards, *Regulation and Repression: The Study of Social Control*, 59.
15. See, for example, Judith Butler, *Gender Trouble: Feminism and the Subversion of Identity*; Davies, *Shards of Glass*; Sandra Bartky, "Foucault, Femininity, and the Modernization of Patriarchal Power."
16. Melucci, "Liberation or Meaning?" 64, 74.
17. Hochschild, *The Managed Heart*, 30–31.
18. Edwards, *Regulation and Repression*, 1.

19. Bartky, "Foucault," 3.
20. Janice Raymond, *A Passion for Friends: Toward a Philosophy of Female Affection*, 3.
21. Zald, and McCarthy, *The Dynamics of Social Movements*, 240.
22. Meridith Edwards, "The Distribution of Income in Households," 131.
23. Guida West and Rhoda Lois Blumberg, eds. *Women and Social Protest*.
24. Joni Seager, *Earth Follies: Feminism, Politics and the Environment*, 271; see also Robyn Lynn, *'Living with Yourself:' Portraits of Female Activism in North Queensland*, 38–39.
25. Tuttle, *Encyclopedia of Feminism*, 178.
26. Eisenstein, *Contemporary Feminist Thought*, 48–51.
27. Kaplan, *Meagre Harvest*, 114–115.
28. See Susan Bordo, *Unbearable Weight: Feminism, Western Culture, and the Body*; Kirsten Dellinger and Christine L. Williams, "Makeup At Work: Negotiating Appearance Rules in the Workplace;" Bartky, "Foucault, Femininity."
29. Dellinger and Williams, "Makeup At Work," 159.
30. The ridicule faced by feminists who reject feminine appearance norms today is reminiscent of that heaped upon first-wave feminists who embraced the notion of dress reform last century. When Elizabeth Cady Stanton and a number of other feminists adopted the bloomer costume in the 1850s, they faced such constant ridicule that after two years it was reluctantly abandoned. Spender, *Women of Ideas*, 248–249.
31. Whittier, *Feminist Generations*.
32. Ibid, 143.
33. Ann Swidler, "Cultural Power and Social Movements."
34. Bulbeck, *Living Feminism*, 147.
35. Candace Clark, "Emotions and Micropolitics in Everyday Life: Some Patterns and Paradoxes of 'Place,'" 316.
36. Ibid, 322.
37. These two aspects of feminist involvement are discussed in Chapter 6 and Chapter 7, respectively.
38. della Porta and Diani, *Social Movements: An Introduction*, 211.
39. Johnston, Laraña and Gusfield, "Identities, Grievances and New Social Movements."
40. Melucci, "Liberation or Meaning? Social Movements, Culture and Democracy," 64, 69.
41. Tarrow, *Power in Movement*, 95.
42. della Porta and Diani, *Social Movements: An Introduction*.
43. Melucci, "Liberation or Meaning? Social Movements, Culture and Democracy," 63.
44. Dana Crowley Jack, *Silencing the Self: Women and Depression*.
45. Ralph Turner and Lewis Killian, *Collective Behavior*, 3rd ed., 363.
46. Kendrick, "Meaning and Participation," 106.

Chapter 6

1. Klandermans, *The Social Psychology of Protest*, 89.
2. The instrumental rationality of movement actors was emphasized by McCarthy and Zald in their seminal paper on resource mobilization theory. For discussion of the "free-rider" problem and Olson's contribution to the issues, see Jenkins, "Resource Mobilization Theory," 536.
3. McCarthy and Zald, "Resource Mobilization and Social Movements," 1216.
4. Bruce Fireman and William A. Gamson, "Utilitarian Logic in the Resource Mobilization Perspective." For further discussion and critique of rational choice theory within RMT see Jenkins, "Resource Mobilization Theory;" Cohen, "Strategy or Identity;" Ferree and Miller, "Mobilization and Meaning;" Touraine, "An Introduction to the Study of Social Movements;" Eric L Hirsch, "Sacrifice for the Cause: Group Processes, Recruitment, and Commitment in a Student Social Movement;" Scott, *Ideology New Social Movements*, 118; Craig Calhoun, "The Problem of Identity in Collective Action;" Herbert Kitschelt, "Resource Mobilization Theory: A Critique"; Buechler, "Beyond Resource Mobilization?" Mark Drakeford, *Social Movements and their Supporters: The Green Shirts in England*.
5. Ferree, "The Political Context of Rationality."
6. Personal Growth Centre, Bulletin No.18.

7. Hanspeter Kriesi, "Support and Mobilization Potential for New Social Movements: Concepts, Operationalizations and Illustrations from the Netherlands," 23.
8. Katzenstein, "Feminism Within American Institutions," 27–54.
9. See Tuttle, *Encyclopedia of Feminism*, 356; Gisela Kaplan, *Contemporary Western European Feminism*; Burgmann, *Power and Protest*, 95–97.
10. Briët et al., "How Women Become Involved," 51.
11. Weeks, *Women Working Together*, 3.
12. The Cockburn Sound Peace Camp was part of a campaign against United States military bases in Australia. It was modeled on Greenham Common and followed a similar camp held at Pine Gap in 1983.
13. For an argument critical of cultural feminism see Alice Echols, "The New Feminism of Yin and Yang." For an alternative view, see Verta Taylor and Leila J. Rupp, "Women's Culture and Lesbian Feminist Activism: A Reconsideration of Cultural Feminism;" Myra Marx Ferree and Beth B. Hess, *Controversy and Coalition: The New Feminist Movement across Three Decades of Change*, 212–216; and Kaplan, Meagre *Harvest*, 59–60.
14. McLean, "Townsville Women's Centre," 236.
15. See Fireman and Gamson, "Utilitarian Logic in the Resource Mobilization Perspective;" Friedman and McAdam "Collective Identity and Activism."
16. Melucci, "Liberation or Meaning?" 52.
17. Randall Collins, "Stratification, Emotional Energy, and the Transient Emotions," 32.
18. Kaplan, *Contemporary Western European Feminism*, 252, refers to the "tremble, tremble, the witches are back" slogan originating in Italy.
19. Taylor and Whittier, "Analytical Approaches to Social Movement Culture."
20. Taylor, "Watching for Vibes," 229.
21. In an analysis of class passivity in the United States, Lee Harrington and William Flint argue that emotional processes are of central importance to the apprehension of efficacy. Drawing on the sociology of emotions they suggest that efficacy, defined as "an individual's belief that he or she has the capacity to effect change," is based on both cognition and emotion: "One must 'know,' one must 'feel,' and one must be aware of the relationship between the two, prior to acting on material resources." C. Lee Harrington and William C. Flint, "Anger, Resentment and Class (In)Action: Explaining Class Passivity Through Micro-Emotional Processes," 19–22.
22. Gamson, "The Social Psychology of Collective Action," 64–65.
23. Jack, *Silencing the Self*.
24. Calhoun, "The Problem of Identity in Collective Action," 61.

Chapter 7

1. Guida West and Rhoda Lois Blumberg eds. *Women and Social Protest*, 5. See also Yvonne Corcoran-Nantes, "Female Consciousness or Feminist Consciousness? Women's Consciousness Raising in Community-Based Struggles in Brazil."
2. See Carol McClurg Mueller, "Collective Consciousness, Identity Transformation, and the Rise of Women in Public Office in the United States;" Buechler, "Beyond Resource Mobilization?" and Joseph R. Gusfield, "The Reflexivity of Social Movements."
3. See Katzenstein, "Feminism Within American Institutions," 33, 34; and Katzenstein, "Discursive Politics and Feminist Activism," 35.
4. Mueller, "Collective Consciousness, Identity Transformation," 98, 99.
5. Ibid, 92.
6. Jocalyn Lawler, *Behind the Screens: Nursing, Somology, and the Problem of the Body*, 202–212.
7. Ibid, 208.
8. Valerie Walkerdine, "Sex, Power and Pedagogy."
9. Carmel Shute, "Unequal Partners: Women, Power and the Trade Union Movement," 166.
10. Evan Willis, *Illness and Social Relations*, 44–53.
11. Broom, *Damned If We Do: Contradictions in Women's Health Care*, 33.
12. Jo VanEvery, *Heterosexual Women Changing the Family: Refusing to be a 'Wife'!*
13. Ibid, 19.
14. These figures do not include one woman who was not available for the follow-up interviews.

15. This does include some households with male children but no adult males.
16. The changes reported here add to more than 18 because some women fit into more than one category.
17. VanEvery, *Heterosexual Women Changing the Family*, 18–27.
18. Ibid, 65.
19. Pat Mainardi, "The Politics of Housework," 341.
20. Michael Bittman, *Juggling Time: How Australian Families Use Time.*
21. VanEvery, *Heterosexual Women Changing the Family*, 54.
22. Bartky, *Femininity and Domination*, 19.
23. Gamson, "The Social Psychology of Collective Action," 60.
24. Carol McClurg Mueller, "Collective Consciousness, Identity Transformation."
25. Katzenstein, "Feminism Within American Institutions," 27–54; Katzenstein, "Discursive Politics and Feminist Activism."
26. Taylor and Rupp, "Women's Culture and Lesbian Feminist Activism," 49.

Chapter 8

1. Klandermans, *The Social Psychology of Protest.*
2. Snow et al., "Frame Alignment Processes."
3. Touraine, "An Introduction to the Study of Social Movements," 778.
4. Melucci, "The Symbolic Challenge of Contemporary Movements."
5. Janeen Baxter, "Gender Inequality in Australian Society," 105.
6. Kevin McDonald, *Struggles for Subjectivity: Identity, Action and Youth Experience,* 208.
7. Young, "Gender as Seriality."
8. Melucci, *Nomads of the Present*, 332.
9. Young, "Gender as Seriality," 722.
10. Ibid, 723–724.
11. Ibid, 728.
12. Ibid, 728.
13. Myra Marx Ferree has coined the term "soft repression" to refer to the type of social control experienced by the women in this study, "Soft Repression: Ridicule, Stigma, and Silencing in Gender-based Movements."
14. Young, "Gender as Seriality," 713–738.

Bibliography

Bail, Kathy, ed. *D.I.Y. Feminism.* St. Leonards, Australia: Allen and Unwin, 1996.

Bartky, Sandra. *Femininity and Domination.* New York and London: Routledge, 1990.

———. "Foucault, Femininity, and the Modernization of Patriarchal Power." *Feminist Social Thought: A Reader.* Edited by Diana Tietjens Meyers. New York: Routledge, 1997.

Basu, Amrita, ed. with assistance from C. Elizabeth McGrory. *The Challenge of Local Feminisms: Women's Movements in Global Perspective.* Boulder, CO: Westview Press, 1995.

Baxter, Janeen. "Gender Inequality in Australian Society." *A Sociology of Australian Society*, 3rd ed. Edited by Jake M. Najman and John S. Western. South Yarra, Australia: Macmillan, 2000.

Billig, Michael. "Rhetorical Psychology, Ideological Thinking, and Imagining Nationhood." *Social Movements and Culture.* Edited by Hank Johnston and Bert Klandermans. London: University College London Press, 1995.

Bittman, Michael. *Juggling Time: How Australian Families Use Time.* Canberra, Australia: AGPS, 1991.

Bordo, Susan. "Postmodern Subjects, Postmodern Bodies." *Feminist Studies* 18 (1992): 159–175.

———. *Unbearable Weight: Feminism, Western Culture, and the Body.* Berkeley: University of California Press, 1993.

Briët, Martien, Bert Klandermans, and Frederike Kroon. "How Women Become Involved in the Women's Movement of the Netherlands." *The Women's Movements of the United States and Western Europe.* Edited by Mary Fainsod Katzenstein and Carol McClurg Mueller. Philadelphia, PA: Temple University Press, 1987.

Brodribb, Somer. *Nothing Mat(t)ers: A Feminist Critique of Postmodernism.* Melbourne, Australia: Spinifex Press, 1992.

Broom, Dorothy. *Damned If We Do: Contradictions in Women's Health Care.* Sydney, Australia: Allen & Unwin, 1991.

Buechler, Steven M. "Beyond Resource Mobilization? Emerging Trends in Social Movement Theory." *The Sociological Quarterly* 34 (1993): 217–35.

———. "New Social Movement Theories." *The Sociological Quarterly* 36 (1995): 441–64.

———. *Social Movements in Advanced Capitalism: The Political Economy and Cultural Construction of Social Activism.* Oxford and New York: Oxford University Press, 2000.

Bulbeck, Chilla. *Living Feminism: The Impact of the Women's Movement on Three Generations of Australian Women.* Cambridge: Cambridge University Press, 1997.

Burgmann, Verity. *Power and Protest: Movements for Change in Australian Society.* St. Leonards, Australia: Allen & Unwin, 1993.

Butler, Judith. *Gender Trouble: Feminism and the Subversion of Identity.* New York: Routledge, 1990.

Caine, Barbara. "International Links." *Australian Feminism.* Edited by Barbara Caine, Moira Gatens, Emma Grahame, Jan Larbalestier, Sophie Watson, and Elizabeth Webby. Melbourne, Australia: Oxford University Press, 1998.

Calhoun, Craig. "The Problem of Identity in Collective Action." *Macro-Micro Linkages in Sociology*. Edited by Joan Huber. Newbury Park, CA: Sage, 1991.

Calhoun, Craig, ed. *Social Theory and the Politics of Identity*. Oxford: Blackwell, 1994.

Castells, Manuel. *The Power of Identity*. Malden, MA: Blackwell, 1997.

Charles, Nickie. "Feminist Practices: Identity, Difference, Power." *Practising Feminism: Identity, Difference, Power*. Edited by Nickie Charles and Felicia Hughes-Freeland. London and New York: Routledge, 1996.

Clark, Candace. "Emotions and Micropolitics in Everyday Life: Some Patterns and Paradoxes of 'Place.'" *Research Agendas in the Sociology of Emotions*. Edited by Theodore D. Kemper. Albany: State University of New York Press, 1990.

Clough, Patricia T. "On the Brink of Deconstructing Sociology: Critical Reading of Dorothy Smith's Standpoint Epistemology." *The Sociological Quarterly* 34 (1993): 169–182.

Cohen, Jean L. "Strategy or Identity: New Theoretical Paradigms and Contemporary Social Movements." *Social Research* 52 (1985): 663–716.

Collins, Randall. "Stratification, Emotional Energy, and the Transient Emotions." *Research Agendas in the Sociology of Emotions*. Edited by Theodore D. Kemper. Albany: State University of New York Press, 1990.

Corcoran-Nantes, Yvonne. "Female Consciousness or Feminist Consciousness? Women's Consciousness Raising in Community-Based Struggles in Brazil." *'VIVA' Women and Popular Protest in Latin America*. Edited by Sarah A. Radcliffe and Sallie Westwood. London: Routledge, 1993.

Curthoys, Ann. "Doing It for Themselves: The Women's Movement Since 1970." *Gender Relations in Australia: Domination and Negotiation*. Edited by Kay Saunders and Raymond Evans. Sydney: Harcourt Brace Jovanovich, 1992.

———. "Australian Feminism Since 1970." *Australian Women: Contemporary Feminist Thought*. Edited by Norma Grieve and Ailsa Burns. Melbourne, Australia: Oxford University Press 1994.

Damousi, Joy. "Marching to Different Drums: Women's Mobilisations 1914–1939." *Gender Relations in Australia: Domination and Negotiation*. Edited by Kay Saunders and Raymond Evans. Sydney, Australia: Harcourt Brace Jovanovich, 1992.

D'Aprano, Zelda. *Zelda*. North Melbourne, Australia: Spinifex Press, 1995.

Davies, Bronwyn. "Education for Sexism: A Theoretical Analysis of the Sex/Gender Bias in Education." *Educational Philosophy and Theory* 21 (1989): 1–19.

———. *Shards of Glass: Children Reading and Writing Beyond Gendered Identities*. St. Leonards, Australia: Allen & Unwin, 1993.

Davies, Bronwyn, and Rom Harré. "Positioning: The Discursive Production of Selves." *Journal for the Theory of Social Behaviour* 20 (1990): 43–62.

della Porta, Donatella. "Social Movements and the State: Thoughts On the Policing of Protest." *Comparative Perspectives on Social Movements*. Edited by Doug McAdam, John D. McCarthy, and Mayer N. Zald. Cambridge: Cambridge University Press, 1996.

della Porta, Donatella, and Mario Diani. *Social Movements: An Introduction*. Oxford: Blackwell, 1999.

Dellinger, Kirsten, and Christine L. Williams. "Makeup At Work: Negotiating Appearance Rules in the Workplace." *Gender & Society* 11 (1997): 151–177.

Diani, Mario. "The concept of social movement." *The Sociological Review* 40 (1992): 1–25.

Donati, Paolo R. "Political Discourse Analysis." *Studying Collective Action*. Edited by Mario Diani and Ron Eyerman. London: Sage, 1992.

Drakeford, Mark. *Social Movements and Their Supporters: The Green Shirts in England*. Houndmills, England: Macmillan, 1997.

Echols, Alice. "The New Feminism of Yin and Yang." *Desire: The Politics of Sexuality*. Edited by Ann Snitow, Christine Stansell, and Sharon Thompson. London: Virago, 1984.

Edwards, Anne R. *Regulation and Repression: The Study of Social Control*. Sydney: Allen & Unwin, 1988.

Edwards, Derek, and Jonathan Potter. *Discursive Psychology*. London: Sage, 1992.

Edwards, Meridith. "The Distribution of Income in Households." *Unfinished Business: Social Justice for Women in Australia*. Edited by Dorothy H. Broom. Sydney, Australia: Allen & Unwin, 1984

Eglash, Ron. *African Fractals: Modern Computing and Indigenous Design.* New Brunswick, NJ: Rutgers University Press, 1999.

Eisenstein, Hester. *Contemporary Feminist Thought.* Sydney, Australia: Allen & Unwin, 1984.

———. *Gender Shock: Practising Feminism on Two Continents.* Sydney, Australia: Allen & Unwin, 1991.

Faludi, Susan. *Backlash: The Undeclared War Against Women.* London: Chatto & Windus,1992.

Ferree, Myra Marx. "The Political Context of Rationality: Rational Choice Theory and Resource Mobilization." *Frontiers in Social Movement Theory.* Edited by Aldon D. Morris and Carol McClurg Mueller. Newhaven, CT, and London: Yale University Press, 1992.

———. "'The Time of Chaos Was the Best:' Feminist Mobilization and Demobilization in East Germany." *Gender & Society* 8 (1994): 597–623.

———. "Soft Repression: Ridicule, Stigma, and Silencing in Gender-based Movements." *Protest and Repression.* Edited by Christian Davenport, Carol Mueller, and Hank Johnston. Minneapolis: University of Minnesota Press, forthcoming.

Ferree, Myra Marx, and Beth B. Hess. *Controversy and Coalition: The New Feminist Movement Across Three Decades of Change.* Rev. ed. New York: Twayne, 1994.

Ferree, Myra Marx, and Frederick D. Miller. "Mobilization and Meaning: Toward an Integration of Social Psychological and Resource Perspectives On Social Movements." *Sociological Inquiry* 55 (1985): 38–61.

Fesl, Eve. "Eve Fesl." *Women Who Do and Women Who Don't Join the Women's Movement.* Edited by Robyn Rowland. London: Routledge and Kegan Paul, 1984.

Fireman, Bruce, and William A. Gamson. "Utilitarian Logic in the Resource Mobilization Perspective." *The Dynamics of Social Movements: Resource Mobilization, Social Control, and Tactics.* Edited by Mayer N. Zald and John D. McCarthy. Cambridge, MA: Winthrop, 1979.

Flax, Jane. *Disputed Subjects: Essays on Psychoanalysis, Politics and Philosophy.* New York: Routledge, 1993.

Fraser, Skye. "Reclaiming Our Power, Using Our Anger: Working in the Field of Sexual Violence." *Women and Violence: Working for Change.* Edited by Ros Thorpe and Jude Irwin. Sydney, Australia: Hale & Iremonger, 1996.

Friedman, Debra, and Doug McAdam. "Collective Identity and Activism: Networks, Choices and the Life of a Social Movement." *Frontiers in Social Movement Theory.* Edited by Aldon D. Morris and Carol McClurg Mueller. Newhaven, CT, and London: Yale University Press, 1992.

Gamson, Joshua. "Messages of Exclusion: Gender, Movements and Symbolic Boundaries." *Gender & Society* 11 (1997): 178–199.

Gamson, William A. "The Social Psychology of Collective Action." *Frontiers in Social Movement Theory.* Edited by Aldon D. Morris and Carol McClurg Mueller. Newhaven, CT, and London: Yale University Press, 1992.

———. *Talking Politics.* Cambridge: Cambridge University Press,1992.

———. "Constructing Social Protest." *Social Movements and Culture.* Edited by Hank Johnston and Bert Klandermans. London: University College of London Press, 1995.

Giddens, Anthony. *New Rules of Sociological Method: A Positive Critique of Interpretive Sociologies.* London: Hutchinson, 1976.

Griffin, Christine. "'I'm Not a Women's Libber, but . . . :' Feminism, Consciousness and Identity." *The Social Identity of Women.* Edited by Suzanne Skevington and Deborah Baker. London: Sage, 1989.

Grosz, Elizabeth A. "The In(ter)vention of Feminist Knowledges." *Crossing Boundaries: Feminisms and the Critique of Knowledges.* Edited by Elizabeth Grosz, Marie deLepervanche, and Barbara Caine. Sydney, Australia: Allen & Unwin, 1988.

Groves, Julian McAllister. "Learning to Feel: The Neglected Sociology of Social Movements." *The Sociological Review* 43 (1995): 435–461.

Gusfield, Joseph R. "The Reflexivity of Social Movements: Collective Behavior and Mass Society Theory Revisited." *New Social Movements: From Ideology to Identity.* Edited by Hank Johnston, Enrique Laraña, and Joseph R. Gusfield. Philadelphia, PA: Temple University Press, 1994.

Habermas, Jürgen. "New Social Movements." *Telos* 49 (Fall 1981): 33–37.

Hanmer, Jalna, and Mary Maynard, eds. *Women, Violence and Social Control.* Houndmills, England: Macmillan, 1987.

Hannigan, John A. "Alain Touraine, Manuel Castells and Social Movement Theory: A Critical Appraisal." *The Sociological Quarterly* 26 (1985): 435–454.

Harding, Sandra, ed. *Feminism and Methodology*. Bloomington: Indiana University Press, 1987.

Harrington, C. Lee, and William C. Flint. "Anger, Resentment and Class (In)Action: Explaining Class Passivity Through Micro-Emotional Processes." Paper presented at Emotion in Social Life and Social Theory Conference, Canberra, Australia, July 1997.

Heimer, Carol A. "Cases and Biographies: An Essay on Routinization and the Nature of Comparison." *Annual Review of Sociology* 27 (2001): 47–76.

Hester, Marianne. *Lewd Women and Wicked Witches: A Study of the Dynamics of Male Domination*. London and New York: Routledge, 1992.

Hirsch, Eric L. "Sacrifice for the Cause: Group Processes, Recruitment, and Commitment in a Student Social Movement." *American Sociological Review* 55 (1990): 243–254.

Hochschild, Arlie Russell. *The Managed Heart: Commercialization of Human Feeling*. Berkeley: University of California Press, 1983.

Horacek, Judy. *Unrequited Love*. Ringwood, Australia: McPhee Gribble, 1994.

Huggins, Jackie. "A Contemporary View of Aboriginal Women's Relationship to the White Women's Movement." *Australian Women: Contemporary Feminist Thought*. Edited by Norma Grieve and Ailsa Burns. Melbourne, Australia: Oxford University Press, 1994.

Hunt, Scott A., and Robert D. Benford. "Identity Talk in the Peace and Justice Movement." *Journal of Contemporary Ethnography* 22 (1994): 488–517.

Irwin, Jude. "The Empty Promise of Multiculturalism for Women." *Women Working Together: Lessons from Feminist Women's Services*. Edited by Wendy Weeks. Melbourne, Australia: Longman Cheshire, 1994.

Jack, Dana Crowley. *Silencing the Self: Women and Depression*. Cambridge, MA, and London: Harvard University Press, 1991.

Jaggar, Alison M. "Love and Knowledge: Emotion in Feminist Epistemology." *Feminist Social Thought: A Reader*. Edited by Diana Tietjens Meyers. New York: Routledge, 1997.

Jay, Nancy. "Gender and Dichotomy." *A Reader in Feminist Knowledge*. Edited by Sneja Gunew. London and New York: Routledge, 1991.

Jenkins, J. Craig. "Resource Mobilization Theory and the Study of Social Movements." *Annual Review of Sociology* 9 (1983): 527–553.

Johnson, Pauline. *Feminism as Radical Humanism*. St. Leonards, Australia: Allen & Unwin, 1994.

———. "Does Postmodern Feminism Have a Future?" *Australian Feminist Studies* 22 (1995): 121–138.

Johnson, Sonia. *From Housewife to Heretic*. Garden City, NY: Anchor Books, 1983.

Johnston, Hank, Enrique Laraña, and Joseph R. Gusfield. "Identities, Grievances, and New Social Movements." *New Social Movements: From Ideology to Identity*. Edited by Hank Johnston, Enrique Laraña, and Joseph R. Gusfield. Philadelphia, PA: Temple University Press, 1994.

Joy, Morny. "Feminism and the Self." *Theory & Psychology* 3 (1993): 275–302.

Kaplan, Gisela. *Contemporary Western European Feminism*. Sydney: Allen & Unwin, 1992.

———. *The Meagre Harvest: The Australian Women's Movement 1950s–1990s*. St. Leonards, Australia: Allen & Unwin, 1996.

Katzenstein, Mary Fainsod. "Feminism Within American Institutions: Unobtrusive Mobilization in the 1980s." *Signs: Journal of Women in Culture and Society* 16 (1990): 27–54.

———. "Discursive Politics and Feminist Activism in the Catholic Church." *Feminist Organizations: Harvest of the New Women's Movement*. Edited by Myra Marx Ferree and Patricia Yancey Martin. Philadelphia, PA: Temple University Press, 1995.

Kendrick, J. Richard Jr. "Meaning and Participation: Perspectives of Peace Movement Participants." *Research in Social Movements, Conflict and Change* 13 (1991): 91–111.

Kennedy, Sally. *Faith and Feminism*. Manly: Studies in the Christian Movement, 1985.

Kitschelt, Herbert. "Resource Mobilization Theory: A Critique." *Research on Social Movements: The State of the Art in Western Europe and the USA*. Edited by Dieter Rucht. Boulder, CO: Westview Press, 1991.

Klandermans, Bert. *The Social Psychology of Protest*. Oxford: Blackwell, 1997.

Klandermans, Bert, and Dirk Oegema. "Potentials, Networks, Motivations, and Barriers: Steps Towards Participation in Social Movements." *American Sociological Review* 52 (1987): 519–531.

Kriesi, Hanspeter. "Support and Mobilization Potential for New Social Movements: Concepts, Operationalizations and Illustrations from the Netherlands." *Studying Collective Action*. Edited by Mario Diani and Ron Eyerman. London: Sage, 1992.

Lawler, Jocalyn. *Behind the Screens: Nursing, Somology, and the Problem of the Body*. Melbourne, Australia: Churchill Livingstone, 1991.

Leeds Revolutionary Feminist Group. "Political Lesbianism: The Case Against Heterosexuality." *Love Your Enemy? The Debate Between Heterosexual Feminism and Political Lesbianism*. London: Onlywomen Press, 1981.

Lynn, Robyn. *'Living with Yourself': Portraits of Female Activism in North Queensland*. Townsville, Australia: CSAWR, James Cook University of North Queensland, 1996.

Mainardi, Pat. "The Politics of Housework." *Voices from Women's Liberation*. Edited by Leslie B. Tanner. New York: New American Library,1970.

Marx, Gary T. "External Efforts to Damage or Facilitate Social Movements: Some Patterns, Explanations, Outcomes and Complications." *The Dynamics of Social Movements: Resource Mobilization, Social Control, and Tactics*. Edited by Mayer N. Zald and John D. McCarthy. Cambridge, MA: Winthrop, 1979.

McAdam, Doug. "Recruitment to High-Risk Activism: The Case of Freedom Summer." *American Journal of Sociology* 92 (1986): 64–90.

———. "Micromobilization Contexts and Recruitment to Activism." *International Social Movement Research* 1 (1988): 125–154.

———. "Gender as a Mediator of Activist Experience: The Case of Freedom Summer." *American Journal of Sociology* 97 (1992): 1211–1240.

McCarthy, John D., and Mayer N. Zald. "Resource Mobilization and Social Movements: A Partial Theory." *American Journal of Sociology* 82 (1977): 1212–1241.

McDonald, Kevin. *Struggles for Subjectivity: Identity, Action and Youth Experience*. Cambridge: Cambridge University Press, 1999.

McLean, Coralie. "Townsville Women's Centre." *Women Working Together: Lessons from Feminist Women's Services*. Edited by Wendy Weeks. Melbourne, Australia: Longman Cheshire, 1994.

Melucci, Alberto. "The Symbolic Challenge of Contemporary Movements." *Social Research* 52 (1985): 789–816.

———. "Getting Involved: Identity and Mobilization in Social Movements." *International Social Movement Research* 1 (1988): 329–348.

———. *Nomads of the Present: Social Movements and Individual Needs in Contemporary Society*. Philadelphia, PA: Temple University Press, 1989.

———. "Liberation or Meaning? Social Movements, Culture and Democracy." In *Emancipations, Modern and Postmodern*. Edited by Jan Nederveen Pieterse. London: Sage, 1992.

———. "The Process of Collective Identity." *Social Movements and Culture*. Edited by Hank Johnston and Bert Klandermans. London: University College of London Press, 1995.

———. *Challenging Codes: Collective Action in the Information Age*. Cambridge: Cambridge University Press, 1996.

Menghetti, Diane. *The Red North: The Popular Front in North Queensland*. Townsville, Australia: History Department, James Cook University of North Queensland, 1981.

Mercer, Jan. "Part 1 The History of the Women's Electoral Lobby." *The Other Half: Women in Australian History*. Edited by Jan Mercer. Ringwood, Australia: Penguin, 1975.

Meyer, David S., and Suzanne Staggenborg. "Movements, Countermovements, and the Structure of Political Opportunity." *American Journal of Sociology* 101 (1996): 1628–1660.

Meyer, David S., and Nancy Whittier. "Social Movement Spillover." *Social Problems* 41 (1994): 277–298.

Mies, Maria. "Women's Research or Feminist Research? The Debate Surrounding Feminist Science and Methodology." *Beyond Methodology: Feminist Scholarship as Lived Research* Edited by Mary Margaret Fonow and Judith A. Cook. Bloomington: Indiana University Press, 1991.

Mitchell, Juliet, and Ann Oakley, eds. *What Is Feminism?* New York: Pantheon Press, 1986.

Modleski, Tania. *Feminism Without Women: Culture and Criticism in a "Postfeminist" Age*. New York: Routledge, 1991.

Mottl, Tahi L. "The Analysis of Countermovements." *Social Problems* 27 (1980): 620–635.

Mueller, Carol McClurg. "Collective Consciousness, Identity Transformation, and the Rise of Women in Public Office in the United States." *The Women's Movements of the United States and Western Europe.* Edited by Mary Fainsod Katzenstein and Carol McClurg Mueller. Philadelphia, PA: Temple University Press, 1987.

Oegema, Dirk, and Bert Klandermans. "Why Social Movement Sympathizers Don't Participate: Erosion and Nonconversion of Support." *American Sociological Review* 59 (1994): 703–722.

Offe, Claus. "Challenging the Boundaries of Institutional Politics: Social Movements Since the 1960s." *Changing Boundaries of the Political: Essays on the Evolving Balance Between the State and Society, Public and Private in Europe.* Edited by Charles S. Maier. Cambridge: Cambridge University Press, 1987.

O'Reilly, Jane. "Click! The Housewife's Moment of Truth (1972)." *Ms*, 12 (2) (spring 2002): 5–8.

O'Shane, Pat. "Is There Any Relevance in the Women's Movement for Aboriginal Women?" *Refractory Girl* (September 1976): 31–34.

Personal Growth Centre. *Bulletin No.18.* Townsville, Australia: Personal Growth Centre, 1992.

Polletta, Francesca. "'It Was Like a Fever . . . ' Narrative and Identity in Social Protest." *Social Problems* 45 (1998): 137–159.

Pringle, Rosemary. *Secretaries Talk: Sexuality, Power and Work.* Sydney, Australia: Allen and Unwin, 1988.

Probert, Belinda. "Women's Working Lives." *Contemporary Australian Feminism.* Edited by Kate Pritchard Hughes. Melbourne, Australia: Longman Cheshire, 1994.

Ram, Kalpana. "Too 'Traditional' Once Again: Some Poststructuralists on the Aspirations of the Immigrant/Third World Female Subject." *Australian Feminist Studies* 17 (1993): 5–28.

Raymond, Janice. *A Passion for Friends: Toward a Philosophy of Female Affection.* Boston: Beacon Press, 1986.

Reade, Katy. "'Struggling to Be Heard': Tensions Between Different Voices in the Australian Women's Liberation Movement in the 1970s and 1980s." *Contemporary Australian Feminism.* Edited by Kate Pritchard Hughes. Melbourne, Australia: Longman Cheshire, 1994.

Rich, Adrienne. "Compulsory Heterosexuality and Lesbian Existence." *Desire: The Politics of Sexuality.* Edited by Ann Snitow. London: Virago, 1983.

Riley, Denise. *Am I That Name? Feminism and the Category "Women" in History.* Minneapolis: University of Minnesota Press, 1988.

Roszak, Betty, and Theodore Roszak. eds. *Masculine/Feminine: Readings in Sexual Mythology and the Liberation of Women.* New York: Harper & Row, 1969.

Rupp, Leila J., and Verta Taylor. *Survival in the Doldrums: The American Women's Rights Movement, 1945–1960.* New York: Oxford University Press, 1987.

Ryan, Barbara. *Feminism and the Women's Movement: Dynamics of Change in Social Movement Ideology and Activism.* New York: Routledge, 1992.

Saunders, Kay, and Raymond Evans, eds. *Gender Relations in Australia: Domination and Negotiation.* Sydney, Australia: Harcourt Brace Jovanovich, 1992.

Sawer, Marian, and Abigail Groves. *Working from Inside: Twenty Years of the Office of the Status of Women.* Canberra, Australia: Australian Government Publishing Service, 1994.

Sawer, Marian, and Marian Simms. *A Woman's Place: Women and Politics in Australia.* Sydney: Allen & Unwin, 1984.

Scott, Alan. *Ideology and the New Social Movements.* London: Unwin Hyman, 1990.

Seager, Joni. *Earth Follies: Feminism, Politics and the Environment.* London: Earthscan Publications, 1991.

Shute, Carmel. "Unequal Partners: Women, Power and the Trade Union Movement." *Australian Women: Contemporary Feminist Thought.* Edited by Norma Grieve and Ailsa Burns. Melbourne, Australia: Oxford University Press, 1994.

Simonds, Wendy. "Feminism On the Job: Confronting Opposition in Abortion Work." *Feminist Organizations: Harvest of the New Women's Movement.* Edited by Myra Marx Ferree and Patricia Yancey Martin. Philadelphia, PA: Temple University Press, 1995.

Smart, Carol, and Barry Smart, eds. *Women, Sexuality and Social Control.* London: Routledge and Kegan Paul, 1978.

Smelser, Neil J. *Theory of Collective Behavior.* London: Routledge and Kegan Paul, 1962.

Smith, Dorothy. "High Noon in Textland: A Critique of Clough." *The Sociological Quarterly* 34 (1993): 183–92.

Smyth, Ailbhe. "A (Political) Postcard from a Peripheral Pre-Postmodern State (of Mind) or How Alliteration and Parentheses Can Knock You Down Dead in Women's Studies." *Women's Studies International Forum* 15, (1992): 331–337.

Snow, David A., and Robert D. Benford. "Ideology, Frame Resonance, and Participant Mobilization." *International Social Movement Research* 1 (1988): 197–217.

Snow, David A., E. Burke Rochford Jr., Steven K. Worden, and Robert D. Benford. "Frame Alignment Processes, Micromobilization, and Movement Participation." *American Sociological Review* 51 (1986): 464–81.

Snow, David A., Louis A. Zurcher Jr., and Sheldon Ekland-Olson. "Social Networks and Social Movements: A Microstructural Approach to Differential Recruitment." *American Sociological Review* 45 (1980): 787–801.

Somers, Margaret R., and Gloria D. Gibson. "Reclaiming the Epistemological 'Other:' Narrative and the Social Constitution of Identity." *Social Theory and the Politics of Identity*. Edited by Craig Calhoun. Oxford: Blackwell, 1994.

Spender, Dale. "What Is Feminism? A Personal Answer." *What is Feminism?* Edited by Juliet Mitchell and Ann Oakley. Oxford: Blackwell, 1986.

———. *Women of Ideas and What Men Have Done to Them*. London: Pandora Press, 1988.

Stacey, Judith. "Are Feminists Afraid to Leave Home? The Challenge of Conservative Pro-Family Feminism." *What Is Feminism?* Edited by Juliet Mitchell and Ann Oakley. Oxford: Blackwell, 1986.

Steuter, Erin. "Women Against Feminism: An Examination of Feminist Social Movements and Anti-Feminist Countermovements." *Canadian Review of Sociology & Anthropology* 29 (1992): 288–306.

Summers, Anne. "Where's the Women's Movement Moving To?" *The Other Half: Women in Australian Society*. Edited by Jan Mercer. Ringwood, Australia: Penguin, 1975.

———. *Damned Whores and God's Police*. Up. ed. Ringwood, Australia: Penguin Books, 1994.

Susan, Barbara. "About My Consciousness Raising." *Voices from Women's Liberation*. Edited by Leslie Tanner B. New York: Signet Books, 1970.

Swidler, Ann. "Cultural Power and Social Movements." *Social Movements and Culture*. Edited by Hank Johnston and Bert Klandermans. London: University College of London Press, 1995.

Sykes, Bobbi. "Black Women in Australia: A History." *The Other Half: Women in Australian Society*. Edited by Jan Mercer. Ringwood, Australia: Penguin, 1975.

Tarrow, Sidney. *Power in Movement: Social Movements, Collective Action and Politics*. Cambridge: Cambridge University Press, 1994.

Taylor, Verta. "Watching for Vibes: Bringing Emotions into the Study of Feminist Organizations." *Feminist Organizations: Harvest of the New Women's Movement*. Edited by Myra Marx Ferree and Patricia Yancey Martin. Philadelphia, PA: Temple University Press, 1995.

———. *Rock-a-by Baby: Feminism, Self-Help, and Postpartum Depression*. New York: Routledge, 1996.

Taylor, Verta, and Leila J. Rupp. "Researching the Women's Movement: We Make Our Own History, but Not Just As We Please." *Beyond Methodology: Feminist Scholarship as Lived Research*. Edited by Mary Margaret Fonow and Judith A. Cook. Bloomington: Indiana University Press, 1991.

———. "Women's Culture and Lesbian Feminist Activism: A Reconsideration of Cultural Feminism." *Signs: Journal of Women in Culture and Society* 19 (1993): 32–61.

Taylor, Verta, and Nancy Whittier. "Collective Identity in Social Movement Communities: Lesbian Feminist Mobilization." *Frontiers in Social Movement Theory*. Edited by Aldon D. Morris and Carol McClurg Mueller. Newhaven, CT: Yale University Press, 1992.

———. "Analytical Approaches to Social Movement Culture: The Culture of the Women's Movement." *Social Movements and Culture*. Edited by Hank Johnston and Bert Klandermans. London: University College of London Press, 1995.

Thiele, Beverly. "Vanishing Acts in Social and Political Thought: Tricks of the Trade." *Feminist Challenges: Social and Political Theory*. Edited by Carol Pateman and Elizabeth Gross. Sydney: Allen & Unwin, 1986.

Touraine, Alain. *The Voice and the Eye: An Analysis of Social Movements*. London: Cambridge University Press, 1981.

———. "An Introduction to the Study of Social Movements." *Social Research* 52 (1985): 749–788.

Turner, Ralph, and Lewis Killian. *Collective Behavior*, 3rd ed. Englewood Cliffs, NJ: Prentice-Hall, 1987.

Tuttle, Lisa *Encyclopedia of Feminism*. London: Arrow Books, 1987.

VanEvery, Jo. *Heterosexual Women Changing the Family: Refusing to be a 'Wife'!* London: Taylor & Francis, 1995.

Walby, Sylvia. "Post-Post-Modernism? Theorizing Social Complexity." *Destabilizing Theory: Contemporary Feminist Debates*. Edited by Michèle Barrett and Anne Phillips. Cambridge, England: Polity Press, 1992.

Walkerdine, Valerie. "Sex, Power and Pedagogy." *Screen Education* 38 (1981):14–24.

Walkerdine, Valerie, and Helen Lucey. *Democracy in the Kitchen: Regulating Mothers and Socialising Daughters*. London: Virago, 1989.

Weedon, Chris. *Feminist Practice and Poststructuralist Theory*. Oxford: Blackwell, 1987.

Weeks, Wendy, ed. *Women Working Together: Lessons from Feminist Women's Services*. Melbourne, Australia: Longman Cheshire, 1994.

West, Guida, and Rhoda Lois Blumberg, eds. *Women and Social Protest*. New York: Oxford University Press, 1990.

Whittier, Nancy. *Feminist Generations: The Persistence of the Radical Women's Movement*. Philadelphia, PA: Temple University Press, 1995.

Willis, Evan. *Illness and Social Relations*. St. Leonards, Australia: Allen & Unwin, 1994.

Yeatman, Anna. "Women and the State." *Contemporary Australian Feminism* Edited by Kate Pritchard Hughes. Melbourne, Australia: Longman Cheshire, 1994.

Young, Iris Marion. "Gender as Seriality: Thinking About Women as a Social Collective." *Signs: Journal of Women in Culture and Society* 19 (1994): 713–738.

Zald, Mayer N., and John D. McCarthy, eds. *The Dynamics of Social Movements: Resource Mobilization, Social Control, and Tactics*. Cambridge, MA: Winthrop, 1979.

Index